Contributions to Management Science

More information about this series at
http://www.springer.com/series/1505

Dennis Schlegel

Cost-of-Capital in Managerial Finance

An Examination of Practices in the German Real Economy Sector

Dennis Schlegel
Stuttgart, Germany

ISSN 1431-1941 ISSN 2197-716X (electronic)
Contributions to Management Science
ISBN 978-3-319-15134-2 ISBN 978-3-319-15135-9 (eBook)
DOI 10.1007/978-3-319-15135-9

Library of Congress Control Number: 2015933649

Springer Cham Heidelberg New York Dordrecht London
© Springer International Publishing Switzerland 2015
This work is subject to copyright. All rights are reserved by the Publisher, whether the whole or part of the material is concerned, specifically the rights of translation, reprinting, reuse of illustrations, recitation, broadcasting, reproduction on microfilms or in any other physical way, and transmission or information storage and retrieval, electronic adaptation, computer software, or by similar or dissimilar methodology now known or hereafter developed.
The use of general descriptive names, registered names, trademarks, service marks, etc. in this publication does not imply, even in the absence of a specific statement, that such names are exempt from the relevant protective laws and regulations and therefore free for general use.
The publisher, the authors and the editors are safe to assume that the advice and information in this book are believed to be true and accurate at the date of publication. Neither the publisher nor the authors or the editors give a warranty, express or implied, with respect to the material contained herein or for any errors or omissions that may have been made.

Printed on acid-free paper

Springer International Publishing AG Switzerland is part of Springer Science+Business Media (www.springer.com)

Acknowledgements

Conducting research on a doctoral level and writing a Ph.D. thesis is a long road. I would like to express my gratitude to the various people who have accompanied and supported me in this process.

First of all, I would like to thank my supervisors, who have made all this possible. I would like to thank my Director of Studies, Dr. Aftab Dean, who has ensured the quality of this thesis with his academic rigour, insisting on high standards of the research. I would like to thank Prof. Claudio Vignali for his advice, inspiration and motivation that he has always given me. I would like to thank Prof. Bernd Britzelmaier, who has always supported me with his outstanding expertise in the field of cost of capital and value-based management.

Moreover, I would like to thank my examiners Dr. Roberta Bampton and Prof. Agyenim Boateng for their valuable comments.

For this research, access to appropriate empirical data was crucial. Obtaining internal data from companies has turned out to be one of the most effortful and time-consuming tasks in this research. Therefore, I would like to express my gratitude to the numerous people who were involved in this process. In particular, I would like to thank the people who supported me in this process by putting me in contact with relevant persons and distributing requests. Moreover, I would like to thank the experts who participated in the semi-structured interviews despite their busy schedules, as well as the numerous respondents who participated in the company survey.

Last but not least, I would like to express my gratitude to my family and friends, who have always supported my decision to pursue a Ph.D. programme.

Dennis Schlegel

Abbreviations

APT	Arbitrage Pricing Theory
BCG	Boston Consulting Group
BU	Business Unit
CAPM	Capital Asset Pricing Model
CCA	Comparable Company Approach
CFROI	Cash Flow Return on Invest
CGU	Cash-generating Unit
CVA	Cash Value Added
DCF	Discounted Cash Flow
EBIT	Earnings Before Interest and Tax
EVA	Economic Value Added
FSE	Frankfurt Stock Exchange
GCF	Gross Cash Flow
GI	Gross Investment
IAS	International Accounting Standard
IFRS	International Financial Reporting Standards
IRR	Internal Rate of Return
MCPM	Market-derived Capital Pricing Model
NBA	Net Business Assets
NDA	Non-depreciable Assets
NOPAT	Net Operating Profit After Tax
NPV	Net Present Value
ROCE	Return on Capital Employed
ROI	Return on Investment
SBU	Strategic Business Unit
SME	Small and medium enterprises
SML	Security Market Line
VBM	Value-Based Management
WACC	Weighted Average Cost of Capital

Contents

1 Introduction 1
  1.1 Background of the Subject 1
    1.1.1 Economic Environment 1
    1.1.2 Cost-of-Capital in Managerial Finance 2
  1.2 About the Research 3
    1.2.1 Research Aim and Objectives 3
    1.2.2 Research Methods 3
    1.2.3 Delimitations of Scope 4
  1.3 Organisation of the Thesis 5
  1.4 Conclusion 6
  References 6

2 Background: Cost-of-Capital in the Finance Literature ... 9
  2.1 Company Cost-of-Capital 10
    2.1.1 Two Perspectives on Cost-of-Capital 10
    2.1.2 The Determination of Cost of Equity 13
    2.1.3 Further Determinants of Cost-of-Capital 21
  2.2 Cost-of-Capital in the Context of Managerial Finance . 23
    2.2.1 Cost-of-Capital in the Finance Literature 23
    2.2.2 Fields of Application of Cost-of-Capital 26
    2.2.3 Agency Theory and Cost-of-Capital Practices 32
  2.3 Cost-of-Capital in the Context of Company Groups 35
    2.3.1 Conceptual and Theoretical Background 35
    2.3.2 Capital Structure of Business Units 41
    2.3.3 Cost-of-Capital of Business Units and Projects .. 44
  2.4 Determination Techniques for the Cost-of-Capital of
      Business Units 44
    2.4.1 Comparable Company Approaches 44
    2.4.2 Analytical Approaches 54
    2.4.3 Practitioner Approaches 60

		2.5	Conclusion	64
		References		65
3	**Previous Results on Cost-of-Capital Practices**			71
	3.1	Previous Studies on Cost-of-Capital Practices		71
		3.1.1	Overview of Previous Studies	71
		3.1.2	Methods Applied in Previous Studies	74
		3.1.3	Limitations in Comparing Studies	76
	3.2	Company Cost-of-Capital		77
		3.2.1	Cost-of-Capital/WACC	77
		3.2.2	Cost of Equity/CAPM	79
	3.3	Cost-of-Capital of Business Units		80
		3.3.1	Block (2003 and 2005)	80
		3.3.2	Steinle et al. (2007)	81
		3.3.3	Petersen et al. (2006)	83
		3.3.4	Geginat et al. (2006)	85
	3.4	Influencing Factors of Company Cost-of-Capital Practices		88
		3.4.1	Overview	88
		3.4.2	Previous Results	88
	3.5	Conclusion		90
		3.5.1	Summary	90
		3.5.2	Research Gaps	91
		3.5.3	Research Propositions	92
		3.5.4	Preliminary Model	93
		3.5.5	Fulfilment of Objectives	94
	References			94
4	**Research Philosophy and Ethics**			97
	4.1	Research Philosophy		97
		4.1.1	Research Philosophy in the Literature	97
		4.1.2	Philosophical Assumptions of This Thesis	101
	4.2	Research Ethics		103
		4.2.1	Background and Importance of Research Ethics	103
		4.2.2	Ethical Considerations in the Expert Interviews	104
		4.2.3	Ethical Considerations in the Company Survey	105
	4.3	Conclusion		105
	References			106
5	**Empirical Research Approach and Methods**			107
	5.1	Mixed Methods Research in the Literature		107
		5.1.1	Introduction and Terminology	107
		5.1.2	Purpose and Typologies	108
		5.1.3	The Debate Around Mixed Methods Research	109
	5.2	Empirical Research Methods of This Research		112
		5.2.1	Overview and Stages	112
		5.2.2	Justification of the Chosen Approach and Methods	113

	5.3	Limitations and Bias	115
	5.4	Conclusion	115
	References	116
6	**Primary Research: Expert Interviews**	**117**
	6.1	Methodological Background	117
		6.1.1 The Nature of Qualitative Research	117
		6.1.2 Approaches to Qualitative Data Analysis	118
		6.1.3 Quality of Qualitative Research	119
	6.2	Research Design	120
		6.2.1 General Approach	120
		6.2.2 Data Collection and Documentation	122
		6.2.3 Sampling Approach	124
		6.2.4 Candidates	128
		6.2.5 Interview Process	128
		6.2.6 Topics and Questions	130
		6.2.7 Data Analysis Approach	131
	6.3	Data Analysis	134
		6.3.1 Step 1: Open Coding	134
		6.3.2 Step 2: Categorisation	134
		6.3.3 Step 3: Conceptualisation	137
	6.4	Findings	138
		6.4.1 Cost-of-Capital Practices	138
		6.4.2 Influencing Factors of Cost-of-Capital Practices	140
	6.5	Conclusion	144
		6.5.1 Summary of Findings	144
		6.5.2 Refined Preliminary Model	144
		6.5.3 Fulfilment of Objectives	144
	References	146
7	**Primary Research: Company Survey**	**147**
	7.1	Research Hypotheses	147
	7.2	Research Design	148
		7.2.1 Total Survey Design Perspective	148
		7.2.2 Sampling	149
		7.2.3 Survey Instrument	156
		7.2.4 Mode and Process of Data Collection	159
		7.2.5 Error and Bias	162
		7.2.6 Data Analysis Approach	167
	7.3	Analysis 1: Sample Characteristics	169
		7.3.1 Test for Normality	169
		7.3.2 Company Characteristics	170
		7.3.3 Respondent Characteristics	171
	7.4	Analysis 2: Cost-of-Capital Practices (Univariate Analysis)	172
		7.4.1 Company Cost-of-Capital	172

	7.4.2	Cost-of-Capital on the Level of Business Units	175
	7.4.3	Performance Measurement and Value-Based Management	178
	7.4.4	Capital Allocation and Capital Budgeting	179
7.5	Analysis 3: Influencing Factors (Bivariate Analysis)		181
	7.5.1	Overview	181
	7.5.2	Size	185
	7.5.3	Industry	195
	7.5.4	Stock Market Listing	195
	7.5.5	Investor Types	197
	7.5.6	Perceived Cost-Benefit	198
	7.5.7	Top Management Background	199
	7.5.8	Corporate Culture	200
	7.5.9	Organisational Structure	201
7.6	Analysis 4: Influencing Factors (Multivariate Analysis)		202
	7.6.1	Analysis of Multicollinearity	202
	7.6.2	Elaboration Analysis	204
7.7	Conclusion		208
	7.7.1	Summary of Findings	208
	7.7.2	Support and Rejection of Hypotheses	209
	7.7.3	Fulfilment of Objectives	211
References			211

8 Conclusion and Contribution to Knowledge ... 215
  8.1 Research Outcome ... 215
    8.1.1 Overview and Synthesis of Previous Literature ... 215
    8.1.2 New Empirical Results on Cost-of-Capital Practices ... 216
    8.1.3 Influencing Factors of Cost-of-Capital Practices ... 219
    8.1.4 Final Model of Cost-of-Capital Practices ... 222
  8.2 Contribution to the Body of Knowledge ... 224
  8.3 Limitations of the Research ... 227
  8.4 Implications for Practice ... 227
  8.5 Implications for Theory and Further Research ... 228
  8.6 Conclusion ... 229
  References ... 229

9 Appendix ... 233
  9.1 List of Codes in Qualitative Data Analysis ... 233
  9.2 Assignment of Codes to Categories in Qualitative Data Analysis ... 236
  9.3 Questionnaire ... 237
  9.4 Descriptive Statistics of Ordinal and Ratio Variables ... 243
  9.5 Relationship Matrix Controlling for Stock Market Listing ... 244
  9.6 Relationship Matrix Controlling for Company Size ... 245

Chapter 1
Introduction

The aim of this chapter is to give a short introduction to the background of the research subject and an overview of the research project. The chapter is organised as follows: First, the current economic environment for companies seeking financing in the capital market is briefly explained, before the importance of cost-of-capital in Managerial Finance is pointed out. Next, the research aim and objectives of the research are formulated, before the choice of research methods is outlined. Subsequently, the scope of the thesis is delimited. Finally, the organisation of the thesis is explained.

1.1 Background of the Subject

1.1.1 Economic Environment

The European Debt Crisis has recently increased public awareness of topics related to capital markets, financing and risk. However, not only are governments faced with an increasingly powerful capital market. Also business firms have to fulfil investors' requirements in order to ensure sustainable financing of their companies in an increasingly competitive, globalised and professional environment.

The situation in the capital market requires companies to yield adequate returns on the capital that is invested in the business, as illustrated in Fig. 1.1: Since the 1990s, there has been an accelerated *globalisation of capital markets*, i.e. a global integration of the financial system and the expansion of capital markets (Clarke 2011). Thus, investors have a large choice of investment opportunities, which creates competition for scarce capital (Laier 2011). Another development that has taken place in the capital market environment is an *increased professionalism* of capital market actors since institutional investors have gained importance (Keay 2011; Pfister 2003). This leads to more active shareholders (Keay 2011) who assert

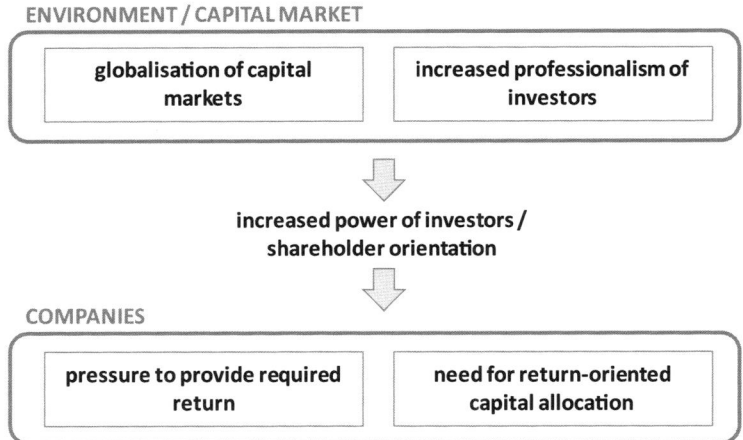

Fig. 1.1 Increased importance of adequate capital returns

their interests. These changes in the environment have led to an increased power of investors and thus to a greater shareholder value orientation (Clarke 2011). Investors are now able to put pressure on companies to provide sufficient return on the capital invested (Laier 2011).

1.1.2 Cost-of-Capital in Managerial Finance

From the point of view of a business firm, the required return of the investors is the cost-of-capital. In order to meet the overall return targets, capital must be efficiently allocated within the company (Laier 2011). From a theoretical standpoint, it is crucial for a business firm to know the appropriate cost-of-capital of an investment in order to make the right investment decisions. A firm only increases shareholder value if it is able to generate returns that exceed the cost-of-capital, i.e. the investors' required return (Ionici et al. 2011; Conroy and Harris 2011).

With the increasing size and complexity of today's company groups and a tendency toward divisionalisation (Horváth 2006), it is important for companies to know not only their overall cost-of-capital, but also the *cost-of-capital of business units or projects* in order to pursue value-enhancing investments (see Sect. 2.2.2.2).

In order to ensure that the required return is generated in the business, the rates should be used in Managerial Finance practices, e.g. as hurdle rates in performance measurement or discount rates in investment appraisal.

For the determination of the overall cost-of-capital of a firm and the cost-of-capital of business units or projects, Finance theory suggests sophisticated methods. These include the well-known Weighted Average Cost-of-Capital (WACC) and

Capital Asset Pricing Model (CAPM) as well as approaches for non-listed entities such as the Comparable Company Approach.

1.2 About the Research

1.2.1 Research Aim and Objectives

The overall aim of this research is to *examine and explain the cost-of-capital practices* of companies in the context of Managerial Finance for the real economy sector in Germany. Previous research (see Sect. 3.1.1) implies that there might be a theory-practice gap, i.e. that the actual cost-of-capital practices of companies are less sophisticated than the theory would suggest.

The following research objectives were formulated in order to provide guidelines for the design and execution of the research:

1. To investigate how companies use and determine cost-of-capital. This includes the question of which of the theoretical cost-of-capital determination models and techniques are applied in practice as well as how hurdle rates and discount rates are applied.
2. To develop a model that allows organisations' cost-of-capital practices to be explained
3. To develop a theory that explains why companies have certain cost-of-capital practices, i.e. to explain the reasons behind the influencing factors

1.2.2 Research Methods

This section provides a short overview of the research methods that are employed in this thesis. The choice of the research methods was based on the research objectives that were stated in the previous section.

First of all, a literature review was conducted in order to gain a comprehensive overview of the field of cost-of-capital. One of the main purposes of the literature review is to identify gaps in the literature and to build a foundation for the design of the empirical research. Next, expert interviews were conducted with 12 management consultants and Finance and Accounting professionals. On the one hand, the expert interviews were important to gain qualitative information on underlying reasons for the cost-of-capital practices of companies that is necessary for theory-building. On the other hand, the expert interviews served as a basis for the design of a company survey that was conducted in a subsequent step.

Table 1.1 explains how the individual parts of the research contribute to achieving the research objectives that were formulated in the previous section. In the course of this thesis, reference will be made to this table after each stage of the

Table 1.1 Research objectives and methods

Research aim	Research objectives	Contribution of literature review	Contribution of expert interviews	Contribution of company survey
Examine and explain cost-of-capital practices	(1) To investigate how companies use and determine cost-of-capital	Synthesise, compare and evaluate previous results; Identify gaps	Gain first exploratory results for the focus population	Gain quantitative results for the focus population
	(2) To develop a model that explains companies' cost-of-capital practices	Identify possible variables from previous empirical results	Identify possible determinants of cost-of-capital practices and relationships between factors	Test factors quantitatively
	(3) To develop a theory that explains companies' cost-of-capital practices		Identify reasons for cost-of-capital practices	

research in order to evaluate whether the objectives of the respective part were reached.

1.2.3 Delimitations of Scope

In a research project with limited time and financial resources, it is necessary to focus and delimit the scope in certain dimensions. Therefore, generalisations from this study might not be possible beyond the delimitations of scope.

First of all, the study is conducted in the *real economy sector*[1] only. This sector has been chosen because it is expected that the theory-practice gap concerning cost-of-capital practices is higher in the real economy sector than in the financial services sector. For instance, Deutsche Bank's former CEO Josef Ackermann announced a return on equity target of 25 %. This example implies that in the financial services sector, there seems to be a focus on a capital return philosophy.

A second delimitation of scope is that the study focuses on *Germany*. The results might not be transferable to other countries. One reason is that there are differences between countries concerning the stock market culture. Germany traditionally

---

[1] In this thesis, the real economy sector is defined as being engaged in the "circulation and exchange of goods and services amongst the members of society" (Empel 2008) as opposed to the financial services sector that includes for instances banks, stock exchanges, asset management and insurances (Fasnacht 2009).

relies more on bank financing in contrast to the more capital-market-oriented Anglo-Saxon countries (Guserl and Pernsteiner 2011). Moreover, there might be other economic as well as cultural differences between countries.

1.3 Organisation of the Thesis

The structure of this thesis is illustrated in Fig. 1.2. Moreover, the figure shows which chapters discuss major milestones such as the formulation of hypotheses.

After the introductory chapter, two chapters (Chaps. 2 and 3) are dedicated to discussing existing literature and previous research. While the first literature review chapter (Chap. 2) primarily serves as a background to the research, the second literature review chapter (Chap. 3) is concerned with the immediate topic of this research. Therefore, research gaps are identified and research propositions formulated as a conclusion to Chap. 3. Moreover, a preliminary model is constructed as a framework for the further research in this thesis.

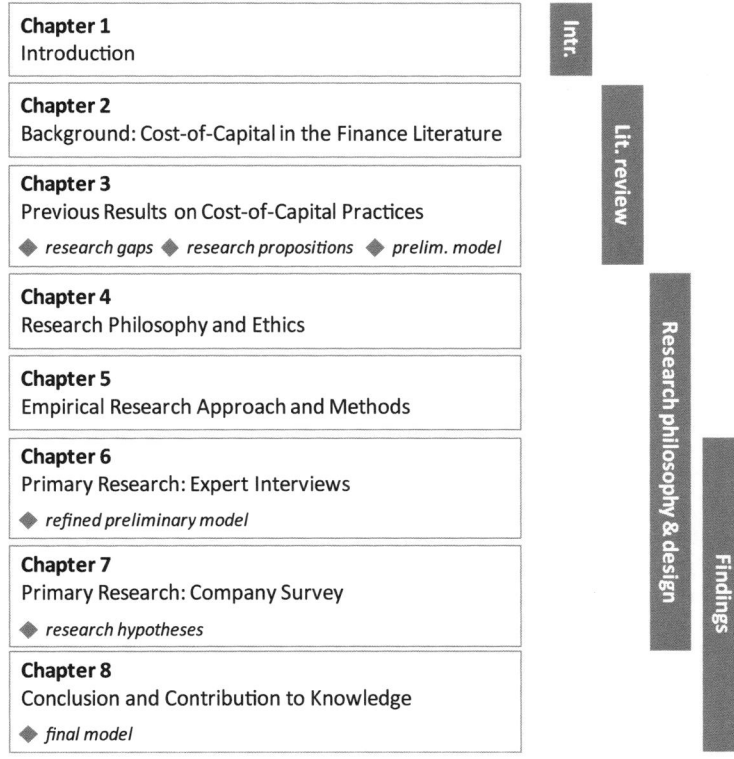

Fig. 1.2 Outline of thesis structure

In Chap. 4, the research philosophy of this thesis and ethical issues associated with this research are discussed.

In Chap. 5, an overview of the overall research approach and the methods used in this thesis is given. Moreover, the mixed methods approach is thoroughly discussed, taking into account relevant literature.

In Chap. 6, details of the methods applied and findings of the expert interviews are discussed. As a result, a refined preliminary model is presented after having identified possible influencing factors of cost-of-capital practices.

In Chap. 7, research hypotheses are derived from the expert interviews' findings and tested with the help of a company survey. After a detailed discussion of the survey design, the data analysis and findings are discussed.

Finally, in Chap. 8, the overall findings and the contribution to knowledge of this research are discussed. This includes the presentation of the final model constructed in this research.

1.4 Conclusion

This chapter has given an overview of the research undertaken for this thesis and an introduction to the research subject. It has shown that due to the external environment, companies are required to offer an adequate return to their investors. In order to pursue value-enhancing investments, they need to know their cost-of-capital. However, according to previous studies, there is a theory-practice gap in cost-of-capital methods.

The aim of this thesis is to examine and explain the cost-of-capital practices of companies. In order to reach the objectives, two empirical methods were used. First, expert interviews were conducted. In a second step, the results from the expert interviews were corroborated with the help of a company survey.

References

Clarke T (2011) The Globalisation of Corporate Governance? Irresistible Market Meet Immovable Institutions. In: Brikk A (ed) Corporate governance and business ethics. Springer, Dordrecht, pp 3–30

Conroy RM, Harris RS (2011) Estimating capital costs: practical implementation of theory's insights. In: Baker HK, Martin GS (eds) Capital structure and corporate financing decisions. Theory, evidence, and practice. Essential perspectives. Wiley, Hoboken, NJ, pp 191–210

Empel M (2008) Financial services in Europe. An introductory overview, 3rd edn. Kluwer Law International, Alphen aan den Rijn, The Netherlands

Fasnacht D (2009) Open innovation in the financial services. Growing through openness, flexibility and customer integration. Springer, Berlin

Guserl R, Pernsteiner H (2011) Finanzmanagement. Grundlagen—Konzepte—Umsetzung. Lehrbuch. Gabler, Wiesbaden

References

Horváth P (2006) Controlling. Handbücher der Wirtschafts- und Sozialwissenschaften. Vahlen, München

Ionici O, Small K, D'Souza F (2011) Cost of capital. An introduction. In: Baker HK, English P (eds) Capital budgeting valuation. Financial analysis for today's investment projects. Wiley, Hoboken, NJ, pp 339–362

Keay AR (2011) The corporate objective. Edward Elgar, Cheltenham, UK

Laier R (2011) Value reporting. Analyse von Relevanz und Qualität der wertorientierten Berichterstattung von DAX-30 Unternehmen. Verlag Gabler, Wiesbaden

Pfister C (2003) Divisionale Kapitalkosten. Theorie und Anwendung. Bank- und finanzwirtschaftliche Forschungen, 349th edn. Haupt, Bern

Chapter 2
Background: Cost-of-Capital in the Finance Literature

The literature review in this thesis is distributed over two chapters. The aim of Chap. 2 is to discuss literature from the field of cost-of-capital. This is necessary as a foundation for the subsequent chapter, which is more application-oriented. In Chap. 3, previous empirical results on companies' cost-of-capital practices are discussed. Research gaps will be identified at the end of that chapter.

This chapter is structured as follows: In Sect. 2.1, the broader field of *company cost-of-capital* is discussed. This includes a brief discussion of traditional seminal papers as a foundation for the rest of the literature review as well as a review of contemporary discussions about general issues of cost-of-capital, such as alternative determination models and the consideration of unsystematic risk. Section 2.2 shows how the field of cost-of-capital relates to the different sub-disciplines of Finance and for which fields of application of *Managerial Finance* it is relevant. In particular, the role of cost-of-capital in internal capital allocation, performance measurement and value-based management is discussed. In Sect. 2.3, a theoretical framework for the determination of cost-of-capital in a *company group context* that is derived from traditional Finance theory is presented as a foundation for the subsequent section. In Sect. 2.4, previous research on the determination techniques for the *cost-of-capital of business units and projects* is discussed thoroughly. This includes a detailed discussion of the techniques as well as the theoretical and empirical methods adopted by other researchers.

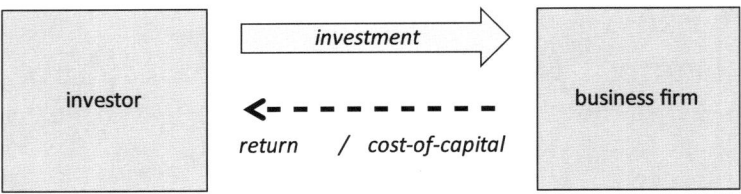

Fig. 2.1 Two perspectives on cost-of-capital (reproduced from Schlegel 2014)

2.1 Company Cost-of-Capital

2.1.1 Two Perspectives on Cost-of-Capital

2.1.1.1 The Investor Perspective

In this section and the next one, it is shown that the *required return* from the point of view of the capital market or investors is the same as the *cost-of-capital* from the point of view of the company (see Fig. 2.1). First, the capital market perspective is discussed. The discussion is limited to the extent that is necessary for an understanding of the subsequent discussion of cost-of-capital.

Required return is expressed as a percentage. For instance, a required return of 12 % means that the investment should at least yield a return of 12 % in order to compensate for the risk. It is generally assumed that investors are risk-averse and that the required return depends on the risk of the investment (Emery et al. 2004), i.e. the higher the risk of an investment, the higher the required return. This relationship between risk and return is illustrated in Fig. 2.2. On the very left there are government bonds of solvent countries such as the U.K. or Germany, which are generally considered as risk-free investments. They yield the risk-free rate.[1] Investments with a higher risk are remunerated with the risk-free rate plus a risk-premium.

Classical Finance theory is mostly based on the assumption of efficient markets (Schall 1972). This means that relationships such as the risk-return relationship outlined above should always hold. Otherwise, arbitrage processes would restore equilibrium (Brealey et al. 2009; Emery et al. 2004): an investment in a company is associated with an opportunity cost for the investors, i.e. they cannot invest that money into another firm (Arnold 2008). If another firm with a comparable risk offered a higher return, investors would withdraw their money and invest it into the other firm. This process would continue until the change in supply and demand at the capital markets associated with these transactions had levelled the returns. Thus, an efficient pricing of securities is ensured.

Risk is defined as the possibility that the actual return differs from the expected return (Watson and Head 2010). From a mathematical or statistical point of view,

---

[1] During the current European Debt Crisis, the assumption of risk-free government bonds can be challenged.

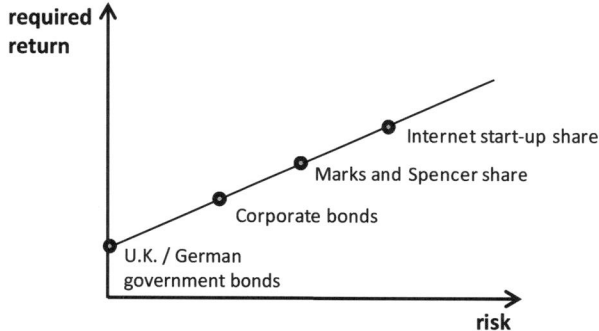

Fig. 2.2 The risk-return relationship (adapted from Arnold 2008)

risk is usually interpreted as follows: Risk is the variance of returns (Markowitz 1952), i.e. the more returns fluctuate, the more risky the investment is considered to be. Thus, for a high-risk investment, there is a certain probability of receiving no return at all or a negative return on the investment. On the other hand, there is also a certain probability of high returns (Arnold 2008).

Markowitz (1952) has shown in his seminal paper called "Portfolio Selection" that part of a stock's variance can be eliminated by diversification, i.e. by investing in portfolios that include different stocks. This effect occurs because the stocks do not always move in the same direction to the same extent. However, not all risk can be diversified, because returns of different stocks have covariances among themselves (Markowitz 1952). This means that they have a tendency to move in the same direction in general. Therefore, Markowitz recommends investing in firms from different industries, since they have lower covariances, particularly if the industries have different economic characteristics (Markowitz 1952).

2.1.1.2 The Business Firm Perspective

From the point of view of a company, cost-of-capital is the rate of return that it has to offer to compensate its investors (shareholders and bondholders) for the capital they provide (Brealey et al. 2009; Arnold 2008; Emery et al. 2004). Following from the risk-return relationship explained in the previous section, the cost-of-capital of a business firm depends on the riskiness of the capital that is invested. Due to an increasing global mobility and flexibility of capital, companies need to ensure that they offer the required return, since they risk losing their investors otherwise. This trend is reinforced by an increased professionalism of capital market actors (Steinle et al. 2007; Pfister 2003).

A company raises capital from various funding sources. The main sources are equity and debt, which both need to be remunerated at their own cost-of-capital, as illustrated in Fig. 2.3.

Standard financial theory suggested calculating the overall cost-of-capital as a weighted average of the cost of using the different capital sources relative to the percentage usage of each source (Britzelmaier 2013; Ionici et al. 2011). This

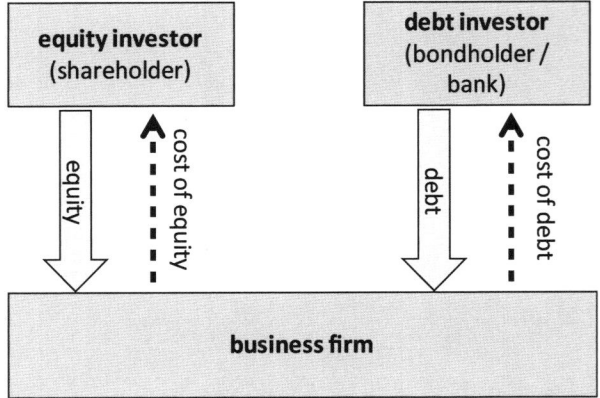

Fig. 2.3 Equity and debt investors (reproduced from Schlegel 2014)

concept is referred to as the *Weighted Average Cost-of-capital (WACC)*. The calculation formula is shown below.[2]

$$WACC = w_{equity} * r_{equity} + w_{debt} * r_{debt}$$

w_{equity} Percentage weight of equity capital
r_{equity} Required return on equity/cost of equity
w_{debt} Percentage weight of debt capital
r_{equity} Required return on debt/cost of debt

Although Miller (2009a, b) has recently criticised the WACC, its use is generally accepted and uncontroversial. However, more difficulties lay in the individual components of the WACC, which are (1) the component weights, (2) the cost of debt, and (3) the cost of equity.

(1) Component Weights (Capital Structure)
Financial theory generally recommends that the component weights should reflect the target capital structure of the company (Baker et al. 2011; Ionici et al. 2011; Britzelmaier 2009; Matschke and Brösel 2007). Sometimes the use of market-value weights is also recommended. However, target weights are generally considered to be superior for the following reasons: First, because cost-of-capital should be forward-looking (Schmalenbach-Gesellschaft 1996) and second, because the market value of equity is volatile, so that the actual weights are not stable and do not permanently reflect target weights (Baker et al. 2011; Pfister 2003).

The use of book-value weights is not considered to be adequate in the literature because book-value weights continue to reflect a situation from the past and ignore

---

[2] In this thesis, no tax considerations are discussed.

current market conditions (depending on the accounting standards that are used) (Baker et al. 2011; Ionici et al. 2011).

(2) Cost of Debt
Determining the cost of debt is simpler than determining the cost of equity for two reasons. First, there is less debate over the correct methodology (Ionici et al. 2011). Second, in case of traditional bank financing, which is very common in Germany (Guserl and Pernsteiner 2011), the interest on the company's debt is contractually agreed (Pfister 2003). In practice, corporate treasurers have a good overview of the company's cost of debt (Ionici et al. 2011).

For traded debt (i.e. bonds), typically the yield-to-maturity adjusted for default probabilities is used (Berk and DeMarzo 2011; Ionici et al. 2011). In the course of this thesis, the issue of cost of debt is not considered any further. A more detailed discussion can be found in standard literature, e.g. Berk and DeMarzo (2011) or Arnold (2008).

(3) Cost of Equity
The cost of equity is probably the WACC's most difficult component to estimate (Conroy and Harris 2011) and there is also extensive debate about the correct methodology for its derivation. Therefore, cost of equity is one focus of the thesis.

The cost of equity depends on the risk of the company's stocks. Financial theory suggests using capital market models to derive the cost of equity from stock price data (see Sect. 2.1.2). The most famous model is the Capital Asset Pricing Model (CAPM).

However, these capital market models can only be directly applied if stock market data is available. That means that for non-listed companies as well as the estimation of cost-of-capital for business units or projects, the models are not applicable. In these cases, there are proxy methods that have to be used. In the field of Managerial Finance, these proxy methods are important because for managerial purposes, it is regularly necessary to work with specific cost-of-capital rates for business units or projects (see Sect. 2.2.2). Thus, these methods are discussed in detail in Sect. 2.4.

2.1.2 The Determination of Cost of Equity

2.1.2.1 The Capital Asset Pricing Model

As mentioned above, the required return (cost-of-capital) depends on the risk of an investment. For the determination of cost of equity, theoretical capital market models can be used that examine the returns on the stock market. In practice, the use of Lintner (1965) and Sharpe's (1964) *Capital Asset Pricing Model (CAPM)* prevails (Young and Saadi 2011; Hoffjan 2009). The CAPM builds, among others, on Markowitz's (1952) model of portfolio selection (Sharpe 1964). A detailed discussion of the analytical derivation is not presented in this thesis, as it can be found in the standard literature, e.g. Berk and DeMarzo (2011).

The basic idea behind portfolio theory and the CAPM is that in an efficient portfolio, an investor can diversify away the firm-specific risk (unsystematic risk).

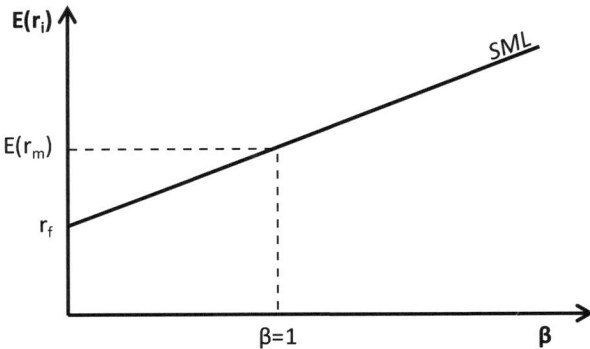

Fig. 2.4 Security market line (adapted from Arnold 2008)

However, unless returns of stocks are perfectly negatively correlated, a complete elimination of all of a stock's risk is not possible (Markowitz 1952). The **systematic risk**, i.e. the general market risk or more technically the part of a stock's risk that is due to the correlation with the market portfolio, cannot be eliminated (Sharpe 1964).

According to the CAPM, an investor is only compensated for the systematic risk that he cannot diversify away (Sharpe 1964).[3] Systematic risk is measured by the beta factor (Perridon and Steiner 2007; Perold 2004). Consequently, the required return on equity depends on the beta factor. The higher the beta factor, the higher the required return. This relationship is expressed in the security market line (SML) shown in Fig. 2.4. If the market is in equilibrium, all securities must lie on this line (Sharpe 1964). In the diagram, it can be seen that a security that is not exposed to systematic risk lies on the very left of the SML and is only compensated with the risk-free rate of return. The market portfolio, i.e. a portfolio consisting of all of an economy's assets, is exposed to average risk and has a beta factor of 1.

The SML can be expressed in the following formula, i.e. the expected return on equity is the risk-free rate plus the market risk premium times the beta factor.

$$E(r_i) = r_f + E(r_m - r_f)\beta_i$$

$E(r_i)$	Expected return on stock i
r_f	Risk-free rate
β_f	Beta factor
$E(r_m - r_f)$	Expected market risk premium (expected return on market portfolio minus risk-free rate)

Beta measures the responsiveness of a stock's returns to changes in the return of the total market (Watson and Head 2010). Stocks with beta factors greater than

---

[3] The notion that investors should only be compensated for systematic risk is increasingly questioned in more recent publications. This issue will be discussed in more detail in Sect. 2.1.2.3.

1 tend to move in the same direction as the overall movement of the market, but to a larger extent. Stocks with beta factors between 0 and 1 also tend to move in the same direction as the overall market, but to a smaller extent (Brealey et al. 2009).

Empirically, beta can be estimated ex post from financial market data. As only the stock's systematic risk and not its total risk is to be measured, the variance of returns is not the correct statistical measure. Instead, the relationship between the stock's return and the market return needs to be examined. This can be done with the help of simple linear regression (Berk and DeMarzo 2011; Watson and Head 2010; Brailsford 2007).

The CAPM has been subject to considerable **criticism**. In spite of this criticism, the CAPM still remains the standard model for cost-of-capital determination, since no workable alternative has yet been found (see Sect. 2.1.2.2). Probably the most prominent opponents of the CAPM for many years have been Fama and French, who presented an alternative model in 1993. In 2004, they published another article on the CAPM, focusing on empirical tests of the model (Fama and French 1993, 2004).

A point of criticism that is frequently raised in secondary literature is that the CAPM itself and also portfolio selection theory, from which it is derived, are based on many *unrealistic simplifying assumptions* (Fama and French 2004; Young and Saadi 2011; Berkman 2013). Examples of such assumptions are that all investors behave rationally according to their utility function, that they have homogeneous expectations and that funds can be borrowed or lent at the same interest rate (Sharpe 1964). The authors are aware that their assumptions are "highly restrictive and undoubtedly unrealistic" (Sharpe 1964, p. 434) and argue that the "proper test of a theory is not the realism of its assumptions but the acceptability of its implications" (Sharpe 1964, p. 434). Moreover, Sharpe (1964) emphasises that their model is an equilibrium model, which means that the tight assumptions are justified. Also Watson and Head (2010) state that the model should be assessed based on its empirical results, since the assumptions might not be far enough away from reality to invalidate the model.

Moreover, the model has other limitations from a theoretical point of view, such as the fact that it is a *one-period model* but investments are usually made for several years (Arnold 2008) and that it assumes that *only one factor* is relevant for the pricing of securities.

However, the most problematic issue about the CAPM is probably not the theory of the model but its empirical application and testing. In empirically applying and testing the model, technical problems occur as well as methodological problems. Moreover, there is considerable empirical evidence that does not support the CAPM, as summarized, for instance, by Dempsey (2013).

First of all, there is a *measurement difficulty* when estimating beta. For instance, beta can be estimated with daily, weekly or monthly financial data, which usually delivers differing results (Arnold 2008). Additionally, the market portfolio that is needed in the regression to estimate beta is not observable, since theoretically not only traded stocks, but all assets of an economy, including physical assets such as consumer durables or real estate, should be included, as pointed out by Roll (1977).[4] Usually, a stock market index is used as a proxy for the market portfolio. Besides that, another problem is that the model deals with expected returns in equilibrium, which are not observable because actual returns differ from theoretically expected returns. To reduce measurement error, a common procedure in empirical tests is to operate with portfolios of shares rather than individual shares (Fama and French 2004).

These technical problems also influence the testability of the CAPM. Another difficulty is that the CAPM is an *ex ante predictive model* (Sharpe 1964), i.e. it is forward-looking. However, it can only be tested with historical data, since future data is obviously not available (Arnold 2008). Watson and Head (2010) point out that if betas are estimated with historical data, the usefulness of the CAPM depends on the stability of betas over time. If betas tend to change a lot, it does not make sense to use past betas as a proxy for future betas. Markowitz (1952) acknowledged this limitation in his model, saying that the "probability distribution of yields (...) is a function of time". Furthermore, in empirical tests, multi-period data is often used, although the CAPM is a one-period model. This also only makes sense if betas are stable over time.

In empirical tests, two main issues are tested. The first is whether the Security Market Line (SML) holds as predicted by the CAPM. This includes testing the intercept, the slope and the linearity of the SML. The second issue is the stability of betas over time (Watson and Head 2010). There are a large number of empirical studies. A detailed discussion of individual studies is not the focus of this thesis. Therefore, summarised results from secondary literature are cited in this paragraph. In general, it can be said that there is no support that the CAPM *completely* explains the observable returns on the stock markets. Known opponents of the model, such as Fama and French (2004), argue that the empirical results of the CAPM are "poor enough to invalidate the way that it is used in applications". However, the general positive relationship between systematic risk and return is confirmed in many studies, although the slope seems to be lower than predicted (Fama and French 2004; Watson and Head 2010), i.e. the risk premium for the systematic risk is less than predicted. On the other hand, the intercept of the SML is found to be higher than predicted, which might be an indication that there are additional factors besides the systematic risk that influence return (Watson and Head 2010; Arnold 2008). For instance, a size effect, i.e. that small companies offer higher actual returns than large companies, is often reported (Brealey et al. 2009; Fama and French 2004). Concerning the stability of betas over time, there are inconclusive

---

[4] The unobtainable market portfolio is only one point of Roll's famous critique. However, most authors only cite this point and do not mention the other (less straight-forward) issue that Roll pointed out: He shows that if the market-portfolio is mean-variance efficient, the CAPM equation must automatically hold (being a mathematical fact). Therefore, he argues that the CAPM is not testable and all empirical tests are invalid unless they concern the only testable hypothesis, which is the mean-variance efficiency of the market portfolio (Roll 1977). Pollard (2008) provides a short mathematical proof of Roll's point.

results (Watson and Head 2010). Another tendency in empirical tests is worth noticing: Apparently, the CAPM is less able to explain the behaviour of returns in later decades of the twentieth century than in the 1950s/1960s/1970s (Arnold 2008).

2.1.2.2 Alternative Models for the Determination of Cost of Equity

In light of the criticism of the CAPM, alternative models have been developed that are supposed to overcome some of the CAPM's flaws. Moreover, there are also a number of extensions to the CAPM as discussed by Berkman (2013). In this thesis, the Arbitrage *Pricing Theory* (*APT*) by Ross (1976), the *three-factor model* by Fama and French (1993), and the more recently presented *Market-derived Capital Pricing Model* (*MCPM*) (McNulty et al. 2002) will be addressed briefly.

A model that has attracted a lot of attention in the academic world is the **Arbitrage Pricing Theory** (**APT**) that was developed by Ross (1976).[5] The theoretical derivation of the APT is different from the CAPM's theoretical background (Ross 1976). However, this is not discussed in this thesis due to the limited relevance to the research question. The most notable difference from the CAPM is that the APT is a multi-factor model, i.e. the expected return does not only depend on one factor, such as systematic risk, but on different factors. This is expressed in the APT formula (Ross 1976) that is shown below.

$$E(r_i) = r_f + \sum_{k=1}^{K} E(r_{mk} - r_f)\beta_{ik}$$

$E(r_i)$	Expected return on stock i
r_f	Risk-free rate
$E(r_m - r_f)$	Expected risk premium on risk factor k (expected return on market portfolio minus risk-free rate)
β_{ik}	Sensitivity of stock i to risk factor k

However, Ross does not name any concrete risk factors. Later studies try to find influencing factors empirically. For instance, Roll and Ross (1984) name inflation, industrial production, risk premiums and the slope of the term structure of interest rates.

Although the theoretical derivation of the APT relies on fewer unrealistic assumptions than the CAPM (Brailsford 2007), general points of criticism concerning all pricing models also concern the APT, for instance that they are backward-looking instead of future-oriented (Câmara et al. 2009). However, the

---

[5] Ross (1976) refers to a working paper from 1971 in which he first presented the theory. However, the article from 1976 is usually cited as the original source, since it is the first journal publication on the APT.

main problem with the APT is that there is no agreement about the factors that make up the model (Young and Saadi 2011; Arnold 2008; Brailsford 2007). Brailsford (2007) additionally points out that even if at one point in time, there was agreement about the factors, one could still not be sure that the factors would remain constant over time in a dynamic environment. The lack of agreement on the factors is probably one of the main reasons why the model is not generally accepted among academics and practitioners.

Another model that is commonly discussed but rarely applied is the **three-factor model** by Fama and French (1993). The authors have empirically tested different risk factors that explain the returns of stocks and bonds. For stocks, they identify three factors, which are an overall market factor, a factor related to firm size and one related to book-to-market ratio (Fama and French 1993).[6]

Several subsequent empirical studies cited by Brailsford (2007) support the model. However, a point of criticism that is often raised in Finance research also applies to the three-factor model: it is based only on empirical data rather than having a theoretical justification. The authors rely on testing risk factors that appeared to be relevant in previous empirical research—among others, in their own previous empirical study (Fama and French 1992). A practical problem that makes an application of the model difficult is to generally identify the risk premium values for the factors, since they will differ in each empirical study (Brailsford 2007). However, for a practical application, it will be necessary to have generally accepted values that can be used for all companies.

A more recent development is **option-based models** that use information from option prices to determine the cost-of-capital. The main advantage of such models is that they are forward-looking and thus overcome one of the major points of criticism of the traditional models—namely the reliance on historical stock data to predict the future. Option market prices reflect the market's expectations of a stock's future volatility and thus are a good indicator for future volatility of the stock (Câmara et al. 2009; McNulty et al. 2002).

A well-known option-based model is the Market-derived Capital Pricing Model (MCPM) presented by McNulty et al. (2002). The authors assume that cost-of-capital is made up of three components, namely *national confiscation risk*, *corporate default risk* and *equity return risk* (see Fig. 2.5). The yield on government bonds is used as a proxy for national confiscation risk and the risk premium of corporate bonds (compared to government bonds) is taken as a proxy for corporate default risk (McNulty et al. 2002). The equity return risk is calculated taking into account the implied volatility derived from the market prices of the stock options (McNulty et al. 2002). It has to be emphasised that the model is different from the CAPM and the APT, since it uses total volatility of an individual stock

---

[6] They use so-called *mimicking portfolios* to find out the determining variables. This is done by sorting the stocks according to their respective values for each variable (e.g. for size) and building two portfolios—one includes the stocks below the median of the respective variable and the other one the stocks above. By comparing the return on the two portfolios, the influence of the variable can be examined (Fama and French 1993).

2.1 Company Cost-of-Capital

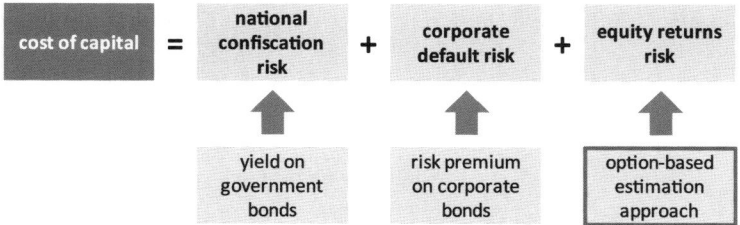

Fig. 2.5 Illustration of the Market-derived Capital Pricing Model (MCPM)

(i.e. systematic and unsystematic risk) and not only its exposure to systematic risk factors. This is a fundamentally different approach. However, a discussion of the exact calculation is beyond the scope of this thesis.

The MCPM is a straightforward approach that is easily understandable and might be useful for application by practitioners. Moreover, it is forward-looking by deriving all of its input variables from current market figures which is indeed a major improvement on the traditional models. However, as the model is quite new, empirical evidence on its usefulness is outstanding. McNulty et al. (2002) present examples of stocks for which their model produced results superior to the CAPM and say they did "similar comparisons of MCPM and CAPM numbers for hundreds of companies in a wide range of industries with the same result" (McNulty et al. 2002). However, this cannot be accepted as scientific empirical evidence, since details on their method, data and results are not disclosed. Another point of criticism against the MCPM that is also brought up by Câmara et al. (2009) is that the model lacks theoretical support.

Another type of approach that appears in the literature from time to time is **implied cost-of-capital**, which means that the cost-of-capital is estimated indirectly. Gebhardt et al. (2001) derived the cost-of-capital from the IRR of a forward-looking residual income model that explains the current market value. Borgman and Strong (2006) used analysts' forecasts of dividends and derived the beta factor from a dividend discount model. These approaches are problematic because they are based on forecasts. Hence, they are not dealt with any further.

Besides these models, there are more recently published studies that are working on improving existing cost-of-capital models. For instance, McGowan and Rifon (2011) developed an international asset pricing model based on the APT, which adjusts indices for foreign exchange effects. Other authors have attempted to develop enhanced versions of the CAPM. For instance, Chong and Phillips (2012) developed a version of the CAPM that integrates downside risk.

As a conclusion to the discussion of alternative models, the following statement can be made: Despite the known limitations of the CAPM, it remains the standard model for the determination of cost-of-capital (see Sect. 3.2). The main reason is that there is no consensus among academics as to which model could replace the CAPM and that there is no workable alternative model for an actual application (Black et al. 2002). Sharpe's impression from the 1960s that there is a "dearth of alternative models leading to similar results" (Sharpe 1964) still seems to be valid.

Although APT seems to be comparatively uncontroversial, the absence of commonly accepted risk factors makes it unsuitable for practical application. Arnold (2008, p. 303) states that "perhaps it will be useful to step back from high academic theory and observe the techniques that some market practitioners use". One promising model that is at its early stage of academic discussion is the MCPM, which might be interesting, although it will have to be examined more thoroughly by academia.

2.1.2.3 Consideration of Unsystematic Risk

As explained above, the CAPM, which is still the prevailing cost-of-capital model, does not take into account unsystematic risk because it can be diversified away. Finance theory generally assumes that investors are diversified. For diversified investors, the correlation with general market movement is more relevant because they cannot diversify this systematic risk.

Recently, an increasing number of authors (Perold 2004; Petersen et al. 2006) have questioned this notion as being a justification for a lower cost of equity. Moreover, with the MCPM, a new model has emerged that does take unsystematic risk into account. The main argument put forward by proponents of a consideration of systematic risk is that the assumption of a well-diversified investor does not describe reality. For instance, Perold (2004) mentions that many workers and executives have a large concentration of investment in their employer due to retirement plans and remuneration based on stock options. Petersen et al. (2006) state that in the valuation of privately held firms, often investors are involved that are insufficiently diversified. McNulty et al. (2002) argue that corporate investors do not try to minimise risk by diversification but rather through good management.

The authors mentioned above focus their argumentation on the question of whether investors are really diversified in reality. However, the actual question of interest in the context of this thesis is whether investors that are *not* diversified should be compensated for the unsystematic risk to which they are exposed.

Perold (2004) argues that the CAPM is still useful. He states that it makes clear to undiversified investors that there is potential for improving their portfolio and that they are not being compensated for part of the risk they are taking. This thesis tries to take the discussion a little further by taking into account the aspect of whether certain types of investors have the possibility to diversify at all. For those that do not have a possibility to diversify, from their individual point of view, it does make sense to take into account unsystematic risk when making rational economic decisions. However, this does not apply to all types of investors. First of all, financial investors at the stock market—also small private investors—do have the possibility to diversify, since today's market liquidity and range of financial products, such as mutual funds, allow everybody to diversify at low cost. Therefore, the author of this thesis follows Perold's (2004) argumentation in this point that the CAPM makes clear to those investors the need to diversify. The second case that was discussed above concerns owners of private businesses. For them, it makes sense to take into account the total risk of individual investments, for instance in new equipment, since they have no possibility to broadly diversify. However, one has to be careful and consider the situation of the natural person at the beginning of the investment chain. For instance, the author of this thesis disagrees with the argumentation by McNulty et al. (2002) that for a listed company that invests in certain assets, the unsystematic risk is relevant even if the company is not well-diversified. From the point of view of corporate management, the company might be undiversified. However, from a theoretical standpoint, the firm's managers are only intermediaries who invest on behalf of the original investor at the beginning of the investment chain. Consequently, the listed company is only a "conduit for shareholders to invest in the firm's assets", as Emery et al. (2004, p. 313) put it. Being only an intermediate level in the investment chain, the company need not be diversified and still only systematic risk is relevant, since the actual investor is supposed to be diversified. Other argumentations are not compatible with Finance theory, especially portfolio theory. The aspect of the investment hierarchy and a company being a portfolio of assets is dealt with in more detail in Sect. 2.3.1.2.

In brief, the discussion can be summarised as follows: There are two competing points of view that are also reflected in the cost-of-capital models. One is the individualistic point of view of a company, reflected in the MCPM, which takes into account unsystematic and systematic risk. The other is the equilibrium view, which regards the economy as a whole reflected in the CAPM. Which of these is more suitable depends on the situation of the investor.

2.1.3 Further Determinants of Cost-of-Capital

Another important direction of research in the field of cost-of-capital, which has gained considerable attention in recent research, is the impact of certain **variables on the cost-of-capital of companies**. Examples of these kinds of studies are listed in Table 2.1. The studies include both empirical and theoretical papers.

Common themes that can be found in the studies are concepts related to information quality (Chen et al. 2011; Yoo and Semenenko 2012), transparency (Barth et al. 2013) and information asymmetry (Armstrong et al. 2011), which will be briefly outlined in the subsequent paragraphs.

In general, many studies that deal with concepts related to information quality and transparency empirically examine the relationship between the information available to the stock market and the cost-of-capital. For instance, Yoo and Semenenko (2012) find that companies which provide higher quality segment reporting to the stock market have lower cost of equity. Barth et al. (2013) present evidence that companies whose earnings are more transparent have lower cost-of-capital. Their explanation is that in a firm with more transparent financial statements, "uncertainty regarding the value of its equity may be lower, and therefore it will enjoy a lower cost of capital" (Barth et al. 2013, p. 207). According to the researchers, the wider theoretical link is that transparency influences the extent of

Table 2.1 Studies on cost-of-capital values and their determinants

Author and year	Variables examined	Relationship identified
Barth et al. (2013)	Earnings transparency	Negative
Lambert et al. (2012)	Information asymmetry	No influence in perfect competition; positive in imperfect competition
Baran and King (2012)	Stock market index revision	Addition: negative Removal: positive
Boubakri et al. (2012)	Political connections of companies	Negative
Yoo and Semenenko (2012)	Quality of segment reporting	Negative
Armstrong et al. (2011)	Information asymmetry	No influence in perfect competition; positive in imperfect competition
Bloomfield and Fischer (2011)	Disagreement among investors	Positive/negative depending on type of disagreement
Chen et al. (2011)	Audit quality	Negative
Hughes et al. (2007)	Information asymmetry	No influence

information asymmetry and thereby reduces the cost-of-capital. In this context, information asymmetry refers to information asymmetry among different investors or traders in the market.[7] Information asymmetry theory is based on the idea that there are private signals in the capital market which have implications for both systematic factors and specific assets. While informed investors use the signals directly, uninformed investors can only draw inferences about the signals from their effect on prices (Hughes et al. 2007).

However, recent studies that examine the impact of information asymmetry on cost-of-capital (Lambert et al. 2012; Hughes et al. 2007) conclude that information asymmetry only influences cost-of-capital under certain conditions.

Hughes et al. (2007) demonstrate theoretically that equilibrium risk premiums on firm level are not influenced by information asymmetry in the market. However, greater information asymmetry about systematic factors, i.e. on the level of the economy, leads to higher uncertainty and hence higher cost-of-capital. The limitation of Hughes et al.'s (2007) examination is the fact that they operate under perfect competition, showing the effect for large economies where the number of risky assets as well as the related private signals approach infinity. Also Lambert et al. (2012) show theoretically that information asymmetry does not make a difference with perfect competition. On the other hand, they also state that with imperfect competition, cost-of-capital is influenced by information asymmetry and hence point out that the degree of competition in a capital market is crucial for the question of whether or not cost-of-capital is influenced by information asymmetry. Armstrong et al. (2011) build on this theoretical foundation and show empirically

---

[7] For information asymmetry in the context of agency theory, please refer to Sect. 2.3.3.

that in imperfect competition, cost-of-capital has a positive relationship with information asymmetry.

As a conclusion to this section, it can be stated that recent studies on determinants of cost-of-capital such as information asymmetry make an important contribution to knowledge. While neo-classical models like the CAPM assume that cost-of-capital is influenced by systematic risk only, they empirically show different determinants supported by theoretical explanations. However, the relevance of these issues for this thesis is limited, as the research aim of this study is not to explain cost-of-capital values at the capital markets. Instead, it is to consider how the resulting cost-of-capital rates are used internally for Managerial Finance purposes.

2.2 Cost-of-Capital in the Context of Managerial Finance

2.2.1 Cost-of-Capital in the Finance Literature

2.2.1.1 Sub-disciplines of Finance

In the literature, no uniform definition of the sub-disciplines of Finance can be found. For instance, Brigham and Houston (2009) and Fabozzi and Drake (2009) divide Finance into three sub-disciplines. In contrast, Besley and Brigham (2008) divide the field into four areas, whereas Khan and Jain (2007) use four sub-categories. Additionally, different authors use different terms for the same area, which is especially the case for the sub-discipline that is referred to as Managerial Finance in this thesis.

However, if one takes a closer look at the different classifications, it turns out that they are actually quite similar. The difference between the authors is merely that some use a more detailed classification than others. Fig. 2.6 shows how the sub-disciplines referred to by the different authors relate to each other.

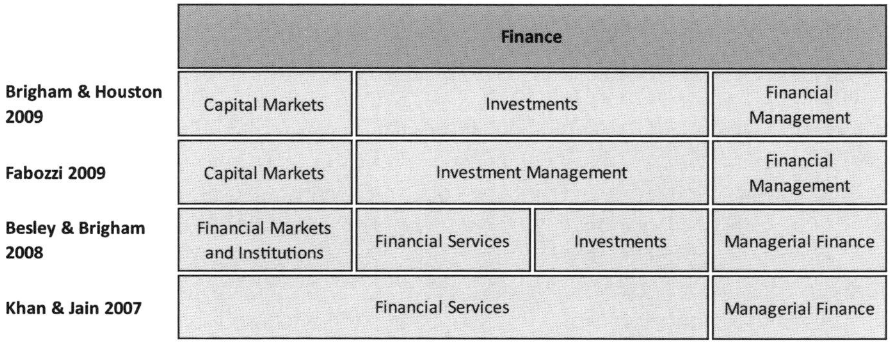

	Finance		
Brigham & Houston 2009	Capital Markets	Investments	Financial Management
Fabozzi 2009	Capital Markets	Investment Management	Financial Management
Besley & Brigham 2008	Financial Markets and Institutions	Financial Services / Investments	Managerial Finance
Khan & Jain 2007		Financial Services	Managerial Finance

Fig. 2.6 Areas of finance—reconciliation of definitions

Fig. 2.7 Classification of finance in this thesis (own illustration based on Brigham and Houston 2009 and Fabozzi and Drake 2009)

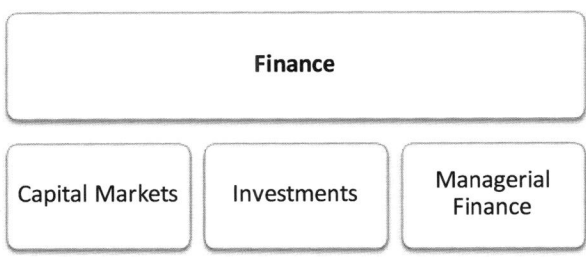

In this thesis, a classification is used that is similar to the one by Brigham and Houston (2009) and Fabozzi and Drake (2009). The three areas shown in Fig. 2.7 will be explained in the remaining part of this section.

(1) Capital Markets
Research in this area is concerned with the financial systems—i.e. financial markets, financial intermediaries and financial regulators—as well as the structure of interest rates and questions of derivative financial instruments (Fabozzi and Drake 2009).

Besley and Brigham (2008) point out the strong relationship between Finance and Economics. This similarity is particularly evident in the area of Capital Markets, but also in the area of Investments whereas Managerial Finance is more related to the field of Business/Management.

(2) Investments
This area focuses on the selection of financial assets—i.e. stocks and bonds, for example—for investment portfolios (Besley and Brigham 2008; Brigham and Houston 2009). This includes research on values, risks and returns of securities (Besley and Brigham 2008) but also activities like setting investment objectives and strategies (Fabozzi and Drake 2009). Many of the famous papers in Finance are concerned with research on value, risk and return—for instance Markowitz's (1952) Portfolio Selection.

(3) Managerial Finance
For this sub-discipline of Finance, there are different names that are used interchangeably by many authors. Probably the most common terms are *Corporate Finance*, *Financial Management*, *Business Finance* and *Managerial Finance*. Although only a few authors provide a clear definition of the terms, there are slight differences, which will be pointed out subsequently. Moreover, the reason why the term *Managerial Finance* has been chosen for this thesis will be explained.

A common element that can be found in many definitions is that this sub-discipline of Finance deals with *financial decisions* of organisations (Lumby and Jones 2011; Brigham and Houston 2009; Bierman 2010; Hillier et al. 2010). Furthermore, the area concerns financial decisions of *business firms*—as opposed to only financial institutions (Besley and Brigham 2008; Khan and Jain 2007). Watson and Head furthermore highlight the management focus in their definition (2010).

While there seems to be no difference between the terms *Financial Management*, *Business Finance* and *Managerial Finance*, strictly speaking the term *Corporate Finance* refers to the financial management of Corporations, which is a common form of organisation in the U.S. (Brealey et al. 2009; Fabozzi and Drake 2009), whereas the other terms include all types of businesses. However, many authors do not stick to the literal meaning of the term and say that Corporate Finance deals with the financial management of all type of businesses (Megginson et al. 2008; Khan and Jain 2007).

In this thesis, the term *Managerial Finance* is used for the following reasons:

- *Corporate Finance* is a term from the U.S., while this thesis is written from a European perspective. Interestingly, the U.S. authors Ross, Westerfield and Jaffe notice this difference and call the International Student Edition of their textbook "Modern Financial Management" (Ross et al. 2008b), while the original U.S. version with exactly the same contents is called "Corporate Finance" (Ross et al. 2008a).
- The term *Financial Management* does not make clear that the area is a sub-discipline of Finance rather than Management.
- The wording is more consistent with the field of Accounting if Managerial Finance rather than Business Finance is used because of the Accounting terminology Managerial vs. Financial Accounting.

2.2.1.2 Cost-of-Capital at the Nexus of Investments and Managerial Finance

This thesis contributes to the field of Managerial Finance. The topic addressed is the cost-of-capital of business units, focusing on the application of cost-of-capital rates for Managerial Finance purposes with a particular emphasis on performance and value-based management as well as capital allocation and capital budgeting.

Although the thesis does contribute to the field of Managerial Finance, it is based on two sub-disciplines of Finance—Managerial Finance and Investments. The reason is that the techniques used to determine the cost-of-capital originate from the field of Investments. Therefore, this literature review contains a substantial part about research on risk and returns, although the actual focus is the application of the techniques from the point of view of a business firm. It can thus be said that the research project is an interdisciplinary approach of different sub-disciplines of Finance.

In Fig. 2.8, this relationship is illustrated graphically. It can be seen that the techniques to estimate cost-of-capital are actually part of the sub-discipline Investments. However, the knowledge is used in various Managerial Finance topics, above all in *capital allocation* and *performance measurement*. The role of cost-of-capital within these two fields of application will be discussed in the next section.

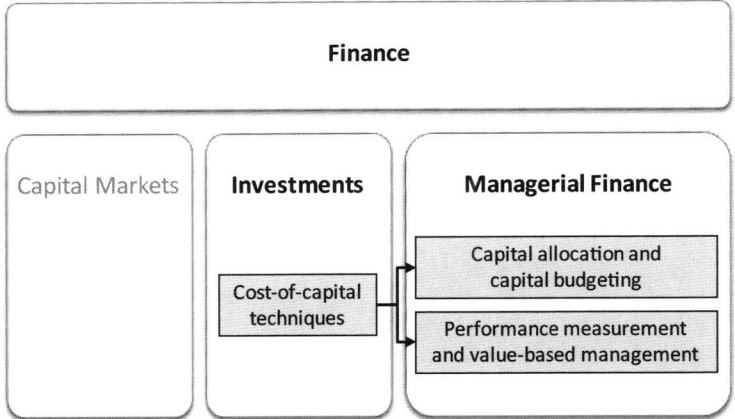

Fig. 2.8 Focus sub-disciplines of finance

2.2.2 Fields of Application of Cost-of-Capital

2.2.2.1 Overview of Fields of Application

Cost-of-capital is used as a discount rate or benchmark return in various fields of application. In Managerial Finance, it especially shows up in two issues: First, as hurdle rates to evaluate investments with the help of *capital budgeting* techniques in the capital allocation process (see Sect. 2.2.2.2). Second, in *performance measurement*, it is used as target returns for profitability measures or as capital charges for value-based measures (see Sect. 2.2.2.3). These two fields are in the focus of this thesis and will be discussed in the following two sections.

Moreover, cost-of-capital rates are used as discount rates for company valuation with the help of the discounted cash flow (DCF) technique (Dempsey 2013). The DCF technique can also be used for a number of other *valuation purposes*, e.g. for the valuation of intangible assets (Schlegel 2008). Since this is not part of the daily operating business, valuation purposes are not taken into further account in this thesis.

Furthermore, cost-of-capital is used in Financial Accounting, for instance according to the *International Financial Reporting Standards* (*IFRS*). In IFRS, cost-of-capital is especially relevant for impairment tests according to IAS 36. This standard requires companies to regularly assess whether certain assets may be impaired. If there is any indication of impairment, the recoverable amount of the asset must be estimated. In this process, valuation techniques that use cost-of-capital as a discount factor are used under certain circumstances (KPMG International 2013; Ng Wee and Hickey 2009). Impairment tests are especially important for goodwill (Kasperzak and Wassermann 2009). As these issues are from a different discipline, they are not further discussed in this thesis.

2.2.2.2 Capital Allocation and Capital Budgeting

One of the most important tasks of Managerial Finance and also an important field of application of cost-of-capital is the **allocation of capital** in internal capital markets. According to Porter (1998, p. 442), the term 'internal capital market' can be defined as "the system by which corporations allocate available capital from both internal and external sources to investment projects within and across business units". Capital allocation is necessary since capital is raised on the corporate level of the company (Conroy and Harris 2011; Harris et al. 1989; Chua et al. 2006) and needs to be invested in different projects, such as research and development projects. In the process of capital allocation, cost-of-capital rates are used as hurdle rates, i.e. minimum returns that an investment project must yield in order to be accepted (Baker et al. 2011).

Taggart (1978) distinguishes between two systems to allocate capital within a company group: the price system and the rationing system. In the *price system*, the central company group management determines hurdle rates based on the cost-of-capital for each business unit. In the next step, the local business unit managers identify potential projects that are able to meet the hurdle rate and report the amount of capital needed back to the headquarters. Finally, the company group raises the required amount of capital from the financial markets. That means that in the price system, no limit is set for the capital that is invested in the business units, since according to Finance theory, an unlimited amount of capital can be obtained from the financial markets if the investments yield the required return. In the *rationing system*, central management applies some form of budgeting to internal capital allocation, which means that the total amount of capital allocated to the business units is limited. Taggart (1978) argues that the rationing system is to be preferred if local managers do not fully perceive the consequences of their actions for the company group as a whole, whereas the price system makes more sense if local management disposes of relevant information that is not known to corporate management.

No matter which system is chosen, a proper determination of cost-of-capital is indispensable. While the total quantity of capital allocated differs among the systems, an analysis of individual projects in terms of their profitability is required irrespective of the system.

It is often emphasised in the literature—even on the textbook level—that a **differentiated treatment of cost-of-capital** rather than using the company cost-of-capital is important if the risk of the business unit or project differs from the average risk of the company (Ionici et al. 2011; Damodaran 2011; Brealey et al. 2009). As early as 1975, Brigham (1975) stressed that a company should use different hurdle rates if its investment projects differ in terms of risk.

What might seem like a mere theoretical accounting problem has serious consequences for business, as the use of incorrect cost-of-capital can result in sub-optimal decision-making and thus failure to maximise shareholder value (Block 2005). If the individual risk of a business unit is not taken into account

Fig. 2.9 Risk and required return of business units (adapted from Brealey et al. 2009 and Brigham and Ehrhardt 2005)

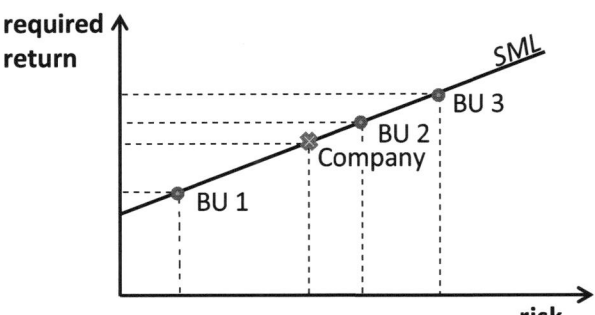

and company cost-of-capital is used as a hurdle rate, this results in a misallocation of capital. Too much capital is allocated to high-risk business units that offer high potential returns because it is not taken into account that the risk is also higher. Low-risk business units that offer lower but less risky returns receive too little capital (Brealey et al. 2009; Arnold 2008). This relationship is often illustrated graphically as shown in Fig. 2.9.

It can be seen that BU 1 in the figure has a lower risk than the other business units and thus also a lower required return according to the SML. This means that the investment projects of the business unit require a lower return in order to be profitable, taking into account the risk. If these projects are evaluated with the company cost-of-capital, many of the projects are rejected, although they would have a positive NPV if they were analysed with the correct cost-of-capital. Consequently, too little capital would be allocated to BU 1 with an undifferentiated treatment of cost-of-capital. In contrast, BU 3 is more risky than the average business unit in the company group and thus requires a higher return. If the investment projects of BU3 are evaluated with the company cost-of-capital, the projects seem more profitable than they actually are because the hurdle rate used is too low. Thus, too much capital would be allocated to BU3 if its investments were analysed with the company cost-of-capital. These examples make clear why a thorough treatment of cost-of-capital is indispensable for an efficient internal capital allocation.

According to Finance Theory, all investments projects should be evaluated with **capital budgeting** techniques that are based on Net Present Value (NPV), such as the Discounted Cash Flow (DCF) approach or Internal Rate of Return (IRR), using the WACC as a hurdle rate (Adjaoud et al. 2011). If the DCF approach is used, future cash flows are discounted with the cost-of-capital. If the discounted cash flows are equal to or exceed the initial cash outflow for the investment, the project should be undertaken (Maher et al. 2012). If the IRR is calculated, the project should be undertaken if the IRR is equal or greater than the cost-of-capital of the project (Maher et al. 2012). In practice, alternative methods such as the payback period of an investment are also used in investment decisions (Arnold and Nixon 2011).

2.2.2.3 Performance Measurement and Value-Based Management

For **performance measurement**, many companies use return measures such as the return on capital employed (ROCE) to measure business performance. Return or profitability indicators are important measures because they compare a profit figure (output) with the capital invested (input) and thus make a statement about the effectiveness with which the capital has been invested (Atrill 2009).[8]

For evaluation, i.e. whether a certain return is adequate or not, or for target setting for return measures, some companies use other companies' returns as a benchmark. Another possibility is to assess the return against the required return demanded by shareholders—which equals the cost-of-capital (Dempsey 2013). Only if a return higher than the cost-of-capital is generated does the company create additional value. This is because the cost-of-capital is not considered as a cost in accounting (Conroy and Harris 2011; Wahlen et al. 2011). According to Baker et al. (2011), many firms even use the cost-of-capital as a benchmark to determine the bonuses that are paid to the management.

In **value-based management** concepts, residual income measures or economic profit measures are used that subtract the cost-of-capital from profit (Britzelmaier 2013; Dempsey 2013). The idea behind this concept is that a company only creates value if the profit exceeds the cost-of-capital (Wahlen et al. 2011; Britzelmaier 2009). This is because shareholders buy shares in the expectation of making profits and additional value is created only if their minimum required return (i.e. the cost-of-capital) is exceeded (Laier 2011).

The idea of deducting the required return on equity was already promoted by Anthony (1973) and other academics long before the concept was refined and commercially exploited by consulting firms (as discussed below). Figure 2.10 outlines the relationship between cost-of-capital and value creation: only part of the profit enhances the value of a company because part of the profit is needed to satisfy the required return of the shareholders.

To calculate economic profit, different accounting measures for profit and capital are used in different concepts. In the author's opinion, it cannot be clearly said which measures are superior from a theoretical perspective as long as the capital measure and the profit measure are defined consistently.[9]

Anthony (1973) demonstrates his concept of cost of equity based on Net Income, Total Equity and Total Assets. Probably the most famous example of an economic profit measure, the Economic Value Added (EVA®), is based on Net Operating Profit After Tax (NOPAT) and Net Business Assets, as shown in the formula below (Stewart 2013).

---

[8] For a detailed discussion and evaluation of return measures, see Schlegel (2011).

[9] For instance, if the capital measure includes debt, the profit measure should be calculated before interest.

Fig. 2.10 Profit, cost-of-capital and value creation (reproduced from Schlegel 2014)

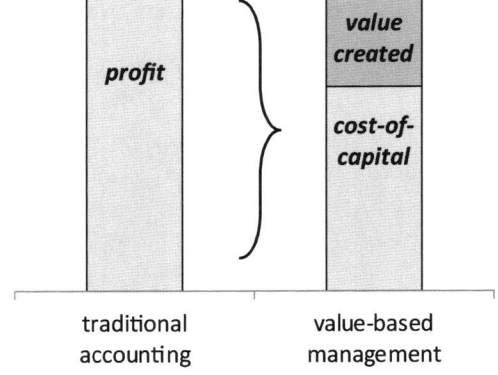

$$EVA = NOPAT - WACC * NBA$$

NOPAT Net Operating Profit After Tax
WACC   Weighted Average Cost-of-Capital
NBA   Net Business Assets

EVA is a registered trademark of the consulting firm Stern, Stewart & Co. As the concept is commercially distributed by Stern, Stewart & Co., a careful interpretation of the proponents' research findings is advisable. Examples of publications by authors affiliated with the company are Stewart (1991), Stern et al. (1996), O'Byrne (1997) and Young and O'Byrne (2000). However, in the meantime, a large body of research by independent academics is available. For a recent literature review and a discussion of research issues concerning EVA, see Sharma and Kumar (2010).

Another value-based measure is the Cash Flow Return on Invest (CFROI). The CFROI uses cash flow related measures. In a first step, the CFROI, which is a cash flow based return measure, is calculated based on a formula similar to an Internal Rate of Return (IRR) calculation. In a second step, this return is contrasted with the cost-of-capital (WACC) in order to calculate the Cash Value Added (CVA), which is an economic profit measure (Britzelmaier 2013).

1. $$NPV = 0 = -GI + GCF \left(\frac{(1 + CFROI)^n}{(1 + CFROI)^n * CFROI} \right) + \frac{NDA}{(1 + CFROI)^n}$$

2. $$CVA = (CFROI - WACC) * GI$$

NPV   Net Present Value
GI   Gross Investment
GCF   Gross Cash Flow
CFROI   Cash Flow Return On Invest
NDA   Non-depreciable Assets
CVA   Cash Value Added
WACC   Weighted Average Cost-of-Capital

Above, it was shown that although there are different value-based measures, the cost-of-capital (WACC) is an important element in all of the main concepts. Any further discussion of individual value-based measures is not the focus of this thesis. For a detailed discussion of the EVA and the CFROI, including a sensitivity analysis of the two measures, see Erasmus and Lambrechts (2006). For a more technical discussion of financial measures, including EVA, see Britzelmaier and Schlegel (2011).

In order to implement an effective value-based management system, managers need to know the wealth-creating potential of their actions (Arnold 2008). This means that value creation needs to be measured not only on an aggregate level of an organisation, but also on lower levels such as the business unit level, in order that effects of market-oriented decisions on value can be evaluated. Therefore, cost-of-capital also has to be determined on a business unit or even a project level, since it is needed to calculate value creation.

Value-based management is a managerial approach with the primary goal of maximising the wealth of shareholders (Arnold 2008). In Managerial Finance theory, the maximisation of shareholder value is often seen as the most important objective of financial management (Erasmus and Lambrechts 2006) and also in business firms it is widely accepted as a fundamental objective of business (Sharma and Kumar 2010; Rappaport 1986). The emphasis of the shareholder perspective in formulating corporate objectives, as advocated by shareholder theory, has often been criticised. Opponents argue that in decision-making, a firm should balance the interests of all stakeholders such as employees and customers (Danielson et al. 2008). Another point of criticism is that shareholder theory encourages short-termism, i.e. the pursuit of a course of action that maximises short-term gains but is suboptimal for the long-term (Danielson et al. 2008; Laverty 1996). Proponents argue that critics are misguided, as exploiting stakeholders and focusing on the short term only is incompatible with the goal of long-term maximisation of shareholder value (Arnold 2008; Danielson et al. 2008). Moreover, Rappaport (1986) points out that enhancing a company's financial position is beneficial for all stakeholders, since they also have financial interests in the company. As this thesis focuses on the technical point of view rather than discussing corporate governance and ethical issues, the discussion of shareholder vs. stakeholder theory is not reviewed in detail.

Besides the further development of value-based measures, recent research about value-based management seems to concentrate on an empirical examination of value-based management and its usefulness in practice. Several authors examine the use and communication of value-based management by companies in practice. For instance, Laier (2011) examines value reporting of German companies by analysing financial statements. Britzelmaier (2010) examines similar research questions among European listed companies. A common question that is investigated is whether companies that use value-based management benefit from it, i.e. whether their financial performance is superior to that of their peers. Recently, this question was examined for German listed companies by Rapp et al. (2011), who conclude that companies using value-based management concepts do indeed show excess returns. Athanassakos (2007) found, with the help of a survey approach, that in Canada, larger companies with younger and more educated managers are more likely to use value-based management concepts. His data also suggests that companies using value-based management outperform their peers. Ryan and Trahan (2007) use longitudinal data in order to find out whether the introduction of value-based management improves economic performance. Although their overall conclusion is that this is the case, the results are somewhat mixed. In the sample, firms that tie executive compensation to value-based measures have lower performance after the introduction of this approach (Ryan and Trahan 2007), while theory would suggest the opposite development.

2.2.3 Agency Theory and Cost-of-Capital Practices

2.2.3.1 Agency Theory and Managerial Finance

The purpose of this section is to discuss the fields of application of cost-of-capital that were outlined in the previous sections in the theoretical context of agency theory.

Agency theory—also referred to as the principal-agent problem—is a concept from neo-institutional economics and became known especially through the publication by Jensen and Meckling (1976). A **principal-agent relationship** is a "contract under which one or more persons (the principal(s)) engage another person (the agent) to perform some service on their behalf which involves delegating some decision making authority to the agent" (Jensen and Meckling 1976, p. 308). The relationship is assumed to have the following characteristics: First, the principal's and the agent's *interests are divergent* and the *agent acts opportunistically*, i.e. is likely to misuse the delegated authority for his own benefit. Second, the agent is able to enforce his own interests, since there is *information asymmetry* in favour of the agent (Britzelmaier 2013; Weber and Schäffer 2006). This creates a reduction of the principal's welfare, which can be classified as different types of agency costs (Jensen and Meckling 1976).

The general principal-agent problem can be found in a number of different settings. In the context of large companies, there is a principal-agent relationship between shareholders and top management. Furthermore, due to delegation and decentralisation, there is a principal-agent relationship at every level within the company (Jensen and Meckling 1976). Thus, principal-agent relationships with multiple tiers are generated, as, for instance, top management is the business unit management's principal and at the same time the shareholders' agent (Scharfstein and Stein 2000).

2.2.3.2 Agency Problems in Capital Allocation and Performance Measurement

Agency theory has implications for both capital allocation and performance measurement. Agency problems in these areas are an important field of investigation, since they result in inefficiencies and decrease of corporate performance.

Concerning **capital allocation**, corporate top management acts as an intermediary—or agent—to invest the shareholders' money (Emery et al. 2004). Thus, responsibility is delegated to a large degree to managers, who are supposed to operate the company in a manner that benefits the shareholders (Arnold and Nixon 2011). Investors have no insight into lower levels, since they invest in the whole company as a portfolio of assets, projects and business units. This is especially the case in public companies where capital is very fluid and individual investors only hold a small share in the company. Here, investors only have a little influence or insight concerning the operations of the company and evaluate its performance based on financial criteria (U.S. National Research Council 1994).

The internal situation is comparable: Top management allocates capital to business units but it is often not involved in daily activities on an operational level. They usually base their decisions on financial information and only get involved on a lower level if certain thresholds are breached (Sutcliff and Donnellan 2007). The delegation of authority to lower hierarchical levels raises the question of how the orientation towards corporate objectives can still be ensured on all organisational levels (Horváth 2006).

Lots of recent research in the area of internal capital markets deals with the examination of inefficiencies in capital allocation as an effect of managerial agency problems. For instance, Gaspar and Massa (2011) as well as Duchin and Sosyura (2011) conduct research on the effect of the personal relationship between the central CEO and divisional managers on capital allocation. Duchin and Sosyura (2011) find that divisional managers who have stronger social connections to the CEO receive more capital. Scharfstein and Stein's (2000) results imply that weaker divisions are often subsidised by stronger ones—which also results in inefficient capital allocation. Other researchers examine the role of incentives and executive compensation in overcoming the agency problems (André et al. 2009; Yong 2007).

While the field of **performance measurement** does not have as many inherent agency problems as capital allocation, it plays an important role in overcoming principal-agent problems in general.

First of all, performance measurement systems help to overcome agency problems by aligning the agent's interests with the principal's interests. This can be done by designing performance-based compensation plans which give managers the right incentives (Brealey et al. 2009). As Brealey et al. (2009, p. 327) state: "Since you get what you reward and you reward what you measure, you get what you measure."

Moreover, performance measurement reduces the information asymmetry between principal and agent and thus mitigates the principal-agent problem.

2.2.3.3 Managerial Risk Preferences

In general, classical theory assumes that investors and other economic actors are risk averse. However, as Laughhunn et al. (1980, p. 1238) point out, risk preferences in reality are probably a "mixture of risk aversion and risk seeking". Research on managerial risk preferences deals with questions concerning the risky choice behaviour of managers.

While the general discussion about risk preferences is not within the scope of this thesis, the consequences of managerial risk preferences from the perspective of agency theory and Managerial Finance are briefly discussed. From this perspective, the issue is problematic if the principal and the agent have different risk preferences. As Karake-Shalhoub and Petty (2002, p. 239) point out, the diverging interests between principals and agents also "get translated into differences in risk preferences". The specific risk behaviour of managers—and hence the extent of the divergence problem—depend on different factors such as their compensation (Gormley et al. 2013). In the following two paragraphs, two examples of diverging risk preferences and their consequences for capital investment and financing decisions are discussed.

One example of diverging risk preferences is the relevance of **unsystematic risk**. As pointed out in Sect. 2.1.2.3, diversified investors are indifferent with regard to unsystematic risk. In contrast, unsystematic risk is relevant for managers, since they are exposed to the idiosyncratic risk of the firm. As Schroeck (2002) points out, managers often invest a large fraction of their personal wealth in the company and their human capital in particular is directly linked with the performance of the company. Therefore, they care about the volatility of cash flow and the default risk of the firm. This difference in risk preferences can lead to agency costs related to unnecessary diversification or suboptimal capital structure, as leverage is too low from a tax shield perspective.

Another example of agency costs related to diverging risk preferences is **investments below the cost-of-capital**. They can occur in a situation where managers are evaluated based on ROI (or other capital return measures) and their business unit's current ROI is below the cost-of-capital. In order to improve the ROI, managers will invest in projects that are below cost-of-capital if they improve the business unit's overall ROI, even if the risk of the project would require a higher ROI (Merchant and Van der Stede 2007).

Overall, it can be summarised that managerial risk preferences can lead to a situation where the agent is either too risk-averse or too risk-seeking from the principal's point of view. This generates agency costs, for instance in the form of inefficiently invested capital.

2.2.3.4 Implications for this Study

As a conclusion to Sect. 2.2.3, it can be summarised that the research concerning principal-agent relationships in Managerial Finance topics deals with the effect of the principal-agent problem on the company's performance, policies and processes.

Previous literature does not address the impact of agency problems on cost-of-capital practices as discussed in this thesis. Nevertheless, the link to cost-of-capital practices can be summarised as follows: agency problems—such as personal relationships between CEOs and divisional managers—undermine a proper application of cost-of-capital practices as suggested by classical Finance theory. Instead of applying objective methods as discussed in this thesis, opportunistic behaviour results in inefficient capital allocation.

As this thesis is written from a technical point of view based on the classical Finance theory perspective, agency theory will not be the focus of this study. However, the findings of this thesis will briefly be discussed in the theoretical context of agency theory in order to establish a theoretical link between the findings and existing theories (cp. Sect. 8.1.4).

2.3 Cost-of-Capital in the Context of Company Groups

2.3.1 *Conceptual and Theoretical Background*

2.3.1.1 Definition of Business Unit

The necessity of using differentiated cost-of-capital rates for different business units was identified above. Up to this point, the term 'cost-of-capital of business units' has been used multiple times. Now a more thorough discussion of what a business unit is follows.

There are different possibilities in terms of how a company group can be divided into organisational units. First of all, there is the *legal* vs. *the management* structure: The primary structure of a company group is determined by the legal ownership structure. However, this statutory structure is overlaid by an operational management structure (Borchers 2006). In *Managerial* Finance and Accounting, the relevant point of view is economic, i.e. the operational structure is relevant. Even in Financial Accounting, with the increased importance of IFRS, a legal view on company groups is increasingly being replaced by a management-oriented view. For instance, IFRS 8 (Operating Segments) requires the reporting of segment data in the way in which they are reported to management—independent from the legal structure. Evidently, for the topic and scope of this thesis, the economic or management point of view as opposed to the legal point of view is also relevant.

However, also from an economic point of view, there are several ways to divide a company group. When differentiating cost-of-capital in a company group, two aspects have to be decided.

First, the *dimension of differentiation*: a company group can be divided into different dimensions. In practice, common dimensions that are reported in (internal or external) financial reports are the following:

- product-lines
- regions
- functions, e.g. marketing, finance etc.

In contemporary company groups, the operational structure is often a multi-dimensional *matrix organisation*, for instance with a functional, a product-oriented and a regional dimension at the same time. Thus, multidimensional performance measurement according to the respective responsibilities must also be done and a decision must be made about the dimension or dimensions into which the cost-of-capital should be differentiated.

Second, the *level of differentiation*: The second aspect refers to the level of differentiation, i.e. if the cost-of-capital is only differentiated on higher and fewer organisational levels or if the differentiation is more detailed. For example, in the region dimension, a company could decide to differentiate cost-of-capital by continents or by individual countries.

Vogel (1998) names minimum requirements which should be fulfilled for the definition of sub-units in the context of value-based management: It must be possible to evaluate them separately, i.e. cash flows (CF) and cost-of-capital must be separately identifiable. Moreover, they must be led by managers with competences and responsibility for the task of value creation. The first of Vogel's requirements is similar to the concept of a *cash generating unit* (*CGU*) from the International Financial Reporting Standards (IFRS), which is used for impairment tests could be applied (Epstein 2010). A CGU is "the smallest identifiable group of assets that generates cash inflows that are largely independent of the cash inflows from other assets" (IAS 36.6).

In this thesis, it is suggested that cost-of-capital should be differentiated by business units. A business unit in this thesis is a *strategic business unit* (*SBU*) as defined in strategic marketing. A SBU is a product-market combination which is strategically independent from other SBUs (Huch et al. 2004). SBUs fulfil both Vogel's requirements and the definition of a CGU. The term *divisional cost-of-capital* can often be found in the literature. This term also means a distinction of cost-of-capital by line of business (Harris et al. 1989) and can thus be used synonymously to *cost-of-capital of business units*.

A differentiation of cost-of-capital by business units consequently means that the suggested dimension of differentiation is the product dimension. There are several reasons why this makes sense from a theoretical point of view:

- Cost-of-capital differentiation only makes sense in a dimension that is a significant determinant for systematic risk because then the cost-of-capital rates differ from each other and therefore a differentiation is necessary. It is uncontroversial that industry affiliation is one of the major determinants of systematic risk. In

multi-industry firms, business units evidently conduct business in different industries, so that the product-lines differ in their systematic risk.
- Another reason that is stated by Harris et al. (1989) is that firms typically delegate authority to managers of business units that are differentiated by product lines. Thus it also makes sense to align value-based performance measurement with decision authority (see Vogel's argument above).

However, depending on the individual circumstances, a cost-of-capital differentiation in a different dimension might also make sense for some companies. A further differentiation of cost-of-capital on a deeper level *within* business units (e.g. for individual investment projects or products) is necessary if the risk of the project is different from the average risk of the business unit. Otherwise, it is sufficient to use the business unit cost-of-capital.

2.3.1.2 The Value Additivity Principle in Investment Theory

One of the theoretical principles upon which the determination of cost-of-capital of business units and projects is based is the value additivity principle. In this section, the general principle is discussed, and in the next section it is transferred to the question of how cost-of-capital and betas can be aggregated from a divisional level to the corporate level. The aggregation of cost-of-capital derived from the value additivity principle is a central premise in many important articles in the field of divisional cost-of-capital, for instance Fuller and Kerr (1981) and Ehrhardt and Bhagwat (1991). In particular, full-information beta approaches that use multiple regression analysis (Ehrhardt and Bhagwat 1991; Cummins and Phillips 2005; Chua et al. 2006) are based on this premise. This means that many of the empirical studies on divisional cost-of-capital also implicitly test the value additivity principle and its assumptions.

The value additivity principle is based on the "law of one price", meaning that one and the same asset should always sell at the same price regardless of the context (Burns 1987). The value additivity principle states that if several assets are packaged together as one unit, the value of this aggregate unit must be the sum of the individual parts. This relationship should hold regardless of how the assets are combined or divided (Burns 1987; Schall 1972). Algebraically, this relation can be easily expressed as follows (Harris et al. 1989; Schall 1972):

$$V = \sum_{j=1}^{n} V_i$$

V   Value of aggregate unit
V_i Value of individual asset i
n   Number of assets

The value additivity principle should hold because of arbitrage processes: if the value of a group of assets was different than the sum of the individual assets' values, traders could earn arbitrage profits. A simple example would be gaining arbitrage profits by assembling assets into a package and selling the package (if the package value was higher than the sum of the individual parts) or buying the package and selling the assets individually (if the package value was lower than the sum of the individual parts) (Burns 1987). For a detailed analytical analysis of arbitrage opportunities if the value additivity principle did not hold, the reader is referred to the explanations by Schall (1972). In efficient capital markets, arbitrage processes would be triggered as soon as the relationship ceases to hold. The arbitrage processes restore equilibrium by shifting demand and supply so that the prices change in the direction that restores the value additivity principle.

Besides the rather generic view presented above, the value additivity principle can be applied to the context of company groups. A company group can also be seen as a portfolio of assets. Consequently, according to the value additivity principle, the company value is the sum of the separate asset values. This relationship should hold for different aggregation levels. For instance, in a company group, there might be intermediate levels such as projects, divisions or business units that should also have the aggregate value of their individual assets (Brealey et al. 2009).

This also means that diversification in a company group should not have an effect on the firm's value. Until the 1960s, the prevalent opinion was that the diversification effect should be considered in corporate investment decisions (Schall 1972). However, today the irrelevancy of investment diversification on the firm level is even taught on a textbook level, for instance in Brealey et al. (2009). The reason why diversification does not add value for investors is that the investors can diversify on their own much more easily and thus are not willing to pay a premium. They can simply buy and sell any amount of shares of different companies, which is much easier and more flexible than a diversification on a firm level (Brealey et al. 2009).[10]

There are only a few studies that explicitly test the value additivity principle. One is by Ang and Clark (1997), who have tested the theory empirically in the banking sector. Their results are in general consistent with the value additivity principle. However, the relationship no longer holds in the later years of their data, which they explain with changes in products, technology and regulatory environment (Ang and Clark 1997). Another empirical test was done by Burns (1987), who also achieves rather mixed results. In his study based on oil security market prices, the value additivity principle does not accurately describe daily prices, but it does fit with average prices. However, Burns (1987) concludes that the results generally support the value additivity principle. A possible explanation for the misfit of daily prices could be that the arbitrage processes are lagged for instance due to

---

[10] Note: At first glance the diversification irrelevancy might seem like a contradiction to portfolio theory. However, also in portfolio theory, the *value* does not increase with diversification. The advantage lies in the reduction of *volatility*.

2.3 Cost-of-Capital in the Context of Company Groups

transaction costs or market imperfections. This would mean that the prices only adjust in the mid-term when the differences are large enough.

Another reason why the value additivity principle might not perform too well in empirical tests is the many (partly unrealistic) assumptions upon which it is based. First of all, it is based on the general assumptions of a perfect and efficient capital market. Additionally, in a company group context, the principle is only applicable under even tighter assumptions, particularly an absence of synergies between the business units (Fuller and Kerr 1981). If there were synergies between business units, an integration of several business units within a company group could increase firm value compared to the aggregate individual values.

2.3.1.3 Value Additivity and Differentiated Cost-of-Capital

As mentioned above, the value additivity principle in the context of company groups states that the aggregated value of a company's business units must equal the total company value—as the aggregated value of individual securities in a portfolio must equal the value of the portfolio as a package. Consequently, the formula of the value additivity principle can be formulated as follows for the case of business units (Fuller and Kerr 1981):

$$V_C = \sum_{i=1}^{n} V_{BU.i}$$

V   Market value of company
$V_{BU\ i}$ Market value of business unit i
n   Number of business units

The value additivity principle is important in the context of divisional cost-of-capital, because it has implications for the relationship between the cost-of-capital of business units or projects and the company cost-of-capital. Technically, cost-of-capital is a return measure. Thus, under the premise of value additivity and the view that a company group is a portfolio of business units, projects and assets, the same statistical principles as in Markowitz's (1952) portfolio selection theory can be applied. Just as in the case of a portfolio of securities, returns can be aggregated by calculating the average cost-of-capital weighted by the market value of the divisions.[11] This relationship is used in statistical tests of business unit betas and also in

---

[11] In practice and empirical research, corporate cost-of-capital is observable for listed companies, whereas the business unit cost-of-capital is not observable, so that the term "aggregate" is not meant to imply that corporate cost-of-capital is calculated from business unit cost-of-capital. The

Table 2.2 Aggregation of business unit cost-of-capital in the literature

Concept	Aggregation weight	Authors
(1) Beta aggregation	Market value of equity	Chua et al. (2006), Ehrhardt and Bhagwat (1991), Fuller and Kerr (1981), Kaplan and Peterson (1998)
(2) Total cost-of-capital aggregation	Market value of equity + debt	Harris et al. (1989)

particular techniques to determine business unit cost-of-capital, which will be addressed in Sect. 2.4.

The aggregation is theoretically applicable to the WACC as a whole or to individual parts of the WACC (for instance cost of debt, cost of equity or the beta factor). However, there are different implications in terms of weights and capital structure of the business units depending on which variables are considered. There is no diversification effect in the aggregation of systematic risk, since systematic risk depends on the correlation of the business unit's return to the overall market development and not to other business units.

In relevant cost-of-capital literature that is based on the value additivity principle, two versions of additivity of business unit cost-of-capital can be identified: The first one is *aggregation of betas* and the second is *aggregation of total cost-of-capital*. Table 2.2 shows which authors rely on which version in their empirical studies.

Total cost-of-capital can be aggregated to the corporate level using the business unit's market value of total capital—i.e. market value of debt and market value of equity—divided by the total company market value as a weight (see formula below) (Harris et al. 1989, p. 75).

$$WACC_C = \sum_{i=1}^{n} \frac{V_{BU\ i}}{V_C} * WACC_{BU\ i}$$

n   Number of business units
$V_{BU\ i}$ Market value of business unit i (equity + debt)
V_C Market value of company (equity + debt)
$WACC_C$ Company cost-of-capital
$WACC_{BU\ i}$ Cost-of-capital of business unit i

If only beta is aggregated, the business unit weight is the business unit's market value of equity divided by the total market value of equity (Brealey et al. 2009; Kaplan and Peterson 1998; Fuller and Kerr 1981).

---

purpose of this section is just to analyse the relationship between business unit and corporate cost-of-capital as a theoretical background to the determination techniques.

$$beta_C = \sum_{i=1}^{n} \frac{E_{BU\ i}}{E_C} * beta_{BU\ i}$$

beta Beta factor
E   Market value of equity
n   Number of business units

Although this is a slightly different procedure, the two approaches are coherent and thus both theoretically valid, since they arrive at the same result, which is also possible to show mathematically.

The explanations above show the relationship between company and business unit cost-of-capital according to the value additivity principle. However, this theory is not without its problems, especially when it comes to empirical testing or a practical application in a business context. First of all, many of the variables used in the model presented above are not observable. This concerns especially market values and betas of business units. This leads to the second problem: If business unit betas and market values are estimated with the help of the proxy methods that are the subject of this thesis, they are very unlikely to match with the empirically determined company cost-of-capital. Moreover, the capital structure of business units is regularly not known because debt is raised on a company group level. This issue will be dealt with in more detail in the subsequent section.

The author of this thesis is not aware of any explicit empirical tests of the value additivity principle in the context of company groups. However, as mentioned above, the theory is often implicitly tested if empirical tests of other models are based on it.

2.3.2 Capital Structure of Business Units

One of the main problems associated with business unit cost-of-capital is that the necessary information to perform the calculations shown in the theoretical framework above is not available on a business unit level but only on the corporate level. This does not only concern betas but also the capital structure to be used as weights in the calculation of the WACC. The reason why capital structure information is usually not available for business units is that financing decisions are made and capital is raised at the corporate level (Conroy and Harris 2011; Harris et al. 1989; Chua et al. 2006). While it is controversial whether capital structure adjustments in the beta factor are necessary (see Sect. 2.4.1.1), the capital structure is always needed for the calculation of the WACC.

In the literature, the following capital structure figures are suggested to be used for business units: (1) the company capital structure, (2) the business unit's target capital structure, (3) the industry capital structure and (4) a combination of company and industry capital structure.

(1) Company Capital Structure

The Schmalenbach-Gesellschaft (1996) considers acceptable the use of *company capital structure* as a proxy for business unit capital structure if the business units are not structured too heterogeneously. In contrast, Bower and Jenks (1972) consider an application of the company's overall financing structure to business units inappropriate. They emphasise the necessity of a differentiated treatment by showing analytically that failure to consider individual debt capacity leads to wrong cost-of-capital rates and thus wrong investment decisions.

(2) Target Capital Structure of Business Units

Another suggestion is the definition of a *target capital structure* for each business unit (Schmalenbach-Gesellschaft 1996; Pfister 2003). This idea originates from the notion that cost-of-capital should be forward-looking and thus also an optimal capital structure that can be realised in future should be used (see Sect. 2.1.1.2). A second argument in favour of this approach is that the observable capital structure is not necessarily the one desired by the company's financial managers, since the market value of equity is very volatile (Pfister 2003). This is a particularly relevant argument considering the high volatility of financial markets in the new millennium. In the definition of a target capital structure of business units, the capital structure of comparable companies (e.g. an industry capital structure) can be included as one factor. Moreover, typically an estimate of the current structure based on market values would be included in the analysis, as well as the financing strategy of the company (Schmalenbach-Gesellschaft 1996).

Although the approach is valid from a theoretical perspective and the argumentation in terms of a future orientation and the volatility of stock markets is evident, it might not be very suitable for practical application. First of all, there is no clear and universal method by which a target capital structure for business units should be determined. Secondly, it is hardly possible to objectively justify a target capital structure, so that there remains a lot of subjectivity and discretion in this determination.

(3) Industry Capital Structure

Another common suggestion in the literature is to use the typical *capital structure in the respective industry*. This approach implicitly assumes that the industry affiliation of a company is a significant determinant of capital structure, i.e. that there are significant differences in capital structure between industries. There are numerous empirical studies that confirm this relationship, although not all studies find that industry is a significant factor (Pfister 2003). Also, some articles that deal with cost-of-capital of business units make the assumption that there is an optimal debt-to-equity ratio for an industry (Kaplan and Peterson 1998; Ehrhardt and Bhagwat 1991). However, there are certainly differences between the companies within one industry, so that some kind of average value has to be calculated.

2.3 Cost-of-Capital in the Context of Company Groups

	company group	business unit A	business unit B
(1) debt according to industry debt ratios		1,000	500
(2) proportion of total company debt		67%	33%
(3) allocation of actual company debt with proportions	1,200 ➡	800	400

Fig. 2.11 Approach to debt allocation (own illustrated based on Chua et al. 2006)

The advantage of this approach is that it is objective and market-oriented (Pfister 2003). Furthermore, it can be integrated into a consistent methodology for the determination of business unit cost-of-capital if betas are applied with the help of the comparable company approach. On the other hand, a major drawback is that the approach completely ignores the company-specific situation. For instance, it might be favourable for a particular company for some reason to have a different overall financing structure than the theoretical optimum suggested by the industry capital structures. The assignment of industry figures to the business units would then mean that they no longer match the overall company target structure. Additionally, in an empirical application of the approach, observed values are used that are subject to volatility and thus do not meet the target structures of the industry and the company (Chua et al. 2006).

(4) Combination of Industry Capital Structure and Company Capital Structure

An approach that integrates *both industry capital structures and company capital structure* is presented by Chua et al. (2006). They argue that both should be taken into account because debt capacity depends on both the firm's inclination to finance with debt and the characteristics of the industry. They allocate corporate debt to the divisions as follows: First, they calculate the amount of debt that each business unit of a firm would be financed with according to the industry average debt ratios. Based on these debt amounts, they calculate which proportion of the company's total debt each business unit would assume. Next, this proportion is used to allocate the company's actual debt to the business units. This procedure is also illustrated in Fig. 2.11.

One of the advantages of the approach can be easily seen in the calculation above: The debt allocated to the business units matches total actual company debt. However, the problem of the determination of capital structure is not solved completely, since equity has not been allocated. Theoretically, equity could be allocated in the same way, but the problem of volatility still remains. This is due to the fact that the model operates with actual capital structure and not target capital structure.

As a conclusion to the treatment of capital structure in the calculation of business unit WACC, it can be said that there is no optimal approach. While using target capital structures is superior from a theoretical point of view, this approach has some weaknesses in terms of practical application. Therefore, an approach that includes some objective method such as industry capital structures is recommendable.

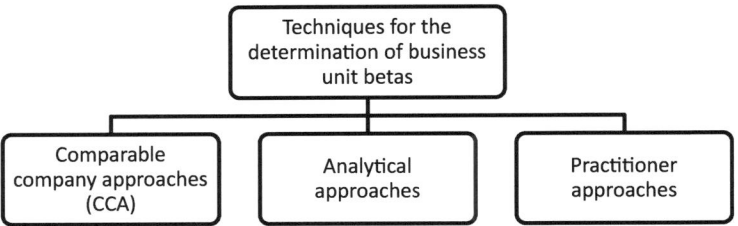

Fig. 2.12 Techniques for the determination of business unit betas (reproduced from Schlegel et al. 2012)

2.3.3 Cost-of-Capital of Business Units and Projects

The main challenge in estimating the cost-of-capital for a business unit is that the capital market data required for a regular determination of beta are not available (Chua et al. 2006; Ingram and Margetis 2010). The reason is that business units are normally not listed on the stock market, but only the company as a whole.

Due to the lack of data to calculate betas, proxy methods have to be used to estimate betas or the complete cost-of-capital rate of a business unit (Cotner and Fletcher 2000). In the literature, the techniques have often been classified as shown in Fig. 2.12 (Krotter 2009; Burger and Ulbrich 2005; Bufka et al. 2004). In the next sections, research concerning the three categories of methods will be discussed in detail.

The comparable company approaches as well as the analytical approaches are used to estimate *betas* of business units only, which can be used to calculate the cost-of-capital rate regularly by applying the CAPM and WACC. In contrast, some practitioner approaches intend to estimate the complete cost-of-capital rate. This has the advantage that no capital structure considerations have to be made for business units. On the other hand, estimating the complete rate is a rougher approach which is less scientific.

2.4 Determination Techniques for the Cost-of-Capital of Business Units

2.4.1 Comparable Company Approaches

2.4.1.1 Discussion of the Technique

The comparable company approach (CCA) was probably first mentioned in 1977 by Brigham and Van Horne (Pfister 2003). The basic idea is to use betas of listed companies that are comparable to the respective business unit as a surrogate for the beta of the business unit.

In German-language secondary literature, a distinction is sometimes made between *pure play betas*, which only use one comparable company, *industry*

2.4 Determination Techniques for the Cost-of-Capital of Business Units

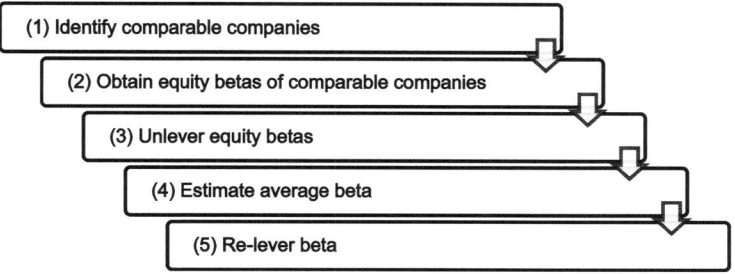

Fig. 2.13 Procedure of the comparable company approach (reproduced from Schlegel 2011)

betas, which use average betas of the respective industry sector, and *peer group betas*, which use several companies that are comparable in different characteristics (Schmalenbach-Gesellschaft 1996). However, there seems to be a confusion of definitions because the term *pure play* is used in original literature to describe companies that only have a single line of business, which does not mean that only one pure play can be used as a comparable company. In this thesis, the term 'pure play approach to cost-of-capital' is used according to the prevailing definition in the original American literature, i.e. using *one or more* companies that are only engaged in *one* line of business as comparable companies. This definition is, for instance, used by Fuller and Kerr (1981) and Chua et al. (2006).

The process of estimating a beta with the comparable company approach consists of five main steps (Bowman and Bush 2006). Below, the comparable company approach is explained and evaluated, taking into account results from empirical research for each step (see Fig. 2.13). An application of the approach in a case study can be found in Schlegel (2011).

(1) Identify Comparable Companies

The first step is to identify companies that are comparable in terms of systematic risk. Usually companies from the same industry are used as comparable companies (Fuller and Kerr 1981; Bowman and Bush 2006). Although this sounds easy, the first step is often a major problem in practice. The reason is that listed pure plays for business units can often not be found, depending on how specific the industry and how developed the capital market of the respective country is (Chua et al. 2006; Cummins and Phillips 2005). In Germany the stock market is comparably narrow (Bufka et al. 2004).

In narrow stock markets, where pure plays are hard to find, enhancements of the comparable company approach are useful that are able to include business units of multi-industry company groups as comparable companies. These approaches build on the relationship that the company beta is the weighted average of business unit betas. If the company betas of several multi-industry firms and the weights of their comparable business units are estimated, the determination of the business unit betas becomes a mere mathematical problem of solving the equations.

Boquist and Moore (1983) use a linear programming approach to solve the problem. However, as there are more comparable business units than companies in their sample, there is no unique optimal solution. Ehrhardt and Bhagwat (1991) propose an approach known as *full-information beta*, which uses multivariate linear regression to solve the problem. A similar approach using WACC instead of betas was applied earlier by Harris et al. (1989). However, empirical tests by Ehrhardt and Bhagwat (1991) and Chua et al. (2006) do not show that beta estimates improve significantly in the full-information approach compared to the standard approach.

Another problem in the selection of comparable companies is that there is a considerable amount of subjective judgment about which companies are comparable. Recently, Ingram and Margetis (2010) presented a method to form groups of comparable companies with the help of cluster analysis.

The third issue to be dealt with in the selection of comparable companies is the number of companies to include in the analysis. The inclusion of more companies reduces the impact of statistical outliers and estimation errors (Brealey et al. 2009; Schmalenbach-Gesellschaft 1996). However, there is a trade-off because the more companies are considered, the less comparable to the business unit they become (Bowman and Bush 2006; Pfister 2003).

(2) Obtain Equity Betas of Comparable Companies
In a second step, the equity betas of the comparable companies are estimated regularly according to the CAPM, as described in Sect. 2.1.2.1.

(3) Unlever Equity Betas and (5) Re-lever Betas
In theory, it is often suggested to adjust equity betas for differences in financial leverage with reference to Modigliani and Miller's (1958) famous propositions (Koller et al. 2005; Brealey et al. 2009). The idea behind adjusting betas for leverage is that the return on equity becomes more risky as debt increases. However, the return on assets—i.e. the return that the company makes from its business—without consideration of the capital structure is constant. Therefore, the measured *equity* betas are transformed into *asset* betas by unlevering them and subsequently transformed back to *equity* betas, taking into account the individual financing of the company.

Apparently, Hamada (1972) was the first to derive a formula for unlevering and relevering betas. Hamada's formula was further refined by Conine and Tamarkin (1985). In the meantime, a number of formulas to adjust betas for leverage based on different theories and assumptions have been presented. A good overview is given by Fernández (2006).

In different cost-of-capital studies, researchers try to measure the impact of leverage adjustment on the estimation accuracy of betas. However, there is no conclusive empirical evidence that adjusted business unit beta estimations are superior to unadjusted comparable company approach estimates. While Chua et al. (2006) find that capital structure adjustments improve beta estimates, Butler et al. (1991, p. 899) state that the "Hamada and Conine models may serve as useful pedagogical tools" but do not provide better beta estimates. Also Fuller and Kerr (1981) find that capital structure has no influence on betas.

(4) Estimate Average Beta

In cases where several comparable companies are used, an average asset beta is calculated after the equity betas have been unlevered. In empirical studies, some authors use the median asset beta (Fuller and Kerr 1981), while others use the arithmetic mean (Bowman and Bush 2006). Another approach could be to use an average weighted by the market values of the comparable companies.

2.4.1.2 Methodology of Empirical Tests

The determination techniques—also analytical and practitioner approaches—are tested with the help of large sample analysis of financial data such as stock price returns or financial statement data. Accounting and finance data can be acquired from large *databases* that are offered by several providers. One of the best-known commercial providers of financial data is COMPUSTAT, which offers historical financial data from 1950 onward for 99 % of all listed companies world-wide. There are also other well-known providers of accounting data, for instance Datastream, Company Analysis, Worldscope, Thomson Financial, Extel Financials, BvD Osiris, BvD BankScope and BvD Amadeus. For financial market data, the Center of Research for Security Prices (CRSP) is the most commonly used source besides COMPUSTAT (Lara et al. 2006).

The studies concerning cost-of-capital discussed below are cross-sectional studies. Typical *statistical methods* that are applied to the data are simple regression (Fuller and Kerr 1981) and multiple regression (Bowman and Bush 2006; Chua et al. 2006; Ehrhardt and Bhagwat 1991). The methods are applied in combination with parametric statistical tests, such as the Student's *t*-test to test the significant of individual factors in a multiple regression model (Ehrhardt and Bhagwat 1991; Bowman and Bush 2006), F-tests to compare the overall fit of different models (Bowman and Bush 2006) and two-tailed binomial tests (Ehrhardt and Bhagwat 1991), as well as non-parametric statistical tests such as the Wilcoxon rank sum test (Chua et al. 2006).

According to Serita (2008), the *advantage* of large sample analysis of financial data in general is that being secondary data, they are relatively easily accessible, which means that models can be tested with different datasets. In terms of databases, the articles discussed in this thesis usually only use one database. However, some authors, for instance Fuller and Kerr (1981), use data from several years for their analysis. Another advantage is the large sample sizes, which provide high levels of confidence, even if sophisticated econometric methods are used (Serita 2008).

One of the drawbacks of large sample analysis is that secondary data are used, which might not be tailored to the specific research problem. This means that proxies that are available in the data might have to be used instead of the required measures. Furthermore no information about the reasons or motivations for decisions and actions is available from the quantitative financial data (Serita 2008). Another problem is that there is a bias depending on which database is used. Lara et al. (2006) conduct research on the effects of database choice on research results in accounting. They run a simple regression of the book value of shareholders' equity and earnings against the market values of the companies over all firms from 14 European countries covered in the respective databases (Lara et al. 2006). The parameters differ substantially across the databases, which the authors explain by the fact that the final sample size varies substantially between the databases (2006). Finally, it can be criticised that the method relies on financial data only, which is often biased due to inherent problems in accounting information (Britzelmaier and Schlegel 2011) and market imperfections in stock market data (Brealey et al. 2009; Schlegel 2011). Due to the large amount of data available, there is a certain danger of finding patterns by chance or by data mining techniques (Brealey et al. 2009) so that deductive hypothesis testing and a sound theoretical foundation are crucial for rigorous research.

As "true" betas of *business units* are not observable, empirical tests of the comparable company approach typically involve a comparison of observable *company* betas of listed companies with the respective proxy betas derived from comparable companies. A major problem with empirical studies is that it is not possible to test the comparable company approach separately from other models or theories it is based on, i.e. if the comparable company approach is rejected, it cannot be said with certainty whether this was due to the comparable company approach itself or due to problems with underlying concepts. Difficulties that might influence empirical tests include the following:

- The comparable company approach is normally tested based on the *CAPM*, which is difficult to test and has a relatively poor empirical record itself.
- Some research designs for the general comparable company approach—especially the one by Fuller and Kerr (1981)—and all research designs for the full-information approach are based on the *value additivity principle*, which is only applicable under tight assumptions.

2.4.1.3 Empirical Tests of the Pure Play Approach

The first empirical test of pure play betas was conducted by Fuller and Kerr (1981) in the U.S. They matched the divisions of 60 multi-divisional companies with 142 pure plays using data from the years 1976, 1977 and 1978.

The researchers used data from Value Line, which is a commercial research and publishing firm that followed 1,700 companies at the time of the analysis. Their *methodology* was to compare regularly observed betas of multi-divisional firms—i.e. the company beta calculated from capital market data with the CAPM—to the company beta aggregated from the business units' betas, estimated with the help of the pure play technique. If there was more than one comparable company, the authors used the median. They then used simple linear regression analysis to check the relationship between the observed company betas and the proxy company betas calculated from the divisions' pure plays (Fuller and Kerr 1981).

2.4 Determination Techniques for the Cost-of-Capital of Business Units

The *findings* were a regression coefficient close to one and a correlation coefficient of 0.78, which corresponds to an r-square of 0.61. The authors also calculated the average relative deviation between the two variables, which was approximately 9 %. The deviations occurred in both directions, i.e. there was no pattern of systematic overestimation or underestimation by the proxy method (Fuller and Kerr 1981). The statistical indicators suggest that there is a strong relationship between the pure play betas and the "real" betas, which seems to empirically confirm the pure play approach as well as the value additivity principle. Consequently, Fuller and Kerr (1981) conclude that the pure play technique is a valid technique for determining betas of business units.

The findings of Fuller and Kerr are an important *contribution* to the field of cost-of-capital of business units because it was the first empirical test of the comparable company approach. The approach and its underlying assumptions—especially the value additivity principle—are theoretically supported, which further increases the credibility of the results. Moreover, it is positive that the authors follow a systematic approach based on criteria to select the pure plays.

Although the results suggest that the pure play approach is empirically valid, a *limitation* is that the authors leave aside the main problem of the approach—the identification of comparable companies. Form the 1,700 companies in the Value Line database, they only chose companies for which good pure plays with similar revenues could be found (Fuller and Kerr 1981). The results might have been less promising if less strict criteria for the selection had been applied, which is often necessary (and done) in practice.

Another empirical test of the CCA has been performed by Bowman and Bush (2006) using data from 2003 of 572 public U.S. companies with revenues larger than US$10 million. Besides testing the standard CCA, the authors also test two models that include additional variables—size, operating leverage, sales growth, dividend payout ratio, price to earnings ratio and book-to-market ratio—and compare the results of the different models. Moreover, a size bias in the selection of comparable companies and the influence of the number of comparable companies on the result are examined.

Due to the complexity and comprehensive nature of the research, the *methodology and findings* are discussed simultaneously for this paper in the following paragraphs (as opposed to sequentially as for the other papers).

The authors use data from the Bloomberg database. They use an industry classification that divides the economy into 73 industries (Bowman and Bush 2006). The test is only performed for 23 industries, as their approach requires a minimum number of companies per industry.

Like Fuller and Kerr (1981), the authors estimate betas with a comparable company approach for *listed* companies, which enables them to compare the beta proxies with the regularly observed betas. For each industry, four companies ("the control group") are used as comparable companies to estimate the betas of the other companies ("the test group"). The arithmetic mean asset beta of the four companies is used as a proxy beta for the companies of the respective industry (Bowman and Bush 2006). First, the companies are assigned to the control group according to the following procedure in order to avoid a size bias in the estimates: the total number of companies is divided into quartiles by size and the median company of each quartile is assigned to the control group (Bowman and Bush 2006).

In a first step, the authors present a new model that estimates the beta of a company depending on the comparable company beta but also on the size of the company, the operating leverage, sales growth, the dividend payout ratio, the price-to-earnings ratio and the book-to-market ratio. In order to estimate the parameters, a multiple regression approach is applied using the regularly observed company beta as the dependent variable and the factors mentioned above, including the comparable company beta, as independent variables (Bowman and Bush 2006).

$$\beta_{ij} = a + b_1\ \beta_{ccj} + b_2\ Size_i + b_3\ OL_i + b_4\ Growth_i \\ + b_5\ Div_i + b_6\ EP_i + b_7\ BTM_i + \varepsilon_{ij}$$

The regression model is found to be significant ($p = 0.001$) with an adjusted r-square of 0.518. Table 2.3 shows the coefficient and the p-value for the factors that are significant according to the t-statistics. Growth, operating leverage and book-to-market ratio are not significant or only marginally significant. It can be seen that the comparable company beta is highly significant with a positive coefficient, as expected. However, the coefficient is different from 1, which means that the comparable company beta alone would be an underestimate (Bowman and Bush 2006). The other significant factors have negative coefficients.

Bowman and Bush also test a variation of the model that only includes those factors that can be easily measured for private companies, with similar results.

In a second step, the models are evaluated by using them to estimate betas for the test companies and comparing the estimates to the observable betas. This is done by calculating the estimation error, i.e. the difference between the estimate and the observation. If the estimate is unbiased, the mean of the distribution errors should be zero or insignificantly different from zero (Bowman and Bush 2006). The estimation errors are compared for the following models:

- The *standard comparable company approach* with the *quartile median size* comparable companies (as explained above). The average estimation error for this approach is -0.0077, which is not significantly different from zero.
- The *standard comparable company approach* using the four *largest companies* from each industry as comparable companies. The reason for this variation is to examine the influence of a size bias in the estimates. It is known from the literature that size is negatively correlated with beta. The problem is that in practice, the public comparable companies that are used are usually larger than the private companies for which the betas are estimated (Bowman and Bush 2006). Indeed, the data shows an average estimation error of -0.479, i.e. a downward bias that is significant ($p = 0.001$) (Bowman and Bush 2006).
- The *new model 1*, which includes the comparable companies and all of the other factors listed above. The average estimation error is 0.0000 (Bowman and Bush 2006), which is obviously not significantly different from zero.

2.4 Determination Techniques for the Cost-of-Capital of Business Units

Table 2.3 Significant factors in the multiple regression (based on Bowman and Bush 2006)

Factor	Coefficient	p-value
Comparable company beta	0.855	0.001
Size	−0.019	0.050
Dividend payout	−0.108	0.050
Earnings-to-price ratio	−3.234	0.001

- The *new model 2*, which only includes those factors that can be measured for private companies with the same result as the new model 1.

To conclude the findings from the comparison of estimation errors, it can be said that the widespread use of the comparable company approach among practitioners is supported by the results. However, the size bias has to be kept in mind when applying the model. The two new models suggested by the authors appear to deliver even better estimates.

Another question that the authors address is how the number of companies included in the average to calculate the industry betas affects the result. Bowman and Bush test this relationship by reducing the number of companies in the control group to 3, 2 and 1 and comparing the estimates. The results suggest that the estimates improve with a larger number of comparable companies (Bowman and Bush 2006).

The article by Bowman and Bush provides a large *contribution to the body of knowledge* because it is a very comprehensive empirical evaluation of the comparable company approach. On the one hand, it provides further evidence for the empirical validity of the standard comparable company approach, which has not been tested in many previous empirical studies. On the other hand, a new model is presented and tested that improves estimates by taking into account other factors to adjust the comparable company betas. Moreover, the authors address issues that are relevant for application in practice: First of all, it is the first study that the author of this thesis is aware of that empirically examines the influence of the number of companies used to calculate the proxy betas. The authors show that the estimates improve as more companies are used. In the literature, a trade-off between less estimation error by including more companies and a better comparability by including less companies is spoken about (Pfister 2003), but no empirical evidence is presented. The second practice-relevant aspect of their research is the bias that is generated because listed comparable companies are often larger than the ones for which the beta is calculated. One the one hand, it is helpful to create awareness of the problem. On the other hand, the authors suggest an alternative model that reduces the bias.

One of the *limitations* of the article is that the alternative models that are proposed lack theoretical foundation. The authors derive the factors of the model from patterns in asset returns that have been noted in previous empirical research (Bowman and Bush 2006) without explaining why the patterns might occur. The problem is that with the large data availability in finance databases, it is possible to find patterns by chance. Therefore, it is important that empirical relationships are substantiated by theories. Concerning the influence of the number of companies included in the mean for the industry betas, it would have been interesting to see where the optimal number of companies is, because it can be expected that the statistical advantage reverses if the number of companies is getting too high. The maximum number of companies that the authors have tested is only 4.

2.4.1.4 Empirical Tests of the Full-Information Approach

Ehrhardt and Bhagwat (1991) introduce and empirically test their full-information approach for divisional beta estimation. With the full-information approach, divisions of multi-divisional firms can be used as comparable companies and not just pure plays that only operate in a single industry. They test the model with data from 1986 for 4,287 U.S. firms.

Methodology As discussed above, the full-information approach is based on the idea that the average of segment betas weighted by the segment values is equal to the company beta. Ehrhardt and Bhagwat reflect this idea in a multiple regression model in which the observable company beta is the dependent variable, the segment weights are the independent variables and the industry betas are the coefficients. The authors use the proportion of segment sales to total sales as a proxy for the segment weights (Ehrhardt and Bhagwat 1991).

$$\hat{a}_i = \sum_{j=1}^{n} \frac{S_j}{S_i} * \hat{a}_j + e_i$$

S   Sales
$\hat{a}_i$ Company beta
$\hat{a}_j$ Industry beta of segment j

The cross-sectional multiple regression is run with a final sample of 4,287 firms using data from the CRSP database. The industry classification is done according to the Standard Industrial Classification (SIC), truncating the four-digit codes to two digits, which is a simplification. Moreover, the estimation errors of the full-information betas are compared to those of the pure play betas. They also cross-validate the results with the help of a hold-out sample.

Findings The regression model is found to be highly significant, with an adjusted r-square of 0.69. Of the 70 industry beta estimates, four are not significant at $a = 0.05$. For the comparison with the pure play approach, 43.9 pure plays per segment (i.e. per industry) could be identified in the data in contrast to 99.8 full-information comparable betas. The authors apply a slightly different approach than Fuller and Kerr (1981) by using the arithmetic mean instead of the median if several

2.4 Determination Techniques for the Cost-of-Capital of Business Units

pure plays can be identified. Thus, for 64 % of the companies, the estimates have a tighter confidence interval in the full-information approach, which is statistically significant in a two-tailed binomial test. However, the difference in the average standard error, which is 18 % lower in the full-information approach, is not significant using a *t*-test. The test with the hold-out sample also produces a mean estimation error that is lower in the full-information approach, which again is not statistically significant (Ehrhardt and Bhagwat 1991).

Ehrhardt and Bhagwat's key *contribution* is above all the introduction of a new estimation technique that can take into account segments of listed companies as comparable companies. This could be helpful in economies with smaller stock markets, such as Germany, where comparable companies are often hard to find. The strength of the approach from a scientific point of view is that it is based on an existing theoretical foundation (the value additivity principle).

However, a major *limitation* is that the researchers cannot provide evidence that the approach produces significantly better results than the less complex pure play approach, which raises the question of whether the approach is necessary at all.

As well as Ehrhardt and Bhagwat (1991) themselves, Chua et al. (2006) have also empirically tested the full information beta approach. Their focus is to discuss different variations of the approach, such as different capital structure adjustments or different divisional weights, and compare them with each other and with the standard pure play approach. They use U.S. data from Research Insight (formerly Compustat) and CRSP from 1991 to 2001 (all companies with complete data).

The general *methodology* of Chua et al. is comparable to the approach followed by Ehrhardt and Bhagwat, i.e. using multiple regression to estimate the industry betas. However, they test 24 cross-sectional regression models with different combinations of the estimation technique for the observable beta, different leverage adjustments and different proxies for the divisional weight (Chua et al. 2006).

In a second step, they compare the accuracy of the different approaches and the pure play betas by testing how well they predict the divisional betas for 1 year ahead. To compare prediction accuracies, the authors use the mean square error measure. In order to make sure that there is any useful information in the methods, they also compare the results against a "naive prediction" beta of 1. They use a Wilcoxon rank sum test on a pair-wise basis to test the statistical significance of the differences (Chua et al. 2006).

The following *findings* have been obtained: The r-squares of the regression models are all between 0.2 and 0.25 which is relatively low compared to the other studies presented above. There are no significant differences in the goodness-of-fit measures between the various models tested (Chua et al. 2006). From the comparison of the prediction accuracy with the help of mean square errors, there are three main findings: First, adjusting for capital structure improves the beta estimates. Second, there are no significant differences when using different proxies for the divisional weight. The third finding—and the most interesting one for this thesis—is that the pure play approach provides better predictions than the full-information approach (Chua et al. 2006).

The most important *contribution* of the article is further evidence on the usefulness of the full-information approach since the results of Erhardt and Bhagwat are quite ambiguous (see above). Furthermore, they test different implementation possibilities for variables where other authors just use one proxy without further discussion—for instance, for the divisional weights.

There are also some *limitations* of the study. First of all, the detailed comparison of the models was only performed for one industry due to data availability issues. The results might not be transferable to other industries. A methodological problem might be that the future betas that the estimates were tested against are also estimates obtained by the same method, since the "real" divisional betas are not observable. That means that if there are systematic errors in the procedure, they are not detected, since they are also included in the comparable figure. Chua et al. (2006) furthermore raise the point that the test period includes the stock market crash from the year 2000, so the results might be distorted.

2.4.2 Analytical Approaches

2.4.2.1 Discussion of the Technique

Analytical approaches were intensely discussed in the 1970s and 1980s. The sheer number of papers published in these two decades shows that lots of attention was devoted to these approaches by academics. The basic idea behind all of the papers is the same. However, the empirical results concerning the approaches are ambiguous and diverse (see Sect. 2.4.2.3) and the practical relevance is very limited (see Sect. 3.3).

The determination of business unit cost-of-capital with analytical approaches, just like the comparable company approaches, is based on the CAPM (Pfister 2003). However, analytical approaches do not directly derive cost-of-capital from share price movements. Instead, fundamental factors—for instance accounting data—that are believed to influence share returns and thus systematic risk are used as a surrogate. The basic idea is that the fundamental factors are influenced by the same underlying events as the systematic risk (see Fig. 2.14). Therefore, they should be correlated with beta. If such a relationship can be shown, it is possible to use the fundamental data to derive systematic risk instead of stock returns. This procedure appears to make sense, since share prices depend on the fundamental factors in the long run (Jähnchen 2009). The relationship should ideally be analysed both theoretically and empirically.

Fig. 2.14 Relationship between fundamental factors and beta

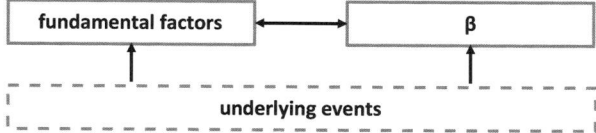

In the literature, analytical approaches are often sub-divided into earning betas, accounting betas and fundamental betas depending on which fundamental factors they use (Steinle et al. 2007; Pfister 2003).

- *Earning betas* use accounting-based profit measures.
- *Accounting betas* also include other accounting-based measures, such as operating leverage, financial leverage or liquidity.
- *Fundamental betas* include different kinds of fundamental factors of the company or its environment.

However, the wording is not used consistently among authors. For instance, Bowman (1979) and Beaver and Manegold (1975) use the term *accounting* beta for a measure derived from *earnings*. In this literature review, the categories are defined as outlined above.

Once a correlation between a fundamental factor and beta has been proven with a large sample, the respective factor can be used as surrogate of stock returns to calculate beta for an individual company. As no stock market data is needed, the approach is also suitable for non-listed business units of a firm. The basic principle is shown in the formula below using the example of earning beta and works the same way as a regular beta calculation.

$$beta_{earning,i} = \frac{cov\,(X_i X_m)}{var(X_m)}$$

beta   Earning beta factor
X_i Profit figure of company / business unit i
X_m Aggregated profit figure of the market / economy

As mentioned above, analytical approaches have not become the prevalent approach to determine cost-of-capital of business units. Notwithstanding, they have some advantages over the comparable company approach:

- Concerning a practical application, the approaches are suitable if **no listed comparable companies** are available. This is especially the case in smaller economies and in economies where the proportion of listed companies is smaller (Pfister 2003).

- Analytical approaches can also be used to **forecast** betas of companies. This is because companies generally do forecast accounting figures and because forecasting accounting data is easier than forecasting stock returns. Jähnchen (2009) presents models to predict betas in his doctoral thesis.
- Pfister (2003) furthermore argues that analytical approaches help to avoid statistical **measurement errors** that occur in a direct measurement of beta.

On the other hand, there are a number of reasons why analytical approaches are less suitable for practical application:

- First of all, there are **too many different fundamental factors** presented in studies and there seems to be no consensus on the relevant factors in empirical studies. Furthermore, it is questionable whether the determinants are the same for different companies (Krotter 2009; Burger and Ulbrich 2005). Pfister (2003) speculates that risk factors might depend on the industry sector.
- Not all factors that are identified in empirical studies can be explained with a sound **theory** (see Sect. 2.4.2.2).
- The assumption that the determinants of systematic risk might depend on the company or industry raises the question of **how a relationship should be verified** for the purpose of determining cost-of-capital. Can a general relationship that is shown in one or several studies be assumed to be correct for the case of a particular company? Or has the relationship to be proven for a particular industry?
- Another practical problem is the **availability of data**. While accounting data should be available for all companies, it is mostly only available monthly or quarterly, while betas are often estimated with monthly or weekly data, so that the time series for a regression might not be long enough (Pfister 2003).
- Moreover, accounting measures are often **biased measures** of a company's true performance and leave room for manipulation (Britzelmaier and Schlegel 2011).

As a conclusion about analytical approaches, it can be said that the basic idea seems to make sense but that the practical applicability is limited, since there is no agreement on the relevant factors and the exact procedure to measure a business unit's cost-of-capital.

2.4.2.2 Theoretical Research

The focus in the discussion of analytical approaches in this thesis is *not* a detailed discussion of each of the possible fundamental factors, but a general discussion of the technique and especially a discussion of the methodology in previous research. In terms of methodology, one can especially distinguish between *theory-based papers* and those based on *empirical data*.

In theory-based papers, the fundamental factors are derived from theoretical models and can subsequently be tested empirically (Pfister 2003). Papers are

2.4 Determination Techniques for the Cost-of-Capital of Business Units

Table 2.4 Theoretical derivation of relationship between beta and other variables

Author	Relationship with systematic risk (β)
Bowman (1979)	*Derived*: firm's leverage, earnings beta *Rejected*: earnings variability, dividends, size, growth
Conine (1982)	*Derived*: business risk (combination of operating leverage, risk in demand, risk in price level, risk in variable costs)
Gordon and Halpern (1974)	*Derived + tested*: earnings beta with growth rates
Lev (1974)	*Derived + tested*: operating leverage

classified as theoretical papers in this thesis if they engage in theory-building regardless of whether the theory is empirically tested in the same paper or not.

Table 2.4 lists examples of theoretical papers and the fundamental factors addressed. Some of the papers are only based on theoretical and analytical considerations and leave the empirical testing to other researchers (Bowman 1979; Conine 1982). Other authors theoretically explain factors and subsequently also empirically test the factors in a deductive approach (Gordon and Halpern 1974; Lev 1974).

Below, the papers by Bowman (1979) and Lev (1974) are briefly discussed as representatives of theoretical papers on analytical approaches.

Bowman (1979) deals with six factors that have shown a relationship with systematic risk (beta) in prior empirical research. He shows a theoretical relationship between leverage and earnings beta in an analytical *methodology*, i.e. by rearranging and combining formulas from existing theoretical models such as the CAPM and Hamada's (1972) leverage formula. His *findings* are that these two factors have a theoretical connection to systematic risk (Bowman 1979) but that other factors (earnings variability, dividends, size and growth) do not have a direct theoretical connection (Bowman 1979).

The *contribution* of the paper is to provide a theoretical basis for the large number of empirical papers that had been published in the years before and to integrate the previous research on the topic into existing accepted theoretical models.

A *limitation* of Bowman's explanations is that the question remains as to why the other factors have shown empirical relationships with systematic risk. He appears to be aware of this shortcoming and explains the limitation with two very general reasons (Bowman 1979, p. 624): The first one is that the "assumptions may not be applicable to the universe being tested". Secondly, he states that there may be measurement errors in empirical tests of the theoretical variables. Although these are valid points, there is still no satisfying explanation for significant relationships that have repeatedly been shown by different researchers. In his analysis, Bowman mainly operates within the boundaries and assumptions of existing theoretical models, where it might be necessary to extend the models or even establish completely new theories.

Lev (1974) analytically shows the relationship between operating leverage—i.e. the proportion of fixed and variable costs—and risk. Additionally, he tests the theory empirically for three homogeneous industries, namely the electrical utility industry, steel and oil production (Lev 1974).

In his *methodology*, Lev first analytically establishes a theoretical relationship between operating leverage and risk by integrating his formula of operating leverage into the CAPM. Subsequently, he tests the relationship empirically. As in the data obtainable from Compustat and CRSP, there is no information on the proportion of fixed and variable costs in total costs of the companies, the costs are split into their fixed and variable components first using a cross-sectional regression between costs and production output for each of the companies in the sample (Lev 1974). In a second step, the proportion of variable costs is used as an independent variable in a cross-sectional regression. The risk measures volatility and beta, which can be directly obtained from the databases, are the dependent variables (Lev 1974).

Lev's *findings* are that there is a positive association between the risk of a stock and the degree of operating leverage, i.e. the higher the proportion of fixed costs, the higher the risk. The theoretical relationship is as follows: There is a connection between a company's earnings (i.e. profit) and the stock returns, which is evident from classical capital market theory. Other things being equal, a higher proportion of fixed costs will cause a higher variability of earnings (Lev 1974). This is because in times with high sales, costs increase less because the variable part of total costs is comparably small and thus profit increases to a larger degree. The other way round, if sales are low in a bad year, if the fixed part is relatively high, total costs remain high and profit decreases to a larger degree. The relationship could also be shown to be significant at the 0.05 level in the cross-sectional regression. However, r-squares are comparably low (Lev 1974).

The *contribution* of the paper is that it analytically derives, theoretically explains and additionally empirically tests the relationship between operating leverage and risk. This is a rigorous deductive approach which only a few papers are able to present.

On the other hand, the paper also has some *limitations*. One is that the regression models implemented have very low r-squares ranging from 0.05 to 0.38. Even Lev himself (1974, p. 636) states that "it is evident that operating leverage is not the only (and may not even be the major) variable contributing to cross-sectional risk differentials". One reason for this might be the separation of total cost into its fixed and variable parts with the help of a regression model, which might be not very accurate. However, without internal data from the companies, it is probably not possible to do a more accurate calculation.

As an **evaluation of theoretical papers** in general, it can be said that the importance of theory to explain reality is uncontroversial (Colquitt and Zapata-Phelan 2007). In the specific case of analytical approaches, theoretical papers help to achieve a deeper understanding of the relationships between variables, instead of just showing a statistical correlation.

However, even the best theory should be subject to empirical testing. Therefore, a combination of theory and empiricism—either in a deductive or an inductive manner—is important. However, this does not necessarily mean that the same author has to deal with both parts.

2.4 Determination Techniques for the Cost-of-Capital of Business Units

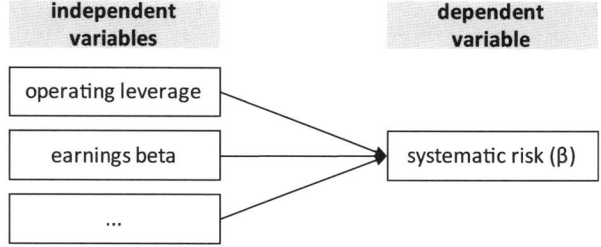

Fig. 2.15 Relationship between fundamental factors and beta

2.4.2.3 Empirical Research

In pure empirical papers on analytical approaches, the factors are determined intuitively or derived from the data (Pfister 2003). Some papers also test existing theories from other authors. As illustrated in Fig. 2.15, the empirical studies are usually based on univariate or multivariate regression using systematic risk (beta) as a dependent variable and the fundamental factors as independent variables (Bildersee 1975; Thompson 1976).

There are probably significantly more empirical papers than theoretical papers on the subject. Most of them are from the U.S. Table 2.5 lists some examples and the variables they have tested.

The table reveals that there are variables that appear several times—for example operating leverage—but also that there is a large variety of variables tested in the studies. The large number of variables shows the problem that was mentioned in the discussion of the analytical approach as a technique to determine cost-of-capital: It is far from clear which factors are relevant or more important than others.

So what is the **value of empirical papers**? On the one hand, theory-based authors claim that many empirical papers are "without theoretical justification" (Conine 1982, p. 199). Considering the large amount of financial data that is available in databases and the enormous computational power of contemporary statistical software, it has to be kept in mind that some of the empirically shown relationships might just have occurred by chance or with the help of data mining techniques. Brealey et al. (2009, p. 221) state in the context of research on stock investments that "if you look long and hard at past returns, you are bound to find some strategy that just by chance would have worked in the past". One of the papers presented above that can be criticised in this point is the one by Bildersee (1975), who uses a stepwise regression to find out the most important independent variables without testing hypotheses of specific relationships between variables (Bildersee 1975).

Because of this problem, it is important that there is a connection to theory. Colquitt and Zapata-Phelan (2007) also point out that many top journals in the field of management require authors to make a contribution to theory. Such a contribution to theory can either be done by *testing theory* or by *building theory*.

On the other hand, it has to be emphasised that not all of the empirical papers listed above operate without a theoretical background. For instance, Beaver and

Table 2.5 Empirical papers on the relationship of accounting variables with beta

Author	Independent variables
Ball and Brown (1969)	Operating income
Beaver et al. (1970)	Payout, growth, leverage, liquidity, size, earnings variability, earnings beta
Beaver and Manegold (1975)	Earnings beta
Bildersee (1975)	Financial leverage, liquidity, efficiency, coverage of fixed obligations
Steiner and Bauer (1992)	Profit variability, accounting beta, sales variability, sales beta, operating profit variability, operating profit beta, equity variability, return on equity beta, debt/equity ratio, financial leverage, machine intensity, operating leverage, dividend yield, balance sheet total, balance sheet total growth
Thompson (1976)	Dividend beta, earnings beta, earnings multiple beta, earnings yield beta, operating income, sales beta, total debt to total assets beta, cash flow to total debt beta, pre-tax interest coverage beta, current ratio beta, working capital to total assets beta, cash and receivables to expenditures for operations beta, dividend variance, earnings variance, earnings multiple variance, earnings yield variance, operating income variance, sales variance, total debt to total assets variance, cash flow to total debt variance, pre-tax interest coverage variance, current ratio variance, working capital to total assets variance, cash and receivables to expenditure for operations variance, dividend payout, growth in assets, growth in sales, growth in earnings, growth measures as mean of the factors, ratio of investments to earnings, return on investment, market volume, different means of annual ratios, size
Toms et al. (2005)	Operating leverage, financial leverage

Manegold (1975) refer to other authors as a theoretical background, although they do not *build* theory and thus their work is classified as empirical paper in this thesis. Furthermore, even if empirical papers have no link to theory at all, they might motivate other researchers to find economic interpretations or build a theory that fits the data. For instance, Bowman's (1979) theoretical paper appears to be motivated by previous empirical papers. This can be understood as a kind of "division of labour" in an inductive approach. In any case, the necessity of empirical research with its statistical power and the importance of testing theories against reality are uncontroversial.

2.4.3 Practitioner Approaches

2.4.3.1 Traditional Practitioner Approaches

Besides the 'academic' approaches presented above, there are a number of techniques that have mainly been developed by practitioners. In this section, the traditionally applied approaches *management interviews* and the *build-up method* are briefly discussed and evaluated. It is concluded that these approaches are to be rejected from a scientific point of view.

Management interviews can be used to make managers estimate the risk of their business unit. A way to make this process more objective is to make managers estimate the risk relative to other industries and to determine the risk based on the betas of the selected industries. This can be made even more effective by not stating the betas in advance (Pfister 2003). The advantage of such an approach is that it can be applied intuitively and is likely to be accepted by the managers. Moreover, only a small amount of publicly available data is needed (industry betas). However, even if a more objective procedure with a relative estimation of risk is chosen, there remains a substantial amount of subjectivity in the approach, since risk is measured by intuition rather than measurable criteria. Additionally, if business unit managers are asked to evaluate the risk, they are not neutral because the cost-of-capital estimate is likely to influence capital allocation to their business unit and the evaluation (and possibly remuneration) by value-based performance measures. They are thus expected to behave opportunistically in the estimation. Therefore, this approach has to be rejected.

In the **build-up method**, different risk surcharges are added to the risk-free rate in order to account for the higher risk. Examples of surcharges are a general equity risk premium, a firm size premium and an industry premium (Pratt 2002). Just like the management interview method, an advantage of this method is its easy application due to its minimal complexity and data requirements. The problem with the method is not the surcharges per se—the CAPM also uses surcharges to the risk-free rate based on beta. The problematic point of the build-up method is that the surcharges are usually added subjectively and lack theoretical justification. Moreover, typically the surcharges include unsystematic risk. This can be argued to be adequate (see Sect. 2.1.2.3) but if unsystematic risk is taken into account, the cost-of-capital figure is not a proxy of a CAPM measure.

2.4.3.2 Criteria-Based Approaches

Besides the traditional approaches discussed above, there are also more systematic methods that have been developed by practitioners or explicitly for a practical application. Two commonly discussed approaches are the ones developed by the *Boston Consulting Group*[12] and *Fuqua Industries* (Gup and Norwood 1982). Both approaches are based on an adjustment of the company total cost-of-capital depending on the specific characteristics of the business units measured in a scoring model.

---

[12] According to Pfister (2003) the approach was first published by Lewis and Stelter (1994) in Germany.

		Value	
Criteria	Low risk	1 2 3 4 5	High risk
Control	Low external influence on return		High external influence on return
Market	Stable, without cycles		Dynamic, cyclical
Competitors	Few, constant market shares		A lot, variable market shares
Products/concepts	Long life cycle, no substitutes		Short life cycle, substitutes
Barriers to entry	High		Low
Cost structure	Low fixed cost		High fixed cost

Fig. 2.16 Scoring model in Boston consulting group approach (reproduced from Bufka et al. 2004)

In the approach used by the **Boston Consulting Group (BCG)**, the management of each business unit is asked to rate the riskiness of the business unit. As shown in Fig. 2.16, the rating is based on six criteria on a scale from 1 (low risk) to 5 (high risk). The reference value of 3 represents the risk of a company group as a whole for each criterion (Pfister 2003).

The values assigned to the criteria are subsequently added up to achieve a total score. This score is divided by 18 in order to calculate a factor by which the company cost-of-capital is multiplied to receive the business unit's cost-of-capital, as shown in the formula below (Pfister 2003). The reason why it is divided by 18 is that a business unit with average risk (i.e. with the company risk) is rated 3 for each of the six criteria ($6 * 3 = 18$). So, the average business unit has a factor of 1, i.e. the company cost-of-capital.

$$WACC_{BU\ i} = WACC_C * \frac{Score\ BU\ i}{18}$$

$WACC_{BU\ i}$ Cost-of-capital of business unit i
$WACC_C$ Company cost-of-capital

The advantage of adjusting the company group cost-of-capital is that no capital structure has to be explicitly assigned to the business units. It is implicitly assumed that the capital structure of the company group applies to all business units—with all its pros and cons. The criteria seem plausible in terms of their ability to explain systematic risk. Indeed, an independent[13] empirical study (Bufka et al. 2004) concludes that the approach is able to explain systematic risk to a certain degree.

On the other hand, it is not clear how the criteria were developed and what the exact theoretical relationship with systematic risk should be. The major problem of

---

[13] One of the study's authors even works for a competitor of Boston Consulting Group (Roland Berger Strategy Consultants) and the method is still evaluated positively, which is an indication of independence.

the approach is probably the assignment of values to the criteria, since the criteria are quite abstract and have to be operationalized. Therefore, considerable subjectivity remains in the approach. From a scientific point of view, it could also be questioned if the relationship between the score and the WACC is really proportional. However, this assumption is probably sufficient.

The approach by Gup and Norwood (1982)—commonly known as the **Fuqua industries approach**—also includes subjective risk assessment based on criteria and a scale from 1 to 5, like the Boston Consulting Group approach. It contains 14 criteria (Gup and Norwood 1982). However, there is also an objective risk assessment that measures the risk based on the variability of profit (NOPAT) compared to the previous year and also to the budgeted profit of the period. The subjective and the objective risk are weighed 50 % each to calculate the final risk class of the business unit (Gup and Norwood 1982).

The risk class of each business unit is translated into a risk index that is multiplied by the company cost-of-capital, as in the BCG approach. However, the difference is that the score is translated into a factor with the help of a table that has been derived from an analysis of comparable companies conducted by Fuqua Industries management (Gup and Norwood 1982).

While this approach might have been suitable for the specific situation of Fuqua Industries, it is very questionable whether it can be transferred to other companies, especially due to the fact that the translation table to derive the multiplication factor from the risk assessment has been compiled specifically for Fuqua Industries. Moreover, the complex calculation of a composite risk measure including its weights and its translation into a risk factor seems arbitrary, since no theoretical or empirical justification is demonstrated by the authors. Also the individual factors in the risk measures can be questioned. For instance, the deviation of profit from plan figures is no valid indicator for risk—or even systematic risk. A deviation might just have been caused because the plan was bad. Furthermore, the points of criticism mentioned for the BCG approach, such as the subjectivity in rating the criteria, are also true for this approach. This rather negative evaluation of the approach is confirmed by the empirical results of Bufka et al. (2004), which are presented in the subsequent section.

2.4.3.3 Empirical Tests of Practitioner Approaches

Practitioner approaches have not been subject to many empirical tests. The only one that the author is aware of is the study by Bufka et al. (2004).The authors empirically test the BCG method and the Fuqua industries method using data from 1997 for 87 German listed companies from the manufacturing sector and also capital-intense firms from the service sector.

The researchers apply the following *methodology*: To measure the criteria (risk factors) that are included in the BCG and the Fuqua industries method, they use data from a questionnaire survey. The consolidated risk measures from the survey are then used as an explanatory variable in four different regression equations. Beta and book-to-market ratio are used as dependent variables. Moreover, the factors company size, stock market trading volume and degree of diversification are included into the model as explanatory variables (Bufka et al. 2004).

The *findings* suggest that the BCG method is useful to estimate betas. In a version of the regression that only includes homogeneous companies (pure plays), the regression has an adjusted r-square of 0.35, which is significant at the 0.01 level. The risk index itself is significant at the 0.05 level (Bufka et al. 2004). However, the Fuqua industries method had to be rejected, since it has a statistically significant negative relationship with beta (2004). In order for the approach to make sense, the relationship should be positive. The authors also ran a regression of the individual criteria that aggregate into the risk measure of the BCG method. Apparently, the results indicate that not all the criteria are relevant. Unfortunately, the exact results are not reported.

The work of Bufka et al. is an important *contribution* to the field of divisional cost-of-capital, since it provides first empirical results on the validity of the heuristic-based methods that have been developed and are used by practitioners.

A *limitation* of the article is that the researchers do not disclose the detailed results of the second regression, which takes into account the individual criteria. This would have been helpful for other researchers and for practitioners to improve the technique.

2.5 Conclusion

In this chapter, a large range of theoretical and empirical literature from the field of cost-of-capital was discussed. First of all, the theoretical background of company cost-of-capital determination with the WACC and the CAPM was dealt with. Moreover, the main fields of applications of cost-of-capital in Managerial Finance—capital allocation and capital budgeting as well as performance measurement and value-based management—were addressed.

One of the main findings in this section was that different hurdle rates must be used for business units or projects that differ from average risk in order that companies can make value-creating decisions. Moreover, the theoretical background of cost-of-capital in the context of company groups was pointed out, before determination techniques for business unit cost-of-capital were discussed in detail.

As explained in the introductory section of this chapter, no identification of research gaps will be made at this point. Instead, research gaps are identified at the end of Chap. 3 for the immediate topic of this thesis.

References

Adjaoud F, Chafri D, Chourou L (2011) Corporate governance and investment decisions. In: Baker HK, English P (eds) Capital budgeting valuation. Financial analysis for today's investment projects. Wiley, Hoboken, NJ, pp 37–56

André J, Brüggen A, Moers F (2009) Divisional rent-seeking, stock options and the quality of internal capital allocation. Working paper available from SSRN

Ang JS, Clark JA (1997) The market valuation of bank shares: with implications for the value additivity principle. Financ Markets Inst Instrum 6(5):1–23

Anthony RN (1973) Accounting for the cost of equity. Harv Bus Rev 51:88–102

Armstrong CS, Core JE, Taylor DJ, Verrecchia RE (2011) When does information asymmetry affect the cost of capital? J Account Res 49(1):1–38

Arnold G (2008) Corporate financial management. Financial Times Prentice Hall, Harlow

Arnold T, Nixon T (2011) Alternative methods of evaluating capital investments. In: Baker HK, English P (eds) Capital budgeting valuation. Financial analysis for today's investment projects. Wiley, Hoboken, NJ, pp 79–94

Athanassakos G (2007) Value-based management, EVA and stock price performance in Canada. Manag Decis 45(9):1397–1411

Atrill P (2009) Financial management for decision makers. Financial Times Prentice Hall, Harlow

Baker HK, Singleton JC, Veit ET (2011) Survey research in corporate finance. Bridging the gap between theory and practice. Oxford University, Oxford

Ball R, Brown P (1969) An empirical evaluation of accounting income numbers. J Account Res 6(2):300–323

Baran L, King THD (2012) Cost of equity and S&P 500 index revisions. Financ Manag 41(2):457–481

Barth ME, Konchitchki Y, Landsman WR (2013) Cost of capital and earnings transparency. J Account Econ 55(2–3):206–224

Beaver W, Manegold J (1975) The association between market-determined and accounting-determined measures of systematic risk: some further evidence. J Financ Quant Anal 10(2):231–284

Beaver W, Kettler P, Scholes M (1970) The association between market determined and accounting determined risk measures. Account Rev 10(2):654–682

Berk JB, DeMarzo PM (2011) Corporate finance. Pearson, Boston, MA

Berkman H (2013) The capital asset pricing model: a revolutionary idea in finance! Abacus 49:32–35

Besley S, Brigham EF (2008) Essentials of managerial finance. Thomson/South-Western, Mason, OH

Bierman H (2010) An introduction to accounting and managerial finance. A merger of equals. World Scientific, Hackensack, NJ

Bildersee JS (1975) The association between a market-determined measure of risk and alternative measures of risk. Account Rev 50(1):81–98

Black C, Parry J, Anderson H, Bennett JA (2002) Are New Zealand chief financial officers the 'country cousins' of their American counterparts? Univ Auckl Bus Rev 4(1):1–11

Block S (2005) Are there differences in capital budgeting procedures between industries? An empirical study. Eng Econ 50(1):55–67

Bloomfield R, Fischer PE (2011) Disagreement and the cost of capital. J Account Res 49(1):41–68

Boquist JA, Moore WT (1983) Estimating the systematic risk of an industry segment: a mathematical programming approach. Financ Manag 12(4):11–18

Borchers S (2006) Beteiligungscontrolling—ein Überblick. Z Plan Unternehmenssteuerung 17:233–255

Borgman RH, Strong RA (2006) Growth rate and implied beta: interactions of cost of capital models. J Bus Econ Stud 12(1):1–11

Boubakri N, Guedhami O, Mishra D, Saffar W (2012) Political connections and the cost of equity capital. J Corp Financ 18(3):541–559

Bower RS, Jenks JM (1972) Divisional screening rates. Financ Manag 4(3):42–49

Bowman RG (1979) The theoretical relationship between systematic risk and financial (accounting) variables. J Financ 34(3):617–630

Bowman RG, Bush SR (2006) Using comparable companies to estimate the betas of private companies. J Appl Financ 16(2):71–81

Brailsford T (2007) Investments concepts and applications. Thomson Australia, Melbourne

Brealey RA, Myers SC, Allen F (2009) Principles of corporate finance. McGraw-Hill, Boston, MA

Brigham EF (1975) Hurdle rates for screening capital expenditure proposals. Financ Manag 4(3):17–26

Brigham EF, Ehrhardt MC (2005) Financial management. Theory and practice. Thomson/South-Western, Mason, OH

Brigham EF, Houston JF (2009) Fundamentals of financial management. South-Western Cengage Learning, Mason, OH

Britzelmaier B (2009) Kompakt-Training wertorientierte Unternehmensführung. Kompakt-Training praktische Betriebswirtschaft. Kiehl, Ludwigshafen (Rhein)

Britzelmaier B (2010) Wertorientierte Unternehmensführung europäischer Kapitalgesellschaften. Eine Untersuchung der Geschäftsberichte der Dow Jones Stoxx 50-Unternehmen. In: Pforzheimer Forschungsberichte, vol 10

Britzelmaier B (2013) Controlling. Grundlagen—Praxis—Umsetzung. Pearson, Munich

Britzelmaier B, Schlegel D (2011) An analysis of dysfunctions and biases in financial performance measures. Glob Bus Econ Rev 13(3/4):269–280

Bufka J, Kemper O, Schiereck D (2004) A note on estimating the divisional cost of capital for diversified companies: an empirical evaluation of heuristic-based approaches. Eur J Financ 10(1):68–88

Burger A, Ulbrich PR (2005) Beteiligungscontrolling. Oldenbourg, München

Burns MR (1987) New evidence on the value additivity principle. J Financ Quant Anal 22(1):65–77

Butler KC, Mohr RM, Simonds RR (1991) The Hamada and Conine leverage adjustments and the estimation of systematic risk. J Bus Financ Account 18(6):885–901

Câmara A, Chung SL, Wang YH (2009) Option implied cost of equity and its properties. J Futur Mark 29(7):599–629

Chen H, Chen JZ, Lobo GJ, Wang Y (2011) Effects of audit quality on earnings management and cost of equity capital: evidence from China. Contemp Account Res 28(3):892–925

Chong J, Phillips MG (2012) Measuring risk for cost of capital: the downside beta approach. J Corp Treas Manage 4(4):344–352

Chua J, Chang PC, Wu Z (2006) The full-information approach for estimating divisional betas: implementation issues and tests. J Appl Finance 16(1):53–61

Colquitt JA, Zapata-Phelan CP (2007) Trends in theory-building and theory-testing: a five-decade case study of the academy of management journal. Acad Manag J 50(6):1281–1303

Conine TE Jr (1982) On the theoretical relationship between business risk and systematic risk. J Bus Finance Account 9(2):199–205

Conine TE Jr, Tamarkin M (1985) Divisional cost of capital estimation: adjusting for leverage. Financ Manag 14(1):54–58

Conroy RM, Harris RS (2011) Estimating capital costs: practical implementation of theory's insights. In: Baker HK, Martin GS (eds) Capital structure and corporate financing decisions. Theory, evidence, and practice. Essential perspectives. Wiley, Hoboken, NJ, pp 191–210

Cotner JS, Fletcher HD (2000) Computing the cost of capital for privately held firms. Am Bus Rev 18(2):27–33

Cummins DJ, Phillips RD (2005) Estimating the cost of equity capital for property-liability insurers. J Risk Insur 72(3):441–478

Damodaran A (2011) Applied corporate finance. Wiley, Hoboken, NJ

Danielson MG, Heck JL, Shaffer DR (2008) Shareholder theory—how opponents and proponents both get it wrong. J Appl Finance 18(2):62–66

Dempsey M (2013) The capital asset pricing model (CAPM): the history of a failed revolutionary idea in finance? Abacus 49:7–23

Duchin R, Sosyura D (2011) Divisional managers and internal capital markets. Ross School of Business Working Paper, vol 1144

Ehrhardt MC, Bhagwat YN (1991) A full-information approach for estimating divisional betas. Financ Manag 20(2):60–69

Emery DR, Finnerty JD, Stowe JD (2004) Corporate financial management. Pearson/Prentice Hall, Upper Saddle River, NJ

Epstein BJ (2010) Wiley IFRS 2010. Interpretation and application of international financial reporting standards. Wiley, Indianapolis, NJ

Erasmus PD, Lambrechts IJ (2006) EVA and CFROI: a comparative analysis. Manag Dyn 15(1):14–26

Fabozzi FJ, Drake PP (2009) Finance: capital markets, financial management, and investment management. Wiley, Hoboken, NJ

Fama EF, French KR (1992) The cross-section of expected stock returns. J Financ 47(2):427–465

Fama EF, French KR (1993) Common risk factors in the returns of stocks and bonds. J Financ Econ 33(1):3–56

Fama EF, French KR (2004) The capital asset pricing model: theory and evidence. J Econ Perspect 18(3):25–46

Fernández P (2006) Levered and unlevered beta. Available at http://www.iese.edu/research/pdfs/DI-0488-E.pdf

Fuller RJ, Kerr HS (1981) Estimating the divisional cost of capital: an analysis of the pure-play technique. J Financ 36(5):997–1009

Gaspar JM, Massa M (2011) The role of commonality between CEO and divisional managers in internal capital markets. J Financ Quant Anal 46(3):841–869

Gebhardt WR, Lee CMC, Swaminathan B (2001) Toward an implied cost of capital. J Account Res 39(1):135–176

Gordon MJ, Halpern PJ (1974) Cost of capital for a division of a firm. J Financ 29(4):1153–1164

Gormley TA, Matsa DA, Milbourn T (2013) CEO compensation and corporate risk: evidence from a natural experiment. J Account Econ 56(2/3):79–101

Gup BE, Norwood SW (1982) Divisional cost of capital: a practical approach. Financ Manag 11(1):20–24

Guserl R, Pernsteiner H (2011) Finanzmanagement. Grundlagen—Konzepte—Umsetzung. Lehrbuch. Gabler, Wiesbaden

Hamada RS (1972) The effect of the firm's capital structure on the systematic risk of common stock. J Financ 27(2):435–452

Harris RS, O'Brien TJ, Wakeman D (1989) Divisional cost-of-capital estimation for multi-industry firms. Financ Manag 18(2):74

Hillier D, Ross SL, Westerfield R, Jaffe JF, Jordan BD (2010) Corporate finance. McGraw-Hill, London

Hoffjan A (2009) Internationales controlling. Schäffer-Poeschel, Stuttgart

Horváth P (2006) Controlling. Vahlens Handbücher der Wirtschafts- und Sozialwissenschaften. Vahlen, München

Huch B, Behme W, Ohlendorf T (2004) Rechnungswesen-orientiertes Controlling. Ein Leitfaden für Studium und Praxis. Physica-Lehrbuch. Physica-Verlag, Heidelberg

Hughes JS, Liu J, Liu J (2007) Information asymmetry, diversification and the cost of capital. Account Rev 82(3):705–729

Ingram M, Margetis S (2010) A practical method to estimate the cost of equity capital for a firm using cluster analysis. Manag Financ 36(2):160–167

Ionici O, Small K, D'Souza F (2011) Cost of capital. An introduction. In: Baker HK, English P (eds) Capital budgeting valuation. Financial analysis for today's investment projects. Wiley, Hoboken, NJ, pp 339–362

Jähnchen S (2009) Kapitalkosten von Versicherungsunternehmen. Fundamentale Betafaktoren als ein Erklärungsbeitrag zur Erfassung der Renditeforderungen der Eigenkapitalgeber. Gabler, Wiesbaden

Jensen MC, Meckling WH (1976) Theory of the firm: managerial behavior, agency costs and ownership structure. J Financ Econ 3:305–360

Kaplan PD, Peterson JD (1998) Full-information industry betas. Financ Manag 27(2):85–93

Karake-Shalhoub Z, Petty JR (2002) Trust and loyalty in electronic commerce: an agency theory perspective. Greenwood, Santa Barbara, CA

Kasperzak R, Wassermann H (2009) "Goodwill-controlling nach IAS 36", Perspektiven des Strategischen Controllings. In: Reimer M, Krystek U (eds) Festschrift für Prof. Dr. Ulrich Krystek. Gabler Research. Gabler, Wiesbaden, pp 119–136

Khan MY, Jain PK (2007) Financial management. Tata McGraw-Hill, New Delhi

Koller T, Goedhart MH, Wessels D, Copeland TE (2005) Valuation. Measuring and managing the value of companies. Wiley, Hoboken, NJ

KPMG International (2013) Kapitalkostenstudie 2012/2013. Steuerung in der Unsicherheit. Available from http://www.kpmg.de

Krotter S (2009) Performance-Messung, Erwartungsänderungen und Analystenschätzungen. Theoretische Konzeption und empirische Umsetzung. Schriften zum Controlling, Finanz- und Risikomanagement, 2nd edn. Frankfurt am Main: Lang, Berlin

Laier R (2011) Value reporting. Analyse von Relevanz und Qualität der wertorientierten Berichterstattung von DAX-30 Unternehmen. Gabler, Wiesbaden

Lambert RA, Leuz C, Verrecchia RE (2012) Information asymmetry, information precision, and the cost of capital. Eur Finan Rev 16(1):1–29

Lara JMG, Osma BG, de Noguer BGA (2006) Effects of database choice on international accounting research. Abacus 42(3/4):426–454

Laughhunn DJ, Payne JW, Crum R (1980) Managerial risk preferences for below-target returns. Manag Sci 26(12):1238–1249

Laverty KJ (1996) Economic short-termism: the debate, the unresolved issues, and the implications for management practice and research. Acad Manag Rev 21(3):825–860

Lev B (1974) On the association between operating leverage and risk. J Financ Quant Anal 9 (4):627–641

Lewis TG, Stelter DM (1994) Steigerung des Unternehmenswertes. Total Value Management. Landsberg/Lech: Verl. Moderne Industrie

Lintner J (1965) The valuation of risk assets and the selection of risky investments in stock portfolios and capital budgets. Rev Econ Stat 47(1):13–37

Lumby S, Jones C (2011) Corporate finance. Theory and practice. Cengage Learning, Andover

Maher M, Stickney CP, Weil RL (2012) Managerial accounting. An introduction to concepts, methods and uses. South-Western Cengage Learning, Mason, OH

Markowitz H (1952) Portfolio selection. J Financ 7(1):77–91

Matschke MJ, Brösel G (2007) Unternehmensbewertung. Funktionen—Methoden—Grundsätze. Gabler, Wiesbaden

McGowan CB, Rifon D (2011) A test for multi-risk premia internation asset pricing model: an arbitrage pricing theory application. J Appl Bus Res 4(2):53–60

McNulty JJ, Yeh TD, Schulze WS, Lubatkin MH (2002) What's your real cost of capital? Harv Bus Rev 80(10):114–121

Megginson W, Smart S, Lucey B (2008) Introduction to corporate finance. Cengage Learning EMEA, London

Merchant KA, Van der Stede WA (2007) Management control systems: performance measurement, evaluation and incentives. Prentice Hall, Essex

Miller RA (2009a) The weighted average cost of capital is not quite right. Q Rev Econ Finance 49:128–138

Miller RA (2009b) The weighted average cost of capital is not quite right: reply to M. Pierru. Q Rev Econ Finance 49:1213–1218

Modigliani F, Miller MH (1958) The cost of capital, corporation finance and the theory of investment. Am Econ Rev 48(3):261–297

Ng Wee L, Hickey L (2009) Asset valuation and impairment. Chart Account J 88(11):41

O'Byrne SF (1997) EVA and shareholder return. Finance Pract Educ 7(1):50–54

Perold AF (2004) The capital asset pricing model. J Econ Perspect 18(3):3–24

Perridon L, Steiner M (2007) Finanzwirtschaft der Unternehmung. Vahlen, München

Petersen C, Plenborg T, Schøler F (2006) Issues in valuation of privately held firms. J Priv Equity 10(1):33–48

Pfister C (2003) Divisionale Kapitalkosten. Theorie und Anwendung. Bank- und finanzwirtschaftliche Forschungen, 349th edn. Haupt, Bern

Pollard M (2008) Mean-variance efficiency and the capital assets pricing model. Available from http://www.docstoc.com/docs/14916930/Mean-Variance-Efficiency-and-the-Capital-Asset-Pricing-Model

Porter ME (1998) On competition. Harvard Business School, Boston, MA

Pratt SP (2002) Cost of capital. Estimation and applications. Wiley, New York, NY

Rapp MS, Schellong D, Schmidt M, Wolff M (2011) Considering the shareholder perspective: value-based management systems and stock market performance. Rev Manag Sci 5(2–3):171–194

Rappaport A (1986) Creating shareholder value. The new standard for business performance. Collier Macmillan, London

Roll R (1977) A critique of the asset pricing theory's tests. Part I: On past and potential testability of the theory. J Financ Econ 4:129–176

Roll R, Ross S (1984) The arbitrage pricing theory approach to strategic portfolio planning. Financ Anal J 4(3):14–26

Ross S (1976) The arbitrage theory of capital asset pricing. J Econ Theory 13(3):341–360

Ross SA, Westerfield R, Jaffe JF (2008a) Corporate finance. McGraw-Hill/Irwin, Boston, MA

Ross SA, Westerfield R, Jaffe JF (2008b) Modern financial management. McGraw-Hill/Irwin, Boston, MA

Ryan HE, Trahan EA (2007) Corporate financial control mechanisms and firm performance: the case of value-based management systems. J Bus Financ Account 34(1–2):111–138

Schall LD (1972) Asset valuation, firm investment, and firm diversification. J Bus 45(1):11–28

Scharfstein DS, Stein JC (2000) The dark side of internal capital markets: divisional rent-seeking and inefficient investments. J Financ 55(6):2537–2564

Schlegel D (2008) The valuation of patents—a comparison of methods. World J Manage Econ 2(3):3–10

Schlegel D (2011) Subsidiary controlling with strategically aligned performance measurement systems. Eul Verlag, Lohmar

Schlegel D (2014) A comparison of global empirical results on company cost-of-capital practices. Int J Bus Glob 12(1):53–62

Schlegel D, Dean A, Britzelmaier B (2012) Cost-of-capital of business units: comparison of methodology in previous empirical research. Int Manag Cases 14(4):117–131

Schmalenbach-Gesellschaft (1996) Wertorientierte Unternehmenssteuerung mit differenzierten Kapitalkosten. Z Betriebswirtsch Forsch 48(6):543–578

Schroeck G (2002) Risk management and value creation in financial institutions. Wiley, Hoboken, NJ

Serita T (2008) On survey data analysis in corporate finance. J Int Econ Stud 22:97–111

Sharma A, Kumar S (2010) Economic value added (EVA)—literature review and relevant issues. Int Econ Finance 2(2):200–220

Sharpe WF (1964) Capital asset prices: a theory of market equilibrium under conditions of risk. J Financ 19(3):425–442

Steiner M, Bauer C (1992) Die fundamentale Analyse und Prognose des Marktrisikos deutscher Aktien. Z Betriebswirtsch Forsch 44(4):347–368

Steinle C, Krummaker S, Lehmann G (2007) Bestimmung von Kapitalkosten in diversifizierten Unternehmungen: Verfahrensvergleiche und Anwendungsempfehlungen. Z Control Manage 51(3):204–218

Stern JM, Stewart B, Chew DH Jr (1996) EVA: an integrated financial management system. Eur Financ Manag 2(2):233–245

Stewart GB (1991) The quest for value. The EVA management guide. HarperBusiness, New York, NY

Stewart GB (2013) Best practice EVA. The definitive guide to measuring and maximizing shareholder value. Wiley, Hoboken, NJ

Sutcliff M, Donnellan MA (2007) CFO insights. Delivering high performance. Wiley, Chichester

Taggart RA (1978) Capital allocation in multi-division firms: hurdle rates vs budgets. J Financ Res 10(3):177–189

Thompson DJ (1976) Sources of systematic risk in common stocks. J Bus 49(2):173–189

Toms S, Salama A, Nguyen DT (2005) The association between accounting and market-based risk measures. University of York Working Paper

U.S. National Research Council (1994) Investing for productivity and prosperity. National Academy Press, Washington, DC

Vogel J (1998) Marktwertorientiertes Beteiligungscontrolling. Shareholder Value als Maß der Konzernsteuerung (Gabler-Edition Wissenschaft). Deutscher Universitäts-Verlag, Wiesbaden

Wahlen JM, Baginski SP, Bradshaw MT, Stickney CP (2011) Financial reporting, financial statement analysis, and valuation. A strategic perspective. South-Western Cengage Learning, Mason, OH

Watson D, Head A (2010) Corporate finance. Principles and practice. Financial Times/Prentice Hall, Harlow

Weber J, Schäffer U (2006) Einführung in das Controlling. Schäffer-Poeschel, Stuttgart

Yong L (2007) Internal capital allocation and executive compensation. University of Texas Working Paper

Yoo J, Semenenko I (2012) Segment information disclosure and the cost of equity capital. J Account Bus Manag 19(1):103–123

Young SD, O'Byrne SF (2000) EVA and value based management. A practical guide to implementation. McGraw-Hill, London

Young SD, Saadi S (2011) Using the capital asset pricing model and arbitrage pricing theory in capital budgeting. In: Baker HK, English P (eds) Capital budgeting valuation. Financial analysis for today's investment projects. Wiley, Hoboken, NJ, pp 363–380

Chapter 3
Previous Results on Cost-of-Capital Practices

Having reviewed the technical cost-of-capital literature in the previous chapter, the aim of this chapter is to discuss previous research on the application of cost-of-capital determination techniques by practitioners and to compare findings from these studies. The findings that are discussed in this chapter will also be referred to in the following chapters in order to compare them with the empirical findings from this research.

First of all, in Sect. 3.1, an overview of previous studies in the field is given and the different methods that are used in these studies are discussed. Moreover, limitations in the process of comparing different studies are addressed. In Sect. 3.2, findings of previous studies concerning the determination and application of company cost-of-capital, i.e. cost-of-capital on the group level, are presented and compared. In Sect. 3.3, previous findings on cost-of-capital of business units will be discussed. In contrast to the articles on company cost-of-capital, these articles are discussed individually in detail, since there are considerably fewer articles than in the case of company cost-of-capital, which makes possible an individual discussion and evaluation of each piece of literature. Finally, in Sect. 3.4, influencing factors of cost-of-capital practices that have been identified in previous studies are discussed.

3.1 Previous Studies on Cost-of-Capital Practices

3.1.1 Overview of Previous Studies

There are a number of previous studies that investigate Managerial Finance practices of companies. While some focus on specific topics within the discipline of corporate finance, others are very general and contain lots of questions about many topics, such as capital budgeting, capital structure and cost-of-capital. There are only a few studies that focus exclusively on cost-of-capital. However, many studies

Table 3.1 Studies on cost-of-capital practices included in the analysis (adapted from Schlegel 2014)

Author and year	Country focus	Industry focus
Al Mutairi et al. (2012)[a]	KW	None
Baker et al. (2011a)	CA	None
Brunzell et al. (2011)	IS, SE, NO, FI, DK	None
Bennouna et al. (2010)	CA	None
Chazi et al. (2010)	BH, KW, OM, SA, QA, AE	None
Correia and Cramer (2008)	ZA	None
Truong et al. (2008)	AU	None
Cohen and Yagil (2007)	DE, UK, JP, US, CA	None
Hermes et al. (2007)	NL, CN	None
Steinle et al. (2007)	DE	None
Geginat et al. (2006)	DE, CH	None
Petersen et al. (2006)	DK	Financial services
Block (2005)	US	None
Brounen et al. (2004)	DE, UK, NL, FR	None
McLaney et al. (2004)	UK	None
Block (2003)	US	None
Black et al. (2002)	NZ	None
Ryan and Ryan (2002)	US	None
Graham and Harvey (2001)	US	None
Arnold and Hatzopoulos (2000)	UK	None

[a]Previously published as Al Mutairi et al. (2009)

with another focus—especially capital budgeting—include questions about cost-of-capital. For this thesis, the author has compiled those studies that contain explicit cost-of-capital questions from a large number of studies on related topics. Only studies published in the year 2000 or later were considered.

The studies that were analysed in detail for this chapter are listed in Table 3.1. For each study, the table indicates the year of publication, the countries that were examined in the study and a possible industry focus. It can be seen that only one of the studies focuses on a specific industry.

Some studies that include details on cost-of-capital practices were excluded from further analysis. They are listed in Table 3.2. The studies by KPMG International (2010, 2012, 2013) were excluded because they deal with cost-of-capital but in the context of International Financial Reporting Standards (IFRS). IFRS require companies to calculate certain positions in the financial statements of a company with specific consideration of cost-of-capital. As this research deals with the topic from a Managerial Finance perspective, behaviours of companies that are enforced by regulation are beyond its scope. Another paper that was excluded is the one by Weißenberger and Blome (2005). They report interesting results concerning the cost-of-capital of business units from a survey of German companies. However, the

3.1 Previous Studies on Cost-of-Capital Practices

Table 3.2 Studies on cost-of-capital practices excluded from the analysis

Author and year	Reason for exclusion
KPMG International (2013)	Scope (Financial Accounting)
KPMG International (2012)	Scope (Financial Accounting)
KPMG International (2010)	Scope (Financial Accounting)
Weißenberger and Blome (2005)	Unclear methodology

Table 3.3 Reproductions of the Graham and Harvey (2001) study

Author	Additional questions
Black et al. (2002)	N/A
Brounen et al. (2004)	Firm's goals and stakeholders
Chazi et al. (2010)	Islamic law
Correia and Cramer (2008)	CAPM parameters

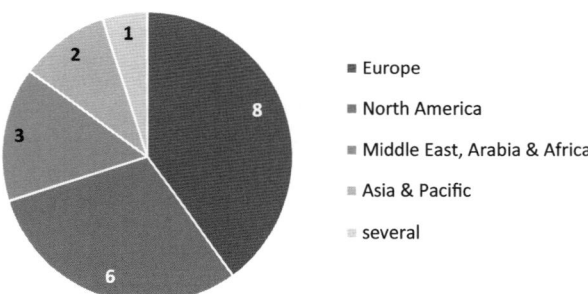

Fig. 3.1 Geographical regions addressed in previous studies

results and the methodology are not described properly so that it is not possible to evaluate and interpret them.

Probably the most famous study of this kind is the one by Graham and Harvey (2001), which won the Jensen price for the best corporate finance paper published in the Journal of Financial Economics in 2001 (Brounen et al. 2004) and has approximately 2,700 citations in Google Scholar.[1] Serita (2008, p. 97) states that the remarkable fact about their research is "that they are more rigorous in testing hypotheses and explaining managers' motives in financial decisions". The survey was replicated by other authors in different countries, often complemented by additional questions (see Table 3.3).

Figure 3.1 shows the distribution of regions addressed in the studies that were analysed. The countries of the studies were aggregated to the regions *Asia and Pacific*, *Europe*, *North America* and *Middle East, Arabia and Africa*. The country in

---

[1] Number of citations by May 2013, http://scholar.google.com/citations?user=cajqjGAAAAAJ&hl=en

which the questions are asked can have an influence on the results, since there are substantial differences between countries and regions in terms of the stage of development of the economy and also the importance of financial markets (Guserl and Pernsteiner 2011). No studies from South America were identified in the literature review. It can be seen that most of the studies originate from Europe and that in contrast to the papers that deal with the development and evaluation of cost-of-capital techniques discussed in Sect. 2.4, there is no prevalence of papers from North America in terms of number of publications.

3.1.2 Methods Applied in Previous Studies

The choice of a research method is supposed to be derived from the research question. For the question of how companies deal with cost-of-capital in practice, internal information from management is needed that is not publicly available. Empirical research in Finance has traditionally focused on large sample analysis of financial data from databases, i.e. secondary data such as stock returns or ratios from financial statements (Bancel and Mittoo 2011; Serita 2008). However, for this type of research question, no such secondary data is available so that new primary data has to be collected. There are basically two ways of collecting the data that is required: questionnaire surveys and interviews with employees of the respective companies.

In previous studies, almost all of the researchers relied on quantitative survey studies using questionnaires. The author is only aware of one paper that applies a quantitative approach using structured interviews (Petersen et al. 2006) and one paper that conducts qualitative interviews (Steinle et al. 2007). According to Serita (2008, p. 98), the first survey study in the field of corporate finance was published by Lintner (1956), who conducted research on the distribution of corporations' incomes among dividends, retained earnings and taxes. However, the method has apparently become more popular in corporate finance research in the last two decades. Since the 1990s, a number of survey studies on corporate finance topics have been published.

The main advantage of survey approaches is that they can produce new data that is unavailable from other sources (Serita 2008; Frank 2007). In contrast to large sample analysis, survey studies can also help to uncover reasons for financial decisions by directly asking financial executives (Serita 2008). This is especially interesting in the case of cost-of-capital of business units because the methods might not be applicable in practice, although they might be suitable from a scientific point of view. For instance, a main problem in comparable company approaches is to find peers (Chua et al. 2006) which is a very individual problem for each of the companies. However, in order to conduct research on reasons for organisational behaviour, a qualitative interview approach might be even more suitable. An advantage of quantitative survey studies over qualitative interview studies is that they can produce statistically robust results.

On the other hand, the survey method is quite controversial in Finance and Accounting research and has been heavily criticised. One of the most common

3.1 Previous Studies on Cost-of-Capital Practices

concerns is measurement errors as well as reliability and validity issues (van der Stede et al. 2008; Frank 2007). Another major problem is that it is difficult to get responses from executives at a senior level and that often inappropriate respondents might fill out the questionnaires (Frank 2007; Serita 2008). Even if adequate individuals can be accessed, the companies might not reveal their true motivations and details of their actions and decisions. Instead, they might deliberately deliver false answers due to strategic, cost and legal considerations as well as agency problems. Therefore, there might be a bias toward "textbook answers" or "politically correct" answers (Bancel and Mittoo 2011; Serita 2008). Moreover, both Frank (2007) and Serita (2008) criticise that generalisations are made from a relatively small number of respondents, as response rates tend to be relatively low. The response rates of the studies listed above are analysed in the next section.

Concerning interview designs in research on cost-of-capital, it can be said that they provide deeper insights to explain the behaviour of organisations compared to survey approaches, which tend to merely describe behaviour. Furthermore, they can include more unexpected details, since it is possible for the interviewer to react to the answers. However, due to time and resource constraints in research, it is not possible to achieve sample sizes as large as in survey approaches.

In Table 3.4, the method and sample size of the papers are listed. It can be seen that most studies follow a quantitative approach. However, there are also papers

Table 3.4 Methods applied in previous studies on cost-of-capital practices

Author and year	Method	Sample size
Al Mutairi et al. (2012)[a]	Quant. survey	80
Baker et al. (2011a)	Quant. survey	214
Brunzell et al. (2011)	Quant. survey	157
Bennouna et al. (2010)	Quant. survey	88
Chazi et al. (2010)	Quant. survey	38
Correia and Cramer (2008)	Quant. survey	28
Truong et al. (2008)	Quant. survey	87
Cohen and Yagil (2007)	Quant. survey	140
Hermes et al. (2007)	Quant. survey	87
Steinle et al. (2007)	Qual. interviews	7
Geginat et al. (2006)	Quant. survey	72
Petersen et al. (2006)	Quant./qual. interviews	39
Block (2005)	Quant. survey	302
Brounen et al. (2004)	Quant. survey	313
McLaney et al. (2004)	Quant. survey	193
Block (2003)	Quant. survey	298
Black et al. (2002)	Quant. survey	26
Ryan and Ryan (2002)	Quant. survey	205
Graham and Harvey (2001)	Quant. survey	392
Arnold and Hatzopoulos (2000)	Quant. survey	96

[a]Previously published as Al Mutairi et al. (2009)

that are purely qualitative (Steinle et al. 2007) or at least include qualitative elements (Petersen et al. 2006).

3.1.3 Limitations in Comparing Studies

In this chapter, the results of different studies are discussed, synthesised and compared. When comparing the results of previous studies, there are a number of differences in terms of methods and content between the studies that one has to be aware of because comparability of the studies is not always given (Baker et al. 2011b). When interpreting the data presented in this chapter, the following differences between the studies should be kept in mind:

- First of all, it is important to recognize that the questions about cost-of-capital that are of interest for this research are asked in **different contexts**, as discussed in Sect. 3.1.1. For instance, some surveys ask about cost-of-capital in general, while others ask about cost-of-capital used in capital budgeting. Therefore, one has to be cautious when analysing and interpreting the results and decide in each case whether the answers are useful for this research or not.
- Many survey studies mention a percentage of companies using a particular technique, for example CAPM. One has to be cautious about how the percentages have been calculated, since some authors refer the positive answers (i.e. the number of companies that do use a certain technique) to the total number of respondents, while others refer the positive answers to a subset of the respondents: for instance, only those that calculate their cost-of-capital at all. From a mathematical point of view, this means that they use **different denominators** for calculating the percentages. In the comparison for WACC and CAPM below, adjustments had to be made so that the figures of different authors were more comparable.
- Moreover, different researchers provide their participants with **different answer possibilities** for the same question. Additionally, some authors allow the selection of multiple answers, while others only allow one. This is, for example, the case for the question concerning techniques used to calculate the cost-of-capital of a business unit (see below).
- Furthermore, **different scales** are used. For instance, Graham and Harvey (2001) and their reproductions use scales indicating how often a certain technique is used, ranging from 0 ("never") to 4 ("always"). In order to convert this scale into a percentage of companies that use a certain technique, the following procedure is adopted by the researchers: they count answers 3 ("almost always") and 4 ("always") as positive, i.e. using the technique. Although this conversion is plausible, the results might be different from those that would be derived using a "yes" and "no" scale.
- Another point is that the **characteristics of the participants**, which may have an influence on the results, are different between the studies. For instance, Brounen

et al. (2004) include in their survey companies with a minimum number of employees of 25, most of which are private companies, while many other authors only include large public companies.
- Although the range of the studies' publication dates is only approximately 10 years, the **point in time** of the survey might have an influence on the result. For instance, there might be certain trends in Managerial Finance and Accounting over time and theoretical development might need some time to be accepted by practitioners. Indeed, there are authors who see a trend toward more sophisticated techniques (Baker et al. 2011b).

The consequence of these differences between the studies is on the one hand that they are not completely comparable and the results have to be interpreted cautiously. On the other hand, it also means that the results of the existing studies are not necessarily transferable to the research questions of this thesis because of the differences in country, context, and participants. Therefore, a new collection of primary data is necessary to address the research problem of this thesis.

3.2 Company Cost-of-Capital

3.2.1 Cost-of-Capital/WACC

This section deals with empirical results concerning company cost-of-capital practices, i.e. the question of how cost-of-capital is estimated on a group level as opposed to a business unit or subsidiary level.

As outlined in the introductory section, finance theory suggests applying **WACC** for the determination of cost-of-capital. Figure 3.2 shows the percentage of companies that use WACC according to different studies. Apparently, most of the companies follow the recommendations of theory and use the WACC to determine their cost-of-capital—the majority of the studies show that more than half of the companies use WACC. The lowest percentage (40 %) is shown in the Croatian study by Dedi and Orsag (2008), while the highest percentage (92 %) has been found in Al Mutairi et al.'s (2009) study in Kuwait.

There is little empirical evidence as to how exactly the WACC approach is applied in terms of weights. Truong et al. (2008) find that 60 % of Australian companies included in the study use target weights, as theory suggests. About half of the companies use market values and half use book values.

Al Mutairi et al. (2012) find that market value weights are most widely used in Kuwait. However, the two studies are not comparable, since there are different answer possibilities. Truong and Partington separate the questions of target vs. current weights and market vs. book values: i.e. all four combinations of the answers are possible. Al Mutairi et al. combine the two aspects and only provide

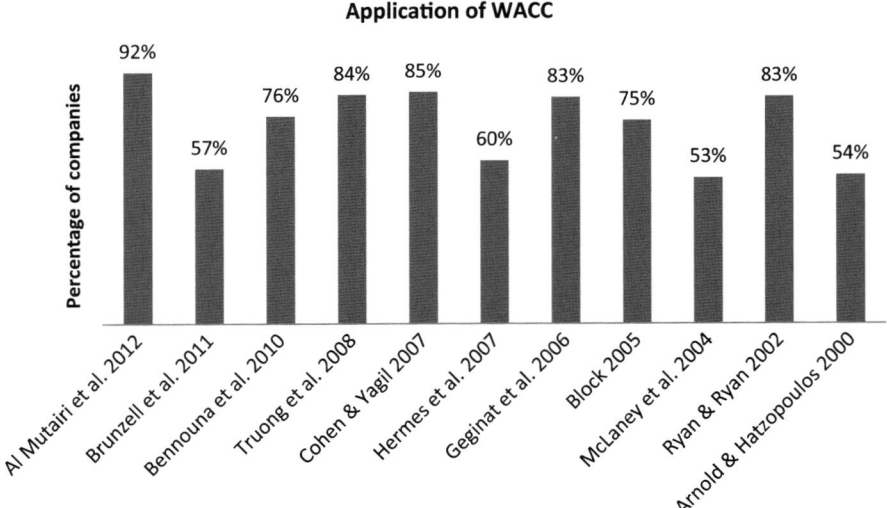

Fig. 3.2 Comparison of previous results on application of WACC (adapted from Schlegel 2014)

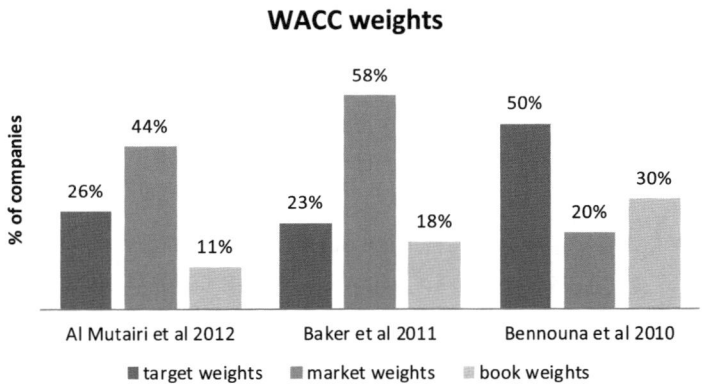

Fig. 3.3 WACC weights applied by practitioners

three possible choices. Baker et al. (2011a) as well as Bennouna et al. (2010) use the same scale as Al Mutairi et al. for their survey of Canadian companies.

In Fig. 3.3, it can be seen that the results of Bennouna et al. (2010) are quite different from those of Al Mutairi et al. (2012) and Baker et al. (2011a), which show a similar distribution. While in the survey by Bennouna et al., half of the companies follow the recommendation of theory and use target weights, smaller percentages use target weights in the other two studies.

3.2 Company Cost-of-Capital

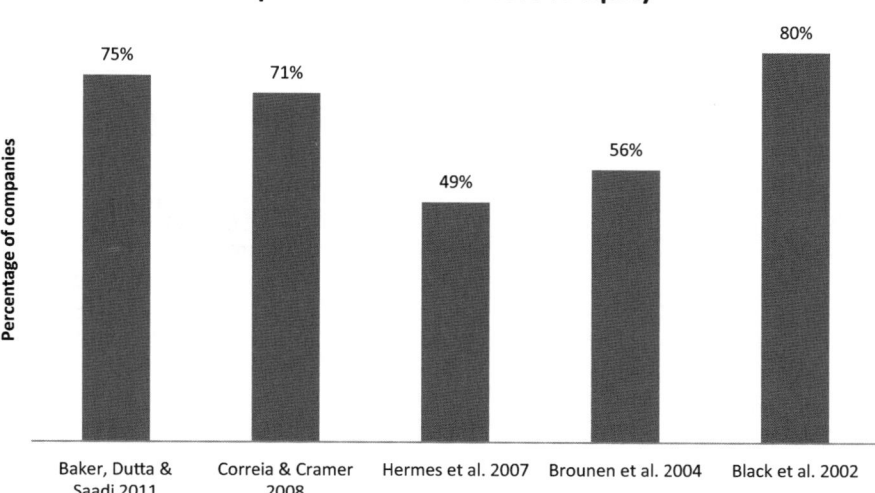

Fig. 3.4 Explicit calculation of cost of equity

The differences between Baker et al. and Bennouna et al. are surprising at first sight, since both surveys were conducted in Canada, only a year apart. There are no obvious differences such as company size in the samples of the two studies.

3.2.2 Cost of Equity/CAPM

In terms of **cost of equity**, the majority of companies seem to explicitly calculate cost of equity according to previous studies (see Fig. 3.4). However, only a few studies ask this type of question.

For the calculation of cost of equity, the CAPM is the most popular model applied. Figure 3.5 reports the percentage of companies in the studies that use the CAPM. The percentage refers to *all* companies taking part in the respective studies, not only those that actually do calculate their cost of equity.

The results of the different studies concerning the use of CAPM have a larger range than in the case of WACC. A possible reason could be that the CAPM is a more sophisticated tool that also requires more prerequisites to be fulfilled (such as stock market listing) than the WACC. Therefore, differences in the characteristics of the sample companies might have a larger effect on the outcome. For instance, some studies only include the largest stock market listed companies, while other studies also include very small companies. Other possible explaining factors could be the country and the context in which the questions were asked.

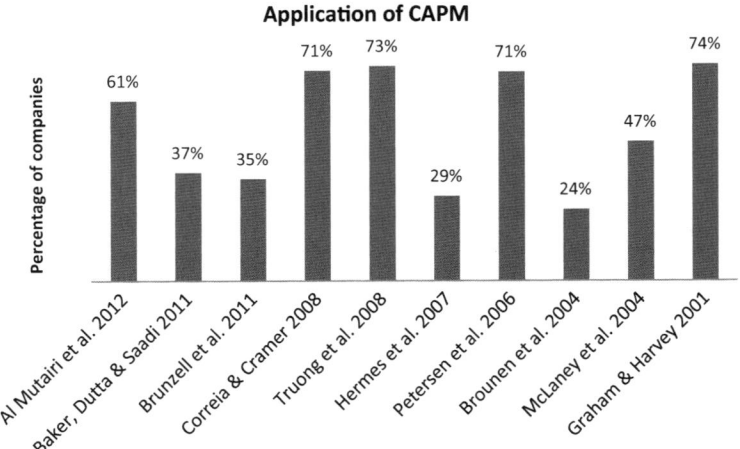

Fig. 3.5 Application of CAPM by practitioners (adapted from Schlegel 2014)

3.3 Cost-of-Capital of Business Units

3.3.1 Block (2003 and 2005)

In two studies published in the years 2003 and 2005, Block conducted a survey among the Fortune 1,000 companies—the 1,000 largest U.S. companies by revenue published by the Fortune magazine. As the two studies are very similar in terms of methodology, they are discussed together in this section. The study published in 2003 is entitled "Divisional cost of capital: A study of its use by major U.S. firms" and focuses on cost-of-capital of business units, subsidiaries and projects. In contrast, the study published in 2005 with the title "Are there differences in capital budgeting procedures between industries? An empirical study" has a broader focus and aims to find differences in capital budgeting between industries. The study also contains some questions about cost-of-capital that are useful for this thesis.

In both studies, a quantitative questionnaire approach was used as a *methodology*. A three-page questionnaire that had been pre-tested in a pilot study was sent to all of the Fortune 1,000 companies. In 2003, 298 companies replied, while in 2005, 302 companies responded to the questionnaire (Block 2003, 2005). In 2003, an additional follow-up telephone survey was conducted in order to make sure that there was no non-response bias in the results (Block 2003).

The following *findings* are reported by the author: One of the questions was whether the respective company uses different cost-of-capital rates for business units, subsidiaries or projects of the firm (Block 2003, 2005). In 2003, 47 % of the companies replied they did. In 2005, the number increased to 51 %.

Of the 298 respondents to Block's (2003) survey, 121 name risk as a primary consideration when using differentiated rates. These 121 companies were asked which technique they use to determine the cost-of-capital of business units. Most of

Fig. 3.6 Determination techniques according to Block (2003)

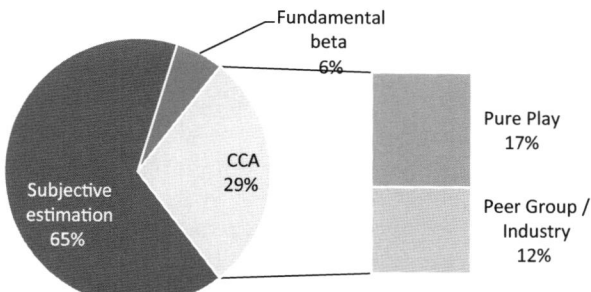

them (65 %) use subjective estimation, while 29 % use a form of the comparable company approach (see Fig. 3.6).

In terms of *contribution to the body of knowledge*, Block's (2003) paper is probably one of the most important publications in the field of application of divisional cost-of-capital techniques by practitioners. It is the only one of the corporate finance surveys dealt with in this literature review that explicitly focuses on divisional cost-of-capital. With his relatively high response rate, Block also has a comparably large sample size in absolute terms.

Like most quantitative survey studies, Block's approach has the *limitation* that specific issues of individual companies cannot be taken into account. Furthermore, no deeper knowledge about the reasons why the companies use or do not use certain techniques is created. Additionally, from the point of view of this thesis, it is questionable whether the results are transferable because the U.S. economy and its financial markets have some characteristics that are different from the German market (Guserl and Pernsteiner 2011).

3.3.2 Steinle et al. (2007)

In Germany, Steinle et al. (2007) conducted research about the importance and determination of cost-of-capital of business units in the context of value-based management. They conducted expert interviews with seven companies from different industries that included both public and private companies. The paper was published in German in the well-known journal *Zeitschrift für Controlling & Management*.

The main *methodology* of the paper is a theoretical comparison of determination techniques for cost-of-capital of business units with the help of a scoring model that included seven criteria such as objectivity, reliability and acceptance. The purpose of the expert interviews that they conducted was to ensure that no important aspects were forgotten in the evaluation of the techniques. Consequently, the researchers applied theoretical sampling (non-probability sampling), which means that they chose a mix of companies from which they expected a broad range of different cost-of-capital practices (Steinle et al. 2007).

Steinle et al. (2007) report the following *findings*: nearly all surveyed companies differentiate their cost-of-capital by business units. However, the degree of differentiation varies among the companies. According to the companies, the primary goal of doing so is an exact determination of required returns for equity. This enables the companies to manage their business units, taking into account the required returns and the risk involved. Additionally, one company stated that by an effective value-based management, the supply of capital from financial markets would be ensured for the future (Steinle et al. 2007).

In terms of the techniques that are applied by the companies to determine the cost-of-capital of their business units, the researchers report that there are different methods among the companies and that many companies also develop their own techniques that take into account their specific situation. The authors only mention details for two of the companies: Bertelsmann—a private publishing company—uses a heuristic-based approach with a comparable low effort to determine business unit cost-of-capital. In contrast, Bayer—a large listed company from the pharmaceutical industry—uses a version of the recently developed MCPM model based on option prices that was discussed in Sect. 2.1.2.2. Bayer has developed an approach that uses the model in a similar way to the comparable company approach. According to the authors, Bayer is the only company from the DAX[2] stock index that uses the MCPM model. However, they do not reference any source for this information. Moreover, one company stated that they include aspects concerning the future into the cost-of-capital figures (Steinle et al. 2007).

The researchers also conducted research on the reasons why some companies do not mathematically determine the cost-of-capital for their business units. The following reasons could be found (Steinle et al. 2007):

- The cost of determining the cost-of-capital rate for business units is higher than the benefit obtained from it, especially if business units are engaged in similar types of business and thus the cost-of-capital rates would only differ slightly.
- Especially for long-term investment projects, companies want to take into account strategic considerations rather than mathematical calculations.

For performance management purposes, a procedure is required that can be communicated, that is understandable and that is accepted by the people who are evaluated by it. Therefore, one company states that they translate the required return into operational performance measures that are accepted by business unit managers (Steinle et al. 2007).

The results of Steinle et al. are a valuable *contribution* to the body of knowledge, since there are very few papers that present empirical results on the application of cost-of-capital of business units in Germany. Furthermore, their qualitative

---

[2] German stock market index.

approach has the advantage that company-specific details can be found, which would not be possible with a structured, standardised survey approach. An example is the MCPM approach by Bayer, which would probably not have been considered in a quantitative survey. Additionally, the qualitative approach has the advantage that it describes not only the approaches of the companies but also the reasons why the companies behave in a certain way.

The *limitations* of the results especially arise from the limited number of companies that were interviewed and the limited scope of the companies included. The research only includes large companies, which might have very different cost-of-capital practices from smaller companies. Furthermore, the presentation of the results is rather condensed. For instance, the authors provide details on the determination techniques for only two of the seven companies. A more detailed report on the results would be helpful for other researchers. Also, in terms of the methodology applied and the questions asked in the interviews, the researchers do not give any details: this makes it hard for other researchers to evaluate the findings. For instance, it is not stated whether the interviews were structured, semi-structured or unstructured. However, the limitations can probably be explained with the fact that the expert interviews were not the main focus of the paper and only served as input for the theoretical comparison of the determination techniques.

3.3.3 Petersen et al. (2006)

Petersen et al. (2006) interviewed 39 Danish Finance professionals, i.e. financial advisors and professionals from the private equity industry, about the methods they use for the valuation of private companies. In the valuation of companies, cost-of-capital rates need to be determined as a discount rate. "Private" in this context refers to companies that are not listed at a stock exchange (Petersen et al. 2006). The cost-of-capital determination in the valuation of private companies poses the same challenges and is achieved using the same techniques as in the case of business units. Therefore, this paper is also useful for the topic of this thesis.

As a *methodology*, the researchers conduct semi-structured interviews, which they refer to as a field study approach (Petersen et al. 2006). With their field study approach, they intend to combine the advantages of case studies and large sample survey studies by using a larger sample than in a case study but at the same time increasing data quality by conducting personal interviews with each of the companies.

To select their sample, the authors first compiled a list of participants from different databases as well as the annual reports and websites of all major banks and financial institutions. Next, they tried to interview all of the participants and reached an acceptance rate of 96 %. They had to filter these companies again because the topic was not applicable to all of them, so that the final sample was 39 companies, which represent 93 % of the private equity companies and 86 % of the financial advisors from the initial list of participants. The researchers explain the

Fig. 3.7 Determination techniques according to Petersen et al. (2006)

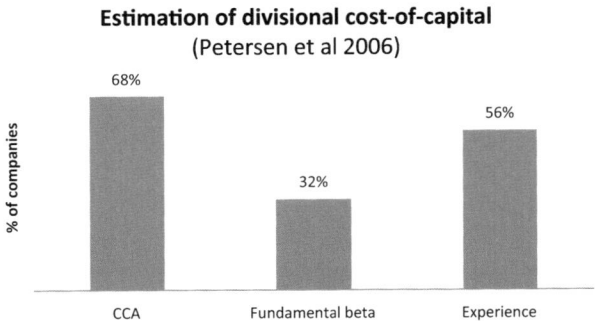

high acceptance rate with the fact that they conduct personal interviews as opposed to mail surveys, which tend have a much lower acceptance rate (Petersen et al. 2006).

The paper contains some *findings* about cost-of-capital determination techniques that are of interest for this thesis. It distinguishes between four categories, namely peer group beta, fundamental beta, experience and other. In Fig. 3.7, it can be seen that using peer betas, i.e. a comparable company approach, is the most popular technique (68 %). But also fundamental beta, i.e. an analytical approach, is used by 32 %. Please note that the percentages refer to the companies that use CAPM (64 % of all participants) and not to the total number of participants, as the techniques are based on the CAPM.

In contrast to Block's studies, the participants in the Petersen et al. study could choose multiple answers, so the sum of the answer possibilities is larger than 100 %. This is because many of the respondents use a combination of several techniques to estimate their beta factors. Often, peer group betas are combined with fundamental betas or with the personal experience of the professionals (Petersen et al. 2006). According to the respondents, the personal experience is especially important for smaller businesses, for which betas cannot be estimated reliably, since it does not make sense to use betas from large listed corporations as substitutes. In this case, a "common-sense approach" might make more sense (Petersen et al. 2006).

The researchers also asked whether the companies adjust for leverage when using betas of comparable companies. The results revealed that of the 17 companies that use peer group betas, 12 companies (70 %) adjust for leverage (Petersen et al. 2006).

Two companies account for unsystematic risk by adding an additional 1–3 % to the cost of equity. In terms of capital structure, 23 participants use the capital structure of listed peers, while 9 participants use the iteration method (Petersen et al. 2006).

In the study by Petersen et al. the objective methods—i.e. comparable company approach and fundamental beta—are a lot more popular than in the Block study. This could be due to the fact that the respondents are Finance professionals and therefore place more importance on sophisticated Finance methods and have a greater knowledge in the field.

The *contribution* of the researchers is especially new empirical results for Denmark, but also some questions—e.g. the inclusion of unsystematic risk—that have not been addressed at all in previous studies in other countries. The advantage of their semi-structured interview approach is that they produce statistically robust results but at the same time are able to include qualitative information such as the reasons why the professionals apply certain methods or find that they are more or less suitable. Furthermore, the paper provides a scientifically clear explanation of the methodology used.

The main *limitation* of the research might be the transferability of the results to other settings—and also to the topic of this thesis—for the following reasons: First, only professionals from the financial services industry were interviewed. Second, the results might not be directly transferable to other countries, although the authors argue that the proportion of private versus public companies is the same as in other important economies such as the U.S. or Germany (Petersen et al. 2006). The application of the techniques by practitioners might be influenced by other determinants as well.

3.3.4 Geginat et al. (2006)

The study by Geginat et al. (2006) was published by one of the largest consultancy firms in Germany, *Roland Berger Strategy Consultants*. All of the authors were employed by the company at the time of the publication. On the one hand, as a researcher one has to be aware of the fact that studies by profit-oriented firms might not be completely independent and one should also carefully check whether the methodology that has been applied is appropriate from a scientific point of view. This is especially important if the study has not been published in a peer reviewed journal, as is the case for this study. On the other hand, studies made by practitioners often deliver valuable insights into business that can also contribute to academic knowledge. Therefore, it was decided to include the study in this literature review.

The authors conducted a survey among large Swiss and German companies about cost-of-capital and strategic decision-making. The survey includes questions about methods to determine cost-of-capital, problems they encounter in the determination and also about which fields of application the companies use cost-of-capital rates for. Furthermore, questions were asked about the importance of capital allocation (Geginat et al. 2006).

The authors adopted the following *methodology*: They sent a questionnaire to the top 500 German companies according to the German magazine *Wirtschaftswoche* and the top 100 companies according to the Swiss magazine *Bilanz*. They received 72 responses which is a response rate of 12 % (Geginat et al. 2006). In their study,

Fig. 3.8 Determination techniques according to Geginat et al. (2006)

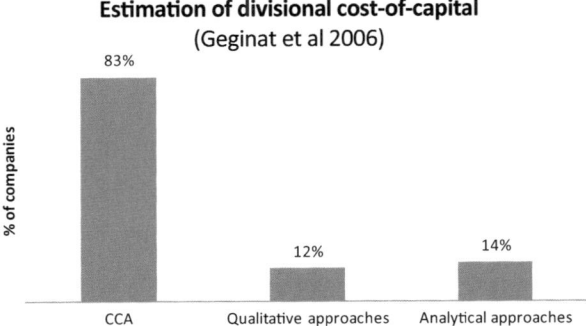

the authors do not further explain according to which criteria the "top" companies for each country were determined by the respective magazines.

One of the authors' *findings* is that 47 % of the companies currently differentiate their cost-of-capital rates by divisions, regions or projects. In the future, 82 % of the respondents are planning to do so. Interestingly, more companies (68 % of those that do differentiate the rates) differentiate by regions than by divisions (65 %) Forty-two percent of the companies differentiate their cost-of-capital rates by projects (Geginat et al. 2006).

In terms of techniques to determine beta in the application of the CAPM, 83 % of the companies use comparable company approaches, 14 % use analytical or other quantitative approaches and 17 % rely on qualitative approaches such as scoring models, as shown in Fig. 3.8 (Geginat et al. 2006). However, it is not further specified by the authors whether the percentages refer to all participants, to the CAPM users or to those that differentiate their cost-of-capital rates.

The authors also conducted research on why some of the companies do not differentiate their cost-of-capital rates. Forty-six percent of the companies stated they did not have enough information available for a differentiated treatment of cost-of-capital. Thirty-eight percent state that all their divisions, regions and projects have the same risk (Geginat et al. 2006). From a theoretical point of view, this would indeed mean that no differentiated cost-of-capital rates are necessary. However, the question is whether the companies' perception is correct that the risk of their divisions is equal. Thirty-two percent state that they had not yet dealt with the topic in depth (Geginat et al. 2006).

Another question addressed by the authors was whether a poor cost-of-capital treatment leads to a misallocation of capital and finally to a decrease in financial performance as suggested by theory (see Fig. 3.9).

One-third of the respondents say that due to a sub-optimal allocation of capital, their financial results deteriorate by at least 10 %, while another third say that it decreases by 5–10 % (2006, p. 8). While this seems to confirm what theory says about cost-of-capital, it is very questionable whether the methodology chosen by the authors to research this question is appropriate and whether the interpretation is correct for the following reasons

3.3 Cost-of-Capital of Business Units

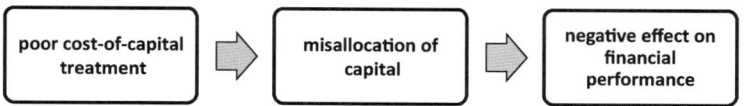

Fig. 3.9 Argumentation chain by Geginat et al. (own illustration based on Geginat et al. 2006)

- First of all, there might be a bias in the way the question was asked. For instance, if respondents are asked "By how much does misallocation of capital decrease the financial result of your company?" there is no neutral formulation of the question. However, the authors do not indicate the exact question, so this aspect cannot be evaluated.
- Second, a survey instrument is probably not appropriate for this question because this assumes that the respondent knows the effect that a misallocation of capital has on their financial performance. This is not possible unless the respondents had made a thorough analysis of the company's financial data beforehand, which is very unlikely. Even with an analysis of financial data, this question is probably hard to answer because the misallocation of capital is a variable that is hard to measure.
- Additionally, in terms of interpretation of the results, the question only concerns the relationship between the two right-hand boxes in the figure above, but the authors assume that the misallocation of capital is caused by the cost-of-capital practices (relationship between the two boxes on the left).

Despite the criticism of one survey question above, the authors made some interesting *contributions* to the field of cost-of-capital: First of all, they delivered new empirical results for large German and Swiss companies. Moreover, some interesting practice-oriented perspectives on the topic were created by including questions such as the importance of capital allocation and the fields of application of cost-of-capital. Additionally, they not only asked how the situation is at the moment, but also how the companies are planning to change certain aspects in their cost-of-capital practices. Interestingly, in contrast to other quantitative survey studies, the authors include reasons why the companies apply certain practices. This might have been possible in this case without a prior qualitative exploratory research because the consultants might have been able to create the answer possibilities from their own professional experience.

On the other hand, there are also some *limitations* to the study. In terms of data analysis, no statistical tests are performed and no relationships between variables are statistically examined. For instance, differences in the cost-of-capital practices between industries are merely described without stating if they are statistically significant (Geginat et al. 2006). Furthermore, there are concerns about the methodology applied to answer certain questions, especially the question of the relationship between misallocation of capital and financial performance that was outlined above. In this example, the authors make conclusions about relationships that are questionable from a statistical point of view and even conclude causal relationships. Moreover, for the purpose of this research project, the results are only partly useful to evaluate the situation in Germany because the authors make no distinction between the Swiss and German companies in their report of the results. They also fail to present descriptive statistics to describe other characteristics of the participants, such as the number of respondents per industry.

3.4 Influencing Factors of Company Cost-of-Capital Practices

3.4.1 Overview

One main theme in the research of this thesis is the question of which factors influence the cost-of-capital practices of companies. Most of the previous studies discussed in this chapter merely analyse their data descriptively, which provides interesting insights into the cost-of-capital practices but delivers little information about the underlying determinants. However, some authors have conducted statistical analyses to test influencing factors. In this section, influencing factors that were identified in the previous studies are summarised. In doing so, only results that are statistically significant at the 0.01 or 0.05 level are taken into account.

Most of the survey studies rely on bivariate analysis of the data. That means that for any given question, the association with each one of the influencing factors is measured pair-wise. The authors use different measures of association or statistical tests: for instance, Chazi et al. (2010) use the Mann Whitney U-test, whereas Baker et al. (2011a) use a t-test. Block (2003) uses the Chi-Squared method. The author is only aware of one paper (Brunzell et al. 2011) that uses a robust probit model to model the dependent variable using multiple determinants. However, the results are not relevant for this thesis.

3.4.2 Previous Results

Table 3.5 shows significant relationships that were identified between the cost-of-capital questions and influencing factors. However, it has to be noted—considering the statistical procedure described above—that the significant relationships were sometimes found only for specific questions or answer possibilities, as a large number of combinations of variables are tested in the studies.

Al Mutairi et al. (2012) find many significant relationships between the question of how the firm's cost-of-capital is calculated and company size as well as the firm's sector. Moreover, there seems to be a weaker relationship between this question and CEO tenure. The same factors are found to influence the question of how the beta factor is estimated. Additionally, this question is significantly related to CEO ownership, stock market listing and CEO education.

3.4 Influencing Factors of Company Cost-of-Capital Practices

Table 3.5 Significant influencing factors in previous studies

	Al Mutairi et al. (2012)	Baker et al. (2011a)	Chazi et al. (2010)	Block (2003)	Graham and Harvey (2001)
Firm size	x	x	x	x	x
Percentage of foreign sales			x		x
Stock market listing					x
Management ownership	x				x
CEO education	x	x			x
CEO tenure	x				
CEO age					x
Leverage					x
Fixed assets ratio				x	
Industry sector	x				x
P/E ratio					x
Investment grade					x
Pay Dividends					x
Regulated entity					x

Baker et al. (2011a) analyse the relationship between different cost-of-capital questions and two determinants: size and CEO education. They find that both of the influencing factors are significantly related to the question of which discount rate is used for evaluating investments projects and to the question of how the cost of equity is calculated with both influencing factors.

Chazi et al. (2010) identify significant relationship between the question of how the cost of equity capital is calculated and the influencing factors size and foreign sales.

Block (2003) reports a significant relationship between the use of different cost-of-capital rates for projects and revenue, i.e. size. Additionally, he reports a positive relationship with fixed assets ratio. A possible explanation could be that a higher fixed assets ratio—i.e. a higher operating leverage—implies higher risk for the company and therefore a higher importance for a proper consideration of cost-of-capital. Moreover, Block (2003) finds a significant relationship between the determination of cost-of-capital of business units with an objective measure (i.e. a comparable company approach or an analytical approach) and the revenue—i.e. size—of the company. This is in line with Graham and Harvey's (2001) finding that larger companies tend to use more sophisticated methods in corporate finance.

Graham and Harvey (2001) have tested relationships with a larger number of influencing factors, which were all found to be significantly correlated to the use of one or more methods to determine cost of equity. For instance, the size factor is significantly related to the use of CAPM, while other factors are related to different techniques to determine cost of equity.

In identifying determinants, it is important to check whether the explanatory variables are correlated. For instance, it could be the case that there is interdependence between size and stock market listing, so that the real reason for the larger companies to use CAPM is not their size but their stock market listing (spurious relationship). Graham and Harvey (2001) analyse the correlation between the determinants in their study. They find that the percentage of foreign sales is indeed a proxy for size, but that the other variables are independent from each other in their study. Also Al Mutairi et al. (2012) describe correlations between control variables. In their data, there are a higher number of correlations.

However, none of the authors attempts to statistically control for the effects of confounding variables. In the statistical analysis of the survey data in this thesis, spurious and suppressed relationships are detected and controlled for using different statistical methods (see Sect. 7.6.2).

3.5 Conclusion

3.5.1 Summary

To summarise, it can be said that there is relatively good knowledge about the use of **company cost-of-capital** determination techniques by practitioners, as there are several studies in different countries that deal with this issue. While the results on WACC are quite uniform, the results on the use of CAPM are more ambiguous. Thus, more research could be conducted on the underlying reasons for the differences.

Less effort has been devoted to research on **cost-of-capital of *business units***. The few studies that exist on this topic indicate that the use of differentiated cost-of-capital rate for business units has arrived in practice—though it is less commonly applied than company cost-of-capital. Still, there are many companies that use the company cost-of-capital rate for their business units.

Concerning the techniques used to determine cost-of-capital for business units, it seems that many companies still rely on a subjective estimation. Among the objective techniques, the comparable company approach seems to be the most important approach. Therefore, it can be concluded that the studies presented above support the notion of a theory-practice gap that is often referred to in the literature (Bennouna et al. 2010; Pfister 2003; Arnold and Hatzopoulos 2000).

3.5.2 Research Gaps

In this study, research on the cost-of-capital practices of companies is conducted. Therefore, no research gaps concerning the development and evaluation of determination techniques as discussed in Chap. 2 are addressed. In the immediate field of this thesis—the cost-of-capital practices of companies that were discussed in this chapter—the following gaps could be identified in the literature review.

1. In terms of company cost-of-capital, there are *mixed results on the application of the CAPM by practitioners.*
2. Furthermore, there are very limited results on the *exact technical application of the models.* This includes, for instance, parameters of the WACC—especially the component weights. Moreover, there are only limited details in previous research about how practitioners set parameters of the CAPM, such as the market return. Additionally, details on the measurement of betas could be interesting—for instance, whether monthly or weekly returns are used by practitioners and which time frames are used.
3. Moreover, there are only limited significant empirical results about the *determinants of cost-of-capital practices.*
4. There are no previous empirical studies that focus in depth on the *real economy sector in Germany.*
5. There are no comprehensive studies for the Managerial Finance topics that are within the scope of this thesis. Most of the previous studies were conducted in the context of capital budgeting. There are only very limited results for the area of *performance measurement and value-based management.*
6. There are only a few studies in general that report *empirical results on the application of cost-of-capital of business units.*
7. While it is generally agreed that there is some kind of theory-practice gap, especially in the area of cost-of-capital of business units and projects, there is little knowledge about the *reasons for this theory-practice gap.* In the studies presented in the literature above, only Steinle et al. (2007) ask this question. In order to further improve the techniques and their acceptance by practitioners, it could be helpful to know why the techniques are rarely applied.
8. Moreover, there is a *lack of theory* to explain the reasons behind differences in the cost-of-capital practices which exist between companies.

Table 3.6 shows which of the research gaps concerning cost-of-capital practices that were identified are dealt with and how this thesis contributes to each issue.

Table 3.6 Research gaps addressed and contribution to the body of knowledge

Research gap		In scope	Contribution
(1)	Mixed results on application of CAPM	Yes	Additional quantitative empirical evidence
(2)	Technical details in application of models (parameters)	No	
(3)	Determinants of cost-of-capital practices	Yes	Development of a model that explains cost-of-capital practices
(4)	Results for real economy sector in Germany	Yes	In-depth investigation by focusing on sector
(5)	Results for area of performance measurement and value-based management	Yes	Focused empirical results in managerial finance context
(6)	Results on *business unit* cost-of-capital	Yes	New empirical results
(7)	Reasons for theory-practice gap	Yes	In-depth explanation of reasons through qualitative inquiry
(8)	Lack of theory to explain determinants/influencing factors	Yes	Development of theory based on qualitative results

Table 3.7 Propositions, hypotheses and model development

Step	Section	Section
Research propositions	Conclusion of literature review chapter	3.5.3
Preliminary model	Conclusion of literature review chapter	3.5.4
Refined preliminary model	Conclusion of expert interviews chapter	6.5.2
Research hypotheses	Beginning of company survey chapter	7.1
Final model	Conclusion/contribution to knowledge chapter	8.1.4

3.5.3 Research Propositions

At this point of the thesis, no formal research hypotheses are formulated. The author feels that the extent of the available literature does not allow the formulation of empirically testable hypotheses at this point.

Instead, research propositions are formulated and a very general preliminary model will be constructed, which will guide the further course of this research. This preliminary model will be further refined after the first empirical results (expert interviews) and converted into testable hypotheses for the company survey. The relevant sections of the thesis are shown in Table 3.7.

There is very little empirical evidence on cost-of-capital practices in Germany and in the context of Managerial Finance. However, taking into account the existing evidence, it is expected that there is a large gap between the companies' practices and what Finance theory suggests. Therefore, the following is proposed:

P1: There is a theory-practice gap in cost-of-capital methods

Especially for the question of whether companies use the CAPM, there are very mixed results (see Sect. 3.2.2). The results range from 24 % of companies using the

3.5 Conclusion

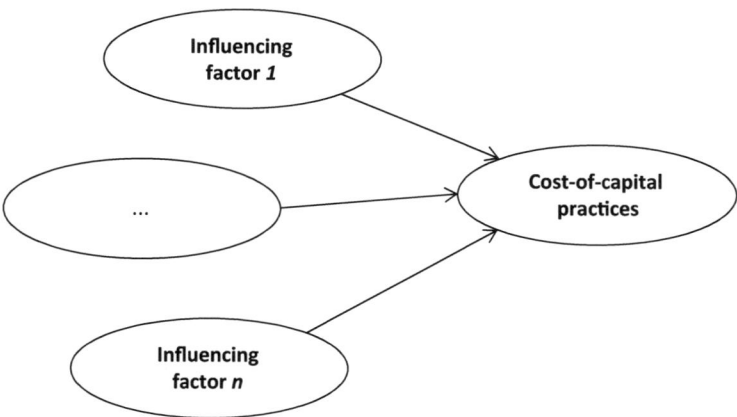

Fig. 3.10 Preliminary model of cost-of-capital practices

CAPM (Brounen et al. 2004) to 74 % (Graham and Harvey 2001). This large variation in the results of different studies might indicate that there are differences in the characteristics of the populations that explain the different cost-of-capital practices. Some previous studies have attempted to find significant influencing factors (see Sect. 3.4). However, there are a limited number of studies and the results are in part inconsistent. Hence, this thesis adopts an exploratory way of investigating determinants of cost-of-capital practices. The following general proposition is formulated:

P2: There are systematic differences between companies that explain differences in cost-of-capital practices (influencing factors).

3.5.4 Preliminary Model

Based on the literature review, the research gaps and the research propositions, the preliminary model of cost-of-capital practices is presented in Fig. 3.10. At this point, the model does not give details about the influencing factors. The preliminary model will guide the expert interviews in order to identify possible influencing factors.

As Saunders et al. (2009, p. 36) state: "Boxes and arrows can add order to a conception (...) but they rarely explain why the relationships have occurred". In his article "What constitutes a good theoretical contribution?" Whetten (1989) also points out that not only is it necessary to provide a description of which factors explain reality and how they are connected, but also an explanation *why* the relationships occur.

Thus, one major objective of this thesis is to find out the underlying reasons for the factors and to develop a theory that explains the relationships shown in the model.

Table 3.8 Objectives and results of literature review

Research aim	Research objectives	Contribution of literature review	Results from literature review
Examine and explain cost-of-capital practices	(1) To investigate how companies use and determine cost-of-capital	Synthesise, compare and evaluate previous results; Identify gaps	• A comprehensive literature review was conducted (Chaps. 2 and 3) • Gaps were identified (Sect. 3.5.1)
	(2) To develop a model that explains the cost-of-capital practices of companies	Identify possible variables from previous empirical results	• There are mixed results concerning influencing factors (Sect. 3.4) • Possible variables will be identified in qualitative research • A simple preliminary model was designed (Sect. 3.5.4)
	(3) To develop a theory that explains the cost-of-capital practices of companies		

3.5.5 Fulfilment of Objectives

The progression of the thesis in terms of the objectives that were determined in the introduction (see Sect. 1.3) is summarised in Table 3.8.

As an interim conclusion, it can be stated that the objectives of the literature review have been reached. In terms of variables for the preliminary model, it was decided that the model needs to be refined after the first primary research findings of this thesis, since the previous results from literature are not detailed enough to construct a model with concrete hypotheses.

References

Al Mutairi M, Tian G, Tan A (2009) Corporate finance practice in Kuwait: a survey to confront theory with practice. In: 22nd Australasian finance and banking conference 2009. Available from SSRN

Al Mutairi M, Tian G, Hasan H, Tan A (2012) Corporate governance and corporate finance practices in a Kuwait stock exchange market listed firm: a survey to confront theory with practice. Corp Gov 12(5):595–615

Arnold G, Hatzopoulos PD (2000) The theory-practice gap in capital budgeting: evidence from the United Kingdom. J Bus Financ Account 27(5/6):603–626

Baker HK, Dutta S, Saadi S (2011a) Corporate finance practices in Canada: where do we stand? Multinatl Financ J 15(3/4):157–192

Baker HK, Singleton JC, Veit ET (2011b) Survey research in corporate finance. Bridging the gap between theory and practice. Oxford University, Oxford

Bancel F, Mittoo UR (2011) Survey evidence on financing decisions and cost of capital. In: Baker HK, Martin GS (eds) Capital structure & corporate financing decisions. Theory, evidence, and practice. Essential perspectives. Wiley, Hoboken, NJ, pp 229–248

Bennouna K, Meredith GG, Marchant T (2010) Improved capital budgeting decision making: evidence from Canada. Manag Decis 48(2):225–247

Black C, Parry J, Anderson H, Bennett JA (2002) Are New Zealand chief financial officers the 'country cousins' of their American counterparts? Univ Auckl Bus Rev 4(1):1–11

Block S (2003) Divisional cost of capital: a study of its use by major U.S. firms. Eng Econ 48 (4):345–362

Block S (2005) Are there differences in capital budgeting procedures between industries? An empirical study. Eng Econ 50(1):55–67

Brounen D, de Jong A, Koedijk K (2004) Corporate finance in Europe: confronting theory with practice. Financ Manag 33(4):71–101

Brunzell T, Liljeblom E, Vaihekoski M (2011) Determinants of capital budgeting methods and hurdle rates in Nordic firms. Account Finance 53(1):85–110

Chazi A, Terra PRS, Zanella FC (2010) Theory versus practice: perspectives of Middle Eastern financial managers. Eur Bus Rev 22(2):195–221

Chua J, Chang PC, Wu Z (2006) The full-information approach for estimating divisional betas: implementation issues and tests. J Appl Finance 16(1):53–61

Cohen G, Yagil J (2007) A multinational survey of corporate financial policies. J Appl Finance 17 (1):57–69

Correia C, Cramer P (2008) An analysis of cost of capital, capital structure and capital budgeting practices: a survey of South African listed companies. Meditari Account Res 16(2):31–52

Dedi L, Orsag S (2008) Capital budgeting practices: a survey of Croatian firms. S East Eur J Econ Bus 2(1):59–67

Frank A (2007) On the value of survey-based research in finance. Alternation 14(1):243–261

Geginat J, Morath B, Wittmann R, Knüsel P (2006) Kapitalkosten als strategisches Entscheidungskriterium. Available at http://www.rolandberger.com/expertise/functional_issues/restructuring/2006-05-03-rbsc-pub-capital.html

Graham JR, Harvey CR (2001) The theory and practice of corporate finance: evidence from the field. J Financ Econ 60(2/3):187–243

Guserl R, Pernsteiner H (2011) Finanzmanagement. Grundlagen—Konzepte—Umsetzung. Lehrbuch. Gabler, Wiesbaden

Hermes N, Smid P, Yao L (2007) Capital budgeting practices: a comparative study of the Netherlands and China. Int Bus Rev 16(5):630–654

KPMG International (2010) Cost of capital and impairment test study 2009. Empirical survey of companies in Germany, the Netherlands, Austria, Switzerland and Spain. Available from: http://www.kpmg.de/WasWirTun/17368.htm

KPMG International (2012) Kapitalkostenstudie 2011/2012. Entwicklungen in volatilen Märkten. Available from http://www.kpmg.de

KPMG International (2013) Kapitalkostenstudie 2012/2013. Steuerung in der Unsicherheit. Available from http://www.kpmg.de

Lintner J (1956) Distribution of incomes of corporations among dividends, retained earnings, and taxes. Am Econ Rev 46(2):97–113

McLaney E, Pointon J, Thomas M, Tucker J (2004) Practitioners' perspectives on the UK cost of capital. Eur J Finance 10(2):123–138

Petersen C, Plenborg T, Schøler F (2006) Issues in valuation of privately held firms. J Priv Equity 10(1):33–48

Pfister C (2003) Divisionale Kapitalkosten. Theorie und Anwendung. Bank- und finanzwirtschaftliche Forschungen, 349th edn. Haupt, Bern

Ryan PA, Ryan GP (2002) Capital budgeting practices of the fortune 1000: how have things changed? J Bus Manage 8(4):355–364

Saunders M, Lewis P, Thornhill A (2009) Research methods for business students. Financial Times Prentice Hall, Harlow

Schlegel D (2014) A comparison of global empirical results on company cost-of-capital practices. Int J Bus Glob 12(1):53–62

Serita T (2008) On survey data analysis in corporate finance. J Int Econ Stud 22:97–111

Steinle C, Krummaker S, Lehmann G (2007) Bestimmung von Kapitalkosten in diversifizierten Unternehmungen: Verfahrensvergleiche und Anwendungsempfehlungen. Z Control Manage 51(3):204–218

Truong G, Partington G, Peat M (2008) Cost-of-capital estimation and capital-budgeting practice in Australia. Aust J Manag 33(1):95–121

van der Stede WA, Young M, Chen CX (2008) Doing management accounting survey research. In: Chapman CS (ed) Handbook of management accounting research. Elsevier, Amsterdam

Weißenberger BE, Blome M (2005) Ermittlung wertorientierter Kennzahlen unter IFRS. University of Gießen Working Paper

Whetten DA (1989) What constitutes a theoretical contribution? Acad Manag Rev 14(4):490–495

Chapter 4
Research Philosophy and Ethics

Before details of the empirical research approach and methods are presented in Chap. 5, it is important to discuss the underlying philosophical assumptions that have consciously and unconsciously guided this research. Hence, the aim of this chapter is to discuss relevant literature concerning research philosophy and the philosophical assumptions adopted by the author. Philosophical discussions concerning mixed methods are not part of this chapter, but will be reviewed in Chap. 5.

Additionally, in this chapter, ethical considerations that have been made in the design of the empirical research are discussed.

Each of the main sections starts with a brief review of relevant literature in order to provide a basis for the discussion of this thesis' assumptions and procedures.

4.1 Research Philosophy

4.1.1 Research Philosophy in the Literature

4.1.1.1 Definition and Importance of Research Philosophy

Thinking about research philosophy involves "examining the nature of knowledge itself, how it comes into being and is transmitted through language" (Patton 2002, p. 92). In the context of research philosophy, the term 'paradigm' is often used. This term has been shaped by Thomas Kuhn (1970) and means "general ways of thinking about how the world works and how we gain knowledge about the world" (Monette et al. 2011, p. 37).

There are two concepts or areas of philosophy that are especially relevant for management research: ontology and epistemology. Ontology is concerned with philosophical assumptions about the nature of reality (Easterby-Smith et al. 2008; Saunders et al. 2009). For epistemology, more diverse definitions can be found in

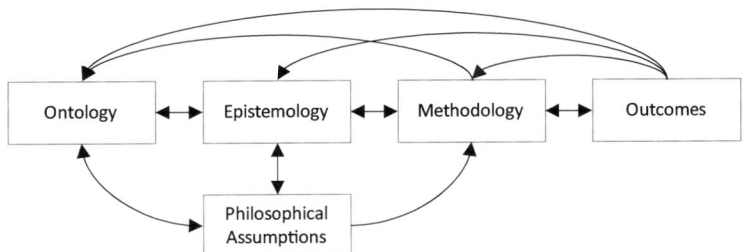

Fig. 4.1 The relationship between philosophy, methodology and outcomes (adapted from Cua and Garret 2009)

the literature. For example, Saunders et al. (2009) and Bryman (2008) state that epistemology concerns the question of what is regarded as acceptable knowledge in a discipline. In contrast, Horrigan (2007) defines the term more widely as the "study or science of knowledge", which is closer to the etymological meaning of the term than the abovementioned definitions by Saunders et al. and Bryman, since the term comes from the Greek *episteme* (=knowledge) and *logos* (=study).

It is important to think about which ontological and epistemological assumptions one makes as a researcher *before* elaborating a methodology, since the research is influenced by the assumptions made (Kanellis and Papadopoulos 2009). In the literature, research is often described as a process that begins with philosophical considerations: Hesse-Biber and Leavy (2011) point out that research is a holistic process in which all elements should be seen as interrelated, i.e. the philosophical perspective influences the choice of methodology and methods design. Also Cua and Garret (2009) see research as a process beginning with ontological and epistemological assumptions. However, they point out that the process is not one-directional but rather complex, since not only do ontology and epistemology have an influence on the methodology, but also the outcomes that were achieved with a certain methodology can in return influence the philosophical assumptions of the researcher (see Fig. 4.1).

Hence, questions of philosophy are central to the research design. As Easterby-Smith et al. (2008) point out, research philosophy can even help to clarify research designs, recognize which designs will work and even identify other designs that have not been used before by the researcher. Moreover, Cua and Garret (2009) emphasise that not only the research design, but also the quality of the research and the outcome are affected by the question of whether the researcher has properly thought through philosophical issues.

4.1.1.2 Positivism vs. Interpretivism

In the literature on research philosophy, a wide range of different philosophical positions and paradigms are discussed. Different authors classify the paradigms in different ways. Commonly, positivism and one or more other extreme poles are

4.1 Research Philosophy

discussed. As Niglas (2001, p. 2) puts it, "it has been quite common to talk about only two big paradigms: positivism and something which denies positivism". For instance, Monette et al. (2011) distinguish between positivist and non-positivist approaches. Saunders et al. (2009) contrast positivism, realism and interpretivism.

It has to be emphasised that the paradigms that are presented in the literature are extreme poles of ideal-typical descriptions of assumptions belonging to a certain paradigm. As Monette et al. (2011, p. 39) point out, "these viewpoints are not necessarily mutually exclusive; people may adopt ideas from more than one of them at the same time". Niglas (2010, p. 216) contends that it is more helpful to view philosophical and methodological issues as a continuum instead of classifying them "into a small number of clearly separate paradigms or movements".

A comprehensive discussion of different paradigms is beyond the scope of this thesis. Therefore, *positivism* and *interpretivism* are briefly contrasted as two extreme poles on a continuum of philosophical directions. The paradigm on which this thesis is based—post-positivism—is addressed in Sect. 4.1.2.1.

Positivism is based on the ontological assumption of objectivity, i.e. the notion that there is an externally existing world and things exist independently of people's beliefs and perceptions about them (Sharma 2010; Monette et al. 2011; Hammersley 2011). According to the positivist tradition, the goal of research is to discover laws about how the world works (Monette et al. 2011) and produce generalizable statements about causal relationships (Kanellis and Papadopoulos 2009). Hence, positivists represent the epistemological position that knowledge is only considered as significant if it has been generated with the help of objective techniques that discover what exists in the external world (Monette et al. 2011; Sharma 2010). This means that the application of methods adopted from the natural sciences is advocated for investigating social reality (Bryman 2008; Kanellis and Papadopoulos 2009).

Positivists expect science to be conducted in a value-free way (David and Sutton 2011; Bryman 2008). That means that the researcher behaves in a passive and neutral role without influence of his cultural, social or moral beliefs or his experience from the past (Kanellis and Papadopoulos 2009). Moreover, David and Sutton (2011, p. 76) state that this requires a "non-normative, non-judgemental detachment of the researcher in relation to what they are studying." This is related to the idea of empiricism, i.e. the need for data which is experienced from the senses as opposed to merely theory-laden evidence (David and Sutton 2011; Kanellis and Papadopoulos 2009).

Based on criticism of the traditional positivist view of the world, different alternatives have emerged. In the literature (Monette et al. 2011; Bryman 2008; Saunders et al. 2009), **interpretivism** is often cited as the opposite pole of positivism. As discussed by Bryman (2008), interpretivism integrates views from different intellectual traditions, assuming a critical position towards the positivist idea that the model of the natural sciences can be applied to the social world. Instead, interpretivists perceive social reality as created from interpretation of human perceptions and the exchange of meanings during a social interaction process (Monette et al. 2011). In terms of epistemology, the emphasis of interpretivism is to gain a deeper *understanding* of human thinking and behaviour and to *interpret* people's actions from their point of view (Bryman 2008).

Proponents of interpretivism argue that positivist research does not take into account the dimension of social reality, i.e. a subjective understanding instead of a superficial explanation of causal relationships (Monette et al. 2011; Bryman 2008). However, as Monette et al. (2011, p. 40) point out, positivists "do not necessarily deny the existence or importance of subjective experiences, but they do question whether the subjective interpretations have scientific validity". The author of this thesis acknowledges that there is a continuum of different traditions and paradigms, which all have a right to exist. The philosophical position on which this thesis is based will be discussed in Sect. 4.1.2. Before that, the link between paradigms and research methods is briefly dealt with.

4.1.1.3 The Link Between Paradigms and Research Methods

Traditionally, there has been the idea that the paradigms are linked to the employment of certain research methods. The positivist position is traditionally more closely related to quantitative methods, whereas interpretivism is associated with qualitative methods (Niglas 2010; Bryman 2008; Monette et al. 2011). As Bryman (2008, p. 22) states, this suggests that the differences between quantitative and qualitative methods are "deeper than the superficial issue of the presence or absence of quantification. For many writers, quantitative and qualitative research differ with respect to their epistemological foundations." This traditional notion of the link between paradigm and methods has led to the discussion about the legitimacy and philosophical foundation of mixed methods research (see Sect. 5.1.3).

However, this traditionally strict view of a direct and exclusive connection between paradigm and methods is increasingly challenged in the contemporary literature. For instance, Monette et al. (2011, p. 39) contend that "it is important not to oversimplify the link between a paradigm and the preferred research methodology (...) because positivists at times use qualitative research." Also Bazeley (2004, p. 4) states that "it is generally recognised that there are no direct or exclusive correspondences between paradigms, methodology and methods." Proponents of the idea that each method can be used appropriately within any research paradigm raise the following points: Today, there is a multiplicity of different approaches and an "overlap and mutual influence between different traditions" (Niglas 2001, p. 2). Therefore, it is argued that the exclusive connection of methods to paradigms is not as strict anymore. Moreover, Niglas (2010, p. 218) argues that the "landscape of social scientific inquiry is continuously changing so that the paradigm system cannot be seen as fixed but as evolving through time."

In this thesis, the position is adopted that there is a certain link between paradigm and methods, but that the paradigms are overlapping and methods can hence be used with different paradigms, as illustrated in Fig. 4.2 by Niglas (2001).

4.1 Research Philosophy

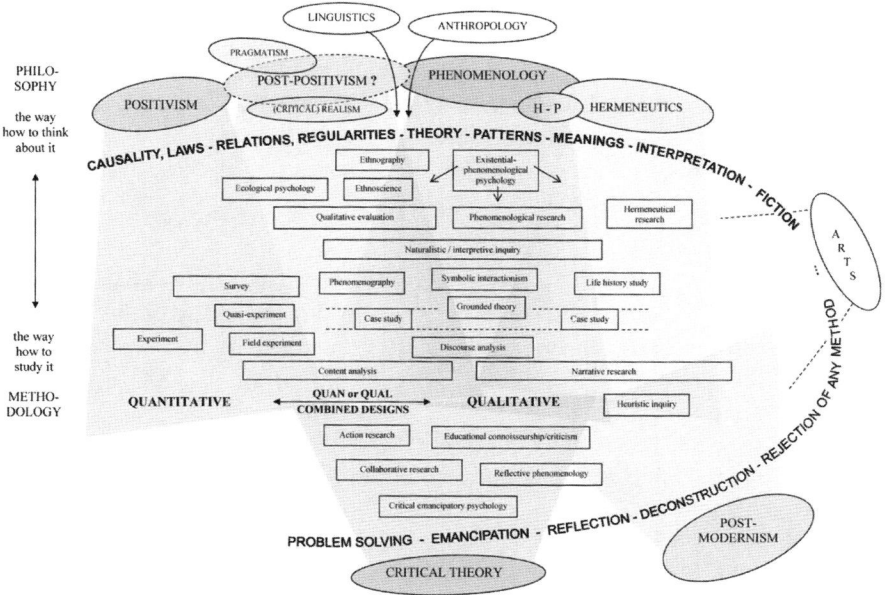

Fig. 4.2 Paradigms and methodology (reproduced from Niglas 2001)

4.1.2 Philosophical Assumptions of This Thesis

4.1.2.1 Post-positivism as Underlying Paradigm

In this research project, a post-positivist research philosophy is adopted. Post-positivism as used in this thesis is a "newer version of positivism" (Niglas 2001, p. 2) that has emerged as a response to the criticism of traditional positivism (Muijs 2004; Sharma 2010). Post-positivism retains the general set of ontological assumptions of positivism, such as the belief in an objective reality (Greene 2007; Muijs 2004).

However, post-positivism recognizes that it is only possible to know or apprehend reality imperfectly (Denzin and Lincoln 2009; Blaxter et al. 2006), since humans are inherently biased in their perception of reality (Sharma 2010). Hence, research can never be certain (Muijs 2004). Instead, research should try to approximate the truth of reality, being aware that it can never be explained fully and that it is shaped by the subjectivity of the observer (Sharma 2010; Muijs 2004).

Although according to the post-positivist epistemology, research can never be certain (Muijs 2004), it is possible to evaluate whether claims are more or less plausible and to test and choose between rival hypotheses (Patton 2002). However, due to the complexity of human behaviour (Sharma 2010), it is problematic to prove causality, i.e. to isolate cause and effect, with certainty (Patton 2002).

In terms of methodology, post-positivism is characterised by less faith in the power of methods (Greene 2007; Patton 2002). Hence, post-positivist research designs regularly rely on using multiple methods "as a way of capturing as much of reality as possible" (Denzin and Lincoln 2009, p. 11). This way, post-positivist research attempts to account for the imperfection of methods and the inherent bias in the perception of reality by triangulating the findings (Sharma 2010).

4.1.2.2 Ontological and Epistemological Assumptions of the Author

On the one hand, the choice of a post-positivist research paradigm is based on the author's personal belief system, which has developed in the course of dealing with Managerial Finance topics in academic and professional environments. On the other hand, the nature of the research area also influences the philosophical assumptions underlying this research.

This thesis conducts research in the context of business firms. From an **ontological point of view**, it is assumed that organisations exist as tangible objects, as described by Bryman (2008). The firms that are investigated are expected to have established rules, regulations and standardised procedures concerning their cost-of-capital practices. In many cases, the procedures might, for instance, be recorded in formal guidelines to which the employees must adhere. Similarly, financial data is stored in information systems, which are also considered as tangible objects. Therefore, it is assumed that the cost-of-capital practices exist externally—independent from the employees' or the researcher's perceptions.

This ontological position is partly based on the nature of the research topic, since the researcher is not primarily concerned with social phenomena such as attitudes or behaviours but with facts that exist externally, independent from the observation.

However, from an **epistemological perspective**, it is probably not possible to completely understand the complex reality of influencing factors and reasons underlying the behaviour of the organisations in terms of their cost-of-capital practices. Therefore, the research and the model that is developed in this thesis can only explain the complex reality with certain confidence, but not with certainty. Moreover, although the researcher attempts to operate from a neutral and value-free position, a human researcher is always subject to certain bias. In this thesis, effort is taken to minimise researcher bias (see Sect. 5.3). However, the author believes that social research can never be completely passive and neutral in a way that the positivist paradigm suggests.

These philosophical assumptions are reflected in the choice of a mixed method approach for this thesis, which helps to reduce bias by triangulating findings by employing different methods. This way, is attempted to construct a model of cost-of-capital practices which more closely approximates reality.

4.2 Research Ethics

4.2.1 Background and Importance of Research Ethics

Every researcher has to ensure that ethical issues and implications in his research have been considered. Although there is a trend towards a formalisation of research ethics, with institutions becoming more active in monitoring the ethical conduct of researchers (Bell and Wray-Bliss 2011), it is the researcher's own responsibility to behave ethically. Unethical behaviour of researchers in the past—such as ethnographic studies in the context of European colonialism and imperialism (Denzin and Lincoln 2009; Bell and Wray-Bliss 2011) or atrocities committed by Nazis in clinical experiments (Bell and Wray-Bliss 2011)—emphasise the importance of considering ethical issues.

According to Gläser and Laudel (2008), the highest precept of social research ethics is that the *people participating in the research* may not be harmed. In the context of organisational research, this does not only apply to the individual human participants in the research, but also to their organisations or businesses. For instance, there must not be any negative effects on the reputation of an organisation due to its participation in the research (Bell and Wray-Bliss 2011). Specifically, the following general responsibilities towards the participants are given in the literature (Bell and Wray-Bliss 2011):

- To avoid physical or psychological harm or risk of harm;
- To fully inform participants about the nature of the research and to request their consent to be involved;
- To maintain privacy and ensure confidentiality or anonymity of data;
- To declare potential conflicts of interests, e.g. due to sources of funding and support or affiliations of the researcher.

Apart from the participants in the research, there is also a responsibility towards *other interest groups* that are directly or indirectly part of the research (Myers 2009). These groups include, for instance, peer researchers. For example, avoiding plagiarism, i.e. the "deliberate copying of someone else's work and presenting it as one's own" (Myers 2009, p. 47) and mentioning all researchers who participated in a project is one ethical responsibility in research (Gläser and Laudel 2008; Bell and Wray-Bliss 2011). Moreover, an honest presentation of the results in the research report is important for audiences, public users of the results and peer researchers (Gläser and Laudel 2008).

In the subsequent two sections, concrete ethical considerations that have been made in each of the two stages of this research project are dealt with.

4.2.2 Ethical Considerations in the Expert Interviews

According to Patton (2002, p. 407), "qualitative methods are highly personal and interpersonal, because naturalistic inquiry takes the researcher into the real world where people live and work, and because in-depth interviewing opens up what is inside people—qualitative inquiry may be more intrusive and involve greater reactivity than surveys, tests and other quantitative approaches."

Generally, due to this nature of interviews, there is an increased risk of people being psychologically harmed. However, in the specific case of this research, the danger has been assessed as less severe for the following reasons: First, the topic of the thesis does not deal with the personal or work situation of the interviewees, but with technical practices of companies, which are more fact-driven than emotion-driven. Second, the people involved in the research are business professionals who are used to similar situations and discussions. Nevertheless, it is essential to inform the participants and respect their rights.

However, besides the aspect of ethical treatment of the participants, it has to be acknowledged that the participants might provide sensitive or confidential information about their companies. Therefore, the researcher also has an ethical obligation toward the companies. In order to inform and protect the participants of the expert interviews, the following measures were taken:

- At the beginning of each interview, the participants were asked if they agreed that the interview would be audio-recorded before the recording device was activated.
- The participants were informed about details concerning the interview process and the usage of the information with the help of an interview information sheet.[1]
- The participants were asked for their *informed consent* to the interview after the points from the information sheet were discussed. This was done orally and recorded (in cases where the participant had agreed to audio recording).
- Names of participants and other personal data as well as company names were only recorded in one electronic file (interview documentation sheet) separately from the interview content. All other files—such as transcripts and data analysis files—only contained the participants' anonymous code numbers.
- In order to ensure data security, the file containing personal information was not sent to any other persons and not stored on third-party servers (e.g. no cloud computing backup was used). Backups were only made on the researcher's physical backup drive.

---

[1] In telephone interviews, the information sheet was read out to the participants by the researcher.

4.2.3 Ethical Considerations in the Company Survey

Also in a company survey, there are similar ethical obligations not only to protect the participants from harm—which is less relevant for this research—but also to ensure that informed consent is obtained and confidentiality of data is ensured (Groves et al. 2009). The following principles were followed in the design and execution of the survey in order to protect the participants:

- Informed consent was obtained on the first page of the web survey: The participants were informed about the objectives of the research and assured that their answers would be treated confidentially and only be analysed and published on an aggregated level. Moreover, contact data for the researcher and supervisors were listed. Only if the participant agreed to these terms could the survey be started.
- Company names and email addresses were optional fields in the survey and could be left empty.
- The link between identifier codes that were used in the data collection process and actual companies was only known personally by the researcher and was stored separately from the answers.
- Data was only analysed on an aggregated level, i.e. no answers for individual companies were analysed.

4.3 Conclusion

In this chapter, the philosophical background of the author and this research was discussed. It was shown that the author adopts a post-positivist research philosophy that advocates the use of multiple methods to triangulate findings that are based on an incomplete human perception of reality and inherently imperfect research methods.

Consequently, in this research, a sequential mixed methods approach is pursued, which consists of qualitative, semi-structured expert interviews followed by a quantitative survey. This enables the researcher to triangulate findings that are achieved with the different methods. In the next chapter, details about the mixed methods approach are discussed.

Furthermore, in this chapter, ethical considerations that were made in the design of the expert interviews and company survey were pointed out. It was explained that the informed consent of the participants was obtained and that measures were taken to ensure the confidentiality of the answers.

References

Bazeley P (2004) Issues in mixing qualitative and quantitative approaches to research. In: Buber R, Gadner J, Richards L (eds) Applying qualitative methods to marketing management research. Palgrave Macmillan, Basingstoke, pp 141–156

Bell E, Wray-Bliss E (2011) Research ethics: regulations and responsibilities. In: Buchanan DA (ed) The SAGE handbook of organizational research methods. Sage, London, pp 78–92

Blaxter L, Hughes C, Tight M (2006) How to research. Open University Press, Berkshire, NY

Bryman A (2008) Social research methods. Oxford University Press, Oxford

Cua FC, Garret TC (2009) Understanding ontology and epistemology in information systems research. In: Cater-Steel A, Al-Hakim L (eds) Information systems research methods, epistemology, and applications. Information Science Reference, Hershey, PA, pp 35–56

David M, Sutton CD (2011) Social research. An introduction. Sage, Los Angeles, CA

Denzin NK, Lincoln YS (2009) Introduction. In: Denzin NK, Lincoln YS (eds) The Sage handbook of qualitative research. Sage, Thousand Oaks, CA, pp 1–32

Easterby-Smith M, Thorpe R, Jackson PR (2008) Management research, 3rd edn. Sage, Los Angeles, CA

Gläser J, Laudel G (2008) Experteninterviews und qualitative Inhaltsanalyse. Als Instrumente rekonstruierender Untersuchungen. VS Verlag für Sozialwissenschaften, Wiesbaden

Greene JC (2007) Mixing methods in social inquiry. Wiley, Chichester

Groves RM, Fowler FJ, Couper MP, Lepkowski JM, Singer E, Tourangeau R (2009) Survey methodology. Wiley, Hoboken, NJ

Hammersley M (2011) Methodology—who needs it? Sage, Los Angeles, CA

Hesse-Biber SN, Leavy P (2011) The practice of qualitative research. Sage, Los Angeles, CA

Horrigan PG (2007) Epistemology: an introduction to the philosophy of knowledge. iUniverse, Lincoln, NE

Kanellis P, Papadopoulos T (2009) Conducting research in information systems: an epistemological journey. In: Cater-Steel A, Al-Hakim L (eds) Information systems research methods, epistemology, and applications. Information Science Reference, Hershey, PA, pp 1–34

Kuhn TS (1970) The structure of scientific revolutions, 2, enlargedth edn. University of Chicago Press, Chicago

Monette DR, Sullivan TJ, DeJong CR (2011) Applied social research. A tool for the human services. Brookscole, Belmont, CA

Muijs D (2004) Quantitative methods in educational research. Sage, London

Myers MD (2009) Qualitative research in business and management. Sage, London

Niglas K (2001) "Paradigms and methodology in educational research". Paper presented at the European conference on educational research, Lille, 5–8 Sept 2001. Available from http://www.leeds.ac.uk/educol/documents/00001840.htm

Niglas K (2010) The multidimensional model of research methodology. An integrated set of continua. In: Tashakkori A, Teddlie C (eds) Sage handbook of mixed methods in social and behavioral research. Sage, Los Angeles, pp 215–236

Patton MQ (2002) Qualitative research and evaluation methods. Sage, London

Saunders M, Lewis P, Thornhill A (2009) Research methods for business students. Financial Times Prentice Hall, Harlow

Sharma B (2010) Postpositivism. In: Mills AJ, Durepos G, Wiebe E (eds) Encyclopedia of case study research. Sage, Los Angeles, pp 701–703

Chapter 5
Empirical Research Approach and Methods

In the previous chapter, the philosophical assumptions of this thesis were explained. It was explained that based on a post-positivist paradigm, a mixed methods approach is pursued.

As mixed methods approaches are not uncontroversial among academics, a brief review of relevant literature and the mixed methods debate is presented. Subsequently, an overview of the methods of this thesis is given.

5.1 Mixed Methods Research in the Literature

5.1.1 Introduction and Terminology

The mixed methods approach is relatively new in social sciences research (David and Sutton 2011). Therefore, some of its aspects, such as a uniform definition and the epistemological foundation, are still under discussion. However, as Bryman (2007, p. 8) states, "there can be little doubt that mixed methods research has moved forward a great deal in recent years". Also Creswell and Plano Clark (2007) mention that in recent years, many researchers have started to advocate mixed methods research as a methodology or design on its own. Johnson and Onwuegbuzie (2004, p. 14) refer to mixed methods research as the "third research paradigm" besides purist quantitative and qualitative approaches.

Moreover, the launch of the *Journal of Mixed Methods Research* and the publication of the *Handbook of Mixed Methods in Social and Behavioral Research* (Tashakkori and Teddlie 2002, 2010) by SAGE is cited as another argument for the increasing importance of mixed methods research by these authors (Creswell and Plano Clark 2007; Bryman 2008).

Some authors criticize that the terminology of mixed methods research is confusing and can be applied to very different approaches to research. They also

Fig. 5.1 Research choices according to Saunders et al. (2009)

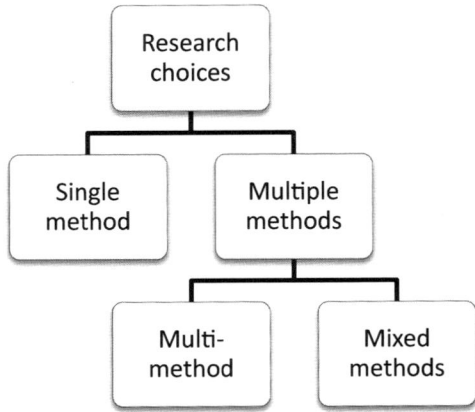

point out that terminology is often used interchangeably: for instance, *mixed methods* and *multiple methods* (David and Sutton 2011; Bazeley 2004). Bazeley (2004, p. 141) states that "it becomes necessary, therefore, to clarify just what is being mixed—and how it is being mixed." However, consensus seems to be growing and the prevailing view in the literature seems to be that the term *mixed methods* refers to mixing *qualitative and quantitative* methods (Ivankova et al. 2006; Saunders et al. 2009; Bryman 2008; Creswell and Plano Clark 2007).

Saunders et al. (2009) provide a clear definition of their understanding of terms that are sometimes confusing (see Fig. 5.1): *Multiple methods* refers to using more than one data collection technique and analysis procedure. Multiple methods can be further classified into a multi-method approach or a mixed methods approach. *Multi-method approach* means using more than one collection and analysis technique, but either only quantitative or only qualitative techniques, whereas the term *mixed methods* is used if both quantitative and qualitative elements are applied.

In the literature, the term *triangulation* is often used in the context of mixed methods research. Niglas (2000, p. 2) criticizes that the term has lost its original meaning and has become "something general and indefinite". Indeed, no generally accepted definition can be found. Some authors use the term as a synonym for mixed methods (Cohen et al. 2007; Krishnaswamy et al. 2006). In this thesis, triangulation is defined in line with Bryman (2008) and David and Sutton (2011): Triangulation means cross-checking or corroborating the result of one method by employing another method in order to achieve greater validity and confidence in the results.

5.1.2 *Purpose and Typologies*

Triangulation is not the only advantage of mixed methods research. In the literature, several purposes and rationales of mixing methods are mentioned: One intention of

5.1 Mixed Methods Research in the Literature

using a mixed methods approach could be to *overcome weaknesses* of individual methods (Krishnaswamy et al. 2006; David and Sutton 2011). On the other hand, Bryman (2008) argues that mixed methods research is not necessarily superior to using a mono method approach because the most important issue is that the research is competently designed and conducted and that it fits the research question.

Bryman (2006) conducted a content analysis of 232 journal articles based on mixed methods research from a 10-year period from 1994 to 2003. The main focus of the study was finding out the rationales for applying mixed methods research. The rationales were coded with 16 codes (Bryman 2006), which are shown in Table 5.1. Section 5.2.2 will refer back to this scheme in order to point out which rationales apply to this thesis.

Apart from the rationales or functions of applying mixed methods research, there are other dimensions out of which typologies of mixed methods approaches are built. According to Niglas (2000), there are two important dimensions that serve as a basis for classification: the *timing* and the *importance* given to divergent methods. In terms of timing, a study can either have a sequential design or a simultaneous design. In terms of importance, the methods can either be given the same weight (equivalent design) or one method can prevail (dominant-less dominant design). Moreover, it can be differentiated in which phase of the inquiry or methodological stage the mixing of methods occurs. More recently, Teddlie and Tashakkori (2006) have introduced a four-dimensional typology of research designs which also takes into account at which stage of the research process the mixing of the methods occurs.

There are several reasons why developing typologies of research designs are important, especially for a relatively new field of research (Teddlie and Tashakkori 2006; Bryman 2006). However, for the purpose of this thesis, a further discussion of the typologies is not necessary. The thesis will be located in the field with the help of the codes describing the rationales for employing mixed methods as shown in Table 5.1.

5.1.3 The Debate Around Mixed Methods Research

While mixing methods can have several advantages, as outlined in the previous section, many researchers express reservations about the approach. The points that are often raised are the following:

- philosophical foundation
- validity concerns and dealing with conflicting findings
- proper integration of findings
- practical issues.

Especially during the 1970s and 1980s—a period that Creswell and Plano Clark (2007, p. 15) refer to as the "paradigm debate period"—there was a strong debate about the **philosophical foundation** of mixed methods research. According to

Table 5.1 Rationales for employing mixed methods research (adapted from Bryman 2008)

No.	Rationale	Description
1	Triangulation	Refers to the traditional view that quantitative and qualitative research may be combined to triangulate findings in order that they may be mutually corroborated
2	Offset	Refers to the suggestion that the research methods associated with both quantitative and qualitative research have their own strengths and weaknesses so that combining them allows the researcher to offset their weaknesses to draw on the strengths of both
3	Completeness	Refers to the notion that the research can bring together a more comprehensive account of the area of enquiry in which he or she is interested if both quantitative and qualitative research are employed
4	Process	Quantitative research provides an account of structures in social life but qualitative research provides sense of process
5	Different research questions	This is the argument that quantitative and qualitative research can each answer different research questions
6	Explanation	One of the two research methods is used to help explain findings generated by the other
7	Unexpected results	Refers to the suggestion that quantitative and qualitative research can be fruitfully combined when one generates surprising results that can be understood by employing the other
8	Instrument development	Refers to contexts in which qualitative research is employed to develop questionnaire and scale items
9	Sampling	Refers to situations in which one approach is used to facilitate the sampling of respondents or cases
10	Credibility	Refers to suggestions that employing both approaches enhances the integrity of findings
11	Context	Refers to cases in which the combination is rationalized in terms of qualitative research, providing contextual understanding coupled with either generalizable, externally valid findings or broad relationships among variables uncovered through a survey
12	Illustration	Refers to the use of qualitative data to illustrate quantitative findings, often referred to putting 'meat on the bones' of 'dry' quantitative findings
13	Utility	Refers to a suggestion, which is more likely to be prominent among articles with an applied focus, that combining the two approaches will be more useful to practitioners and others
14	Confirm and discover	This entails using qualitative data to generate hypotheses and using quantitative research to test them within a single project
15	Diversity of views	This includes two slightly different rationales—namely, combining researchers' and participants' perspectives through quantitative and qualitative research respectively and uncovering relationships between variables through quantitative research while also revealing meanings among research participants through qualitative research
16	Enhancement	This entails a reference to making more of or augmenting either quantitative or qualitative findings by gathering data using a qualitative or quantitative research approach

Bryman (2008), there are two version of the paradigm argument against integrating qualitative and quantitative methods. The first version of the argument is the idea that different *methods are associated with certain epistemological positions* or paradigms and thus cannot be combined, since they are philosophically incompatible (Bryman 2008; Bazeley 2004). The second version of the philosophy argument is that *quantitative and qualitative research are separate paradigms* (Bryman 2008). However, proponents of the mixed methods approach argue that research methods do not necessarily carry with them certain philosophical implications and that they can be employed for a large variety of tasks (Bryman 2008). As Bryman (2008, p. 605) states, "the problem with the argument is that it rests (...) on contentions about the interconnectedness of method and epistemology in particular that cannot—in the case of social research—be demonstrated."

According to Niglas (2000), there are three different positions among researchers concerning the philosophy debate. Academics with a *strong paradigmatic view* consider combining qualitative and quantitative methods unacceptable. Researchers with a *weak paradigmatic view* are somewhat tolerant towards combining methods under certain circumstances. For instance, Easterby-Smith et al. (2008, p. 71) argue that they have "reservations about mixing methods when they represent very distinct ontologies" but that "the researcher may get away with using mixed methods where the overall direction and significance of the two sources are fairly similar". The third position, the *pragmatist* position, advocates the use of mixed methods, arguing that the most important issue to consider is the understanding about the phenomenon under investigation, independent from any philosophical considerations.

As discussed in Sect. 4.1.1.3, in this thesis it is argued that there is a certain link between paradigm and methods, but that the paradigms are overlapping and methods can hence be used with different paradigms. From the post-positivist perspective that is adopted in this thesis, it makes sense to triangulate findings because human perceptions of reality are always incomplete (see Sect. 4.1.2.1).

Another issue that is sometimes raised concerning mixed methods research relates to **validity concerns**, i.e. the question of whether qualitative and quantitative elements of a study that are combined really measure the same thing. For instance, David and Sutton (2011) state that there might be differences due to data collection and measurements, since in quantitative research, closed-ended questions are often used, whereas in qualitative research more open-ended questions are used. This might lead to the problem that different concepts or constructs are measured, although the intention is to measure the same thing with different methods. If this is the case, this leads to the additional (more practical) problem of how the researcher should deal with a situation in which different kinds of data deliver **contradictory results** about the (apparently) same phenomenon (Easterby-Smith et al. 2008; Niglas 2000).

However, the validity concerns are not an inherent problem of the mixed methods approach. Bazeley (2004, p. 9) points out that "validity stems more from the appropriateness, thoroughness and effectiveness with which those methods are applied". This view is shared by the author of this thesis. If the validity of the individual methods that are employed is ensured, they should indeed measure the same thing.

Another point of criticism that is sometimes pronounced is that in most mixed methods studies, there is **no real integration** of the findings from the different components. Instead, the quantitative and qualitative parts are often treated as separate domains and presented in parallel in a largely independent way (Bryman 2007). However, it would be desirable to merge the analyses of the quantitative and qualitative data. As Creswell and Plano Clark (2007) argue, it is not sufficient to collect and analyse the different types of data but mix the datasets in some way in order that they deliver more complete information than each component would on its own. By renouncing a real integration of data and findings, researchers often do not fully exploit the potential of the data they have collected (Bryman 2007).

In his article "Barriers to Integrating Quantitative and Qualitative Research", Bryman (2007) presents the findings from a study in which he interviewed 20 mixed methods researchers in order to find out the reasons for the lack of integration. He reports that there are indeed barriers to integrating the quantitative and qualitative components. He identified eight barriers to integrating the components. The barriers include, for example, methodological preferences of individual researchers and skill specialisms in research teams, as well as timing and publication issues in research projects (Bryman 2007). In this thesis, the results of qualitative and quantitative research will be integrated in the final chapter.

Apart from the methodological concerns against mixed methods research, academics also state **practical issues** that argue against applying mixed methods. First, it is argued that mixed methods research projects are more expensive and time-consuming than mono-method research projects and thus require more resources (David and Sutton 2011; Bryman 2008). Moreover, not all researchers have the necessary skills and training to conduct both quantitative and qualitative research (Bryman 2008).

5.2 Empirical Research Methods of This Research

5.2.1 Overview and Stages

In this thesis, a sequential mixed methods research design is employed. In a first stage, semi-structured qualitative expert interviews will be conducted in order to identify key issues and themes concerning the cost-of-capital practices of companies. These issues and themes will then be tested for their robustness to the real economy sector through a survey instrument. The survey will be conducted with a selective sample that is chosen based on criteria of sector (real economy) and location (Germany). The two stages of the empirical research design are illustrated in Fig. 5.2 and explained below. The reasons for choosing a mixed methods approach are discussed in Sect. 5.2.2.

5.2 Empirical Research Methods of This Research

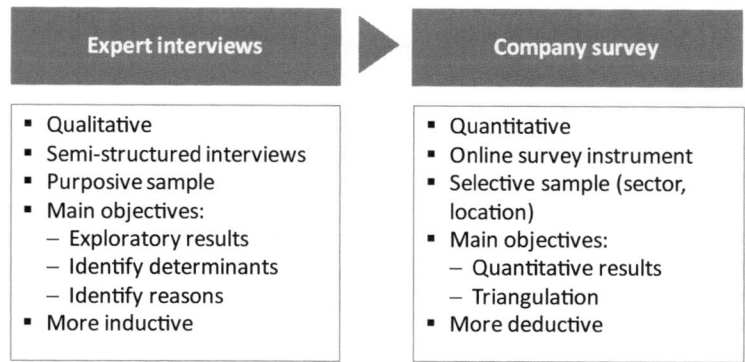

Fig. 5.2 Overview of research design

(1) Expert Interviews

In the first stage, qualitative semi-structured expert interviews are conducted with management consultants and Finance and Accounting professionals from companies. The main objective of this stage is to gain exploratory insights into the cost-of-capital practices of the focus sector and location. This includes the identification of determinants of the cost-of-capital practices. Additionally, the qualitative design is used to identify underlying reasons for the companies' behaviour, which can be used at a later stage to interpret the overall results.

The expert interviews are more inductive than the survey. However, as the questions were partly derived from the literature review, a certain deductive character remains. The results from the qualitative stage are then used to formulate hypotheses at the beginning of stage 2.

(2) Company Survey

In the second stage, a quantitative company survey is conducted with German-based companies from the real economy sector. To collect the data, an online survey instrument is used.

The main objective of this stage is to quantitatively test the results from the qualitative research. Thus, this stage has a deductive character.

5.2.2 *Justification of the Chosen Approach and Methods*

In the previous section, the stages of the empirical research for this thesis were briefly presented. This section justifies why a mixed methods research design is suitable for the objectives of this research. This is done by pointing out which rationales of applying mixed methods research that Bryman (2006) identified in his research (see Sect. 5.1.2) apply to this thesis. The points are sorted according to their importance for this thesis as perceived by the author.

(1) Instrument Development

Although the expert interviews also have their own contribution to the research objectives, one major purpose of the qualitative stage is to provide a basis for the development of the survey instrument. Questions concerning the influencing factors of cost-of-capital practices, in particular, were developed on the basis of the interviews. Moreover, with the help of the exploratory results from the interviews, the adequate level of detail for the cost-of-capital questions could be assessed. Because of the theory-practice gap in cost-of-capital, there is a certain risk to ask questions that are too detailed if companies have very rudimentary practices.

(2) Confirm and Discover

This point refers to "using qualitative data to generate hypotheses and using quantitative research to test them within a single project" (Bryman 2008, p. 609). As pointed out above, the qualitative stage of this research has a more exploratory character because due to research gaps in the area, it was not possible to generate hypotheses directly from the literature review. Instead, research propositions were formulated and detailed hypotheses were formulated after the findings from the expert interviews.

(3) Triangulation

Moreover, the traditional idea of across-method triangulation (Johnson et al. 2007; Bryman 2008), i.e. combining quantitative and qualitative methods in order to mutually corroborate the results, also applies to this thesis.

(4) Offset

This point refers to the common idea (David and Sutton 2011; Krishnaswamy et al. 2006) that combining quantitative and qualitative methods "allows the researcher to offset their weaknesses to draw on the strengths of both" (Bryman 2008, p. 609). For this thesis, the following issues are particularly relevant: In pure quantitative designs, there is the danger of missing out on phenomena if the hypotheses that are tested are not comprehensive (Johnson and Onwuegbuzie 2004), whereas qualitative research is able to identify important factors. In contrast, a disadvantage of qualitative research is that the results produced are often not generalizable (Myers 2009; Johnson and Onwuegbuzie 2004). Here, quantitative research can help to test and validate theories constructed in the qualitative stage (Johnson and Onwuegbuzie 2004).

(5) Explanation

Another point that applies to this thesis is that "one of the two research methods is used to help explain findings generated by the other" (Bryman 2008, p. 609). In this case, the strengths of the qualitative methods to explain *how and why* certain phenomena occur (Johnson and Onwuegbuzie 2004) are used. More precisely, in the expert interviews, underlying reasons for the occurrence of influencing factors are investigated. For instance, the reason why the often-cited size factor in Finance practices occurs (see Sect. 6.4.2) was identified. Thus, using findings from the qualitative stage of the research, this thesis is able to make a contribution to theory.

5.3 Limitations and Bias

Every research project has its limitations, since there are no perfect research designs. Therefore, it is important in any research report to disclose possible limitations and biases in order that the reader can assess the boundaries of the research (Marshall and Rossman 2011).

First of all, as pointed out in the introductory chapter (Sect. 1.2.3), there are explicit **delimitations of scope** in this research project. This study focuses on the real economy sector in Germany in the context of Managerial Finance. Therefore, the results might not be transferable to other sectors, countries or contexts.

Moreover, from a post-positivist perspective, in any study there will be bias, i.e. systematic error that is consciously or unconsciously introduced in the research design (Harden and Thomas 2010). One important form of bias is **researcher bias**, which is the tendency to obtain results that are consistent with what the researcher wants to find. Researcher bias is especially a threat in qualitative research but also in quantitative research. One of the reasons for researcher bias is the researcher's personal views and perspectives (Johnson 2012).

One measure to reduce researcher bias is a critical self-reflection by the researcher in order to become aware of possible biases and attempt to control them (*reflexivity*) (Johnson 2012). One possible bias of the author of this thesis might be his professional background. He works as a Finance and Accounting consultant and has his own experiences with the topic from his clients. Therefore, he has to be careful not to mix his own experiences with findings from the research, especially with statements from the interviewees. Another measure against researcher bias that is suggested in literature (Johnson 2012) is *investigator triangulation*, i.e. the use of multiple researchers. This was not possible in this Ph.D. research project. However, the researcher has regularly put his methodology and findings forward for discussion with supervisors, colleagues and peer researchers. Moreover, because of the mixed methods approach, the results were cross-checked due to *data and methods triangulation*.

Besides the general researcher bias, there might be **bias in the individual research methods**, i.e. in details of the expert interviews or the survey. Efforts are made to reduce this bias by using multiple methods and mutually corroborating the findings from the qualitative and the quantitative stage. Individual measures to reduce bias in each stage of the research are discussed in the respective chapters (see Sects. 6.1.3 and 7.2.5).

5.4 Conclusion

In this chapter, the mixed methods research literature was discussed, before an overview of the methods applied in this research was given. Furthermore, clarification was provided as to why the two methods are used sequentially: expert interviews are conducted first, and then a company survey is used to quantitatively test the findings.

Details on the research design and the findings of these two stages are discussed separately in the next two chapters.

References

Bazeley P (2004) Issues in mixing qualitative and quantitative approaches to research. In: Buber R, Gadner J, Richards L (eds) Applying qualitative methods to marketing management research. Palgrave Macmillan, Basingstoke, pp 141–156

Bryman A (2006) Integrating quantitative and qualitative research: How is it done? Qual Res 6(1):97–113

Bryman A (2007) Barriers to integrating quantitative and qualitative research. J Mixed Methods Res 1(1):8–22

Bryman A (2008) Social research methods. Oxford University Press, Oxford

Cohen L, Manion L, Morrison K (2007) Research methods in education. Routledge, London

Creswell JW, Plano Clark VL (2007) Designing and conducting mixed methods research. Sage, Thousand Oaks, CA

David M, Sutton CD (2011) Social research. An introduction. Sage, Los Angeles

Easterby-Smith M, Thorpe R, Jackson PR (2008) Management research, 3rd edn. Sage, Los Angeles

Harden A, Thomas J (2010) Mixed methods and systematic reviews. Examples and emerging issues. In: Tashakkori A, Teddlie C (eds) Sage handbook of mixed methods in social and behavioral research. Sage, Los Angeles, pp 749–774

Ivankova NV, Creswell JW, Stick SL (2006) Using mixed-methods sequential explanatory design: from theory to practice. Field Methods 18(3):3–20

Johnson B (2012) Educational research, 4th edn. Sage, Thousand Oaks, CA

Johnson RB, Onwuegbuzie AJ (2004) Mixed methods research: a research paradigm whose time has come. Educ Res 33(7):14–26

Johnson RB, Onwuegbuzie AJ, Turner LA (2007) Toward a definition of mixed methods research. J Mixed Methods Res 1(2):112–133

Krishnaswamy KN, Sivakumar AI, Mathirajan M (2006) Management research methodology. Integration of principles, methods and techniques. Pearson, New Delhi

Marshall C, Rossman GB (2011) Designing qualitative research. Sage, Los Angeles

Myers MD (2009) Qualitative research in business and management. Sage, London

Niglas K (2000) Combining quantitative and qualitative approaches. Paper presented at the European conference on educational research, Edinburgh. http://www.leeds.ac.uk/educol/documents/00001544.htm. Accessed 20–23 Sept 2000

Saunders M, Lewis P, Thornhill A (2009) Research methods for business students. Financial Times Prentice Hall, Harlow

Tashakkori A, Teddlie C (2002) Handbook of mixed methods. Sage, London

Tashakkori A, Teddlie C (2010) Sage handbook of mixed methods in social and behavioral research. Sage, Los Angeles

Teddlie C, Tashakkori A (2006) A general typology of research designs featuring mixed methods. Res Sch 13(1):12–28

Chapter 6
Primary Research: Expert Interviews

In this chapter, results of the qualitative research undertaken are presented. The main purpose of this stage of the research was to gain an exploratory insight into cost-of-capital practices and identify factors that influence the cost-of-capital practices of companies.

The chapter starts with a short explanation of the methodological background of qualitative research, taking into account relevant literature (Sect. 6.1). In the next section, the empirical research design of the expert interviews is discussed (Sect. 6.2). The next section (Sect. 6.3) documents the analysis of the qualitative data that has been undertaken with the help of matrices and a concept map. Finally, the findings of the expert interviews are discussed (Sect. 6.4). The chapter ends with a brief conclusion and the presentation of the refined preliminary model of cost-of-capital practices.

6.1 Methodological Background

6.1.1 The Nature of Qualitative Research

Quantitative and qualitative approaches are distinguished based on the types of data they use. Qualitative approaches use non-numeric or textual data as opposed to numeric data (Miles and Huberman 1994; Bazeley 2004).

Research with qualitative data has certain features which can be helpful for this stage of the research: One advantage is that instead of just examining a numerical relationship between certain issues, research using qualitative data is able to extract meaning from the content of the data (David and Sutton 2011). As Denzin and Lincoln (2009, p. 3) say, "qualitative researchers study things in their natural settings, attempting to make sense of, or interpret, phenomena in terms of the meanings people bring to them". In this research, one important objective is to 'make sense' of the cost-of-capital practices of companies. Therefore, a qualitative element is required, which allows researchers "to see and understand the context within which decisions and actions take place" (Myers 2009, p. 5).

Furthermore, qualitative research is a more cyclical process. This means that the focus of the research can be changed during the process because the collection and analysis of data are not completely separate phases of the research (David and Sutton 2011). This is especially helpful for this thesis because the qualitative part has an exploratory character. The cyclical process makes it possible to include new issues that have arisen in previous interviews into the next round of interviews. However, one has to be careful not to be distracted by less important issues that are found in the data (David and Sutton 2011). This danger is minimized in this thesis by not making a round of data analysis after each individual interview. Instead, the data is only analysed after several interviews have been conducted.

6.1.2 Approaches to Qualitative Data Analysis

A variety of different methods for analysing qualitative data are discussed in methodology literature (Silverman 2011; Rapley 2011; Myers 2009). One important differentiation between the methods is whether they follow an **inductive** or a **deductive approach** (Saunders et al. 2009). Deductive approaches involve analysing the data with the help of codes or categories that have been developed before the collection of the data. In contrast, inductive approaches develop the codes from the data (David and Sutton 2011). In this section, two main forms of qualitative data analysis, content analysis (deductive) and grounded analysis (inductive), will be discussed and compared briefly in order to lay the ground for the development of an analysis method for this thesis.

Content analysis is an approach that can be used for different kinds of qualitative data with the main goal of reducing material. It is a deductive approach, which means that the codes and categories are usually derived from theory and not developed from empirical material (which does not mean that codes cannot be adapted due to findings from the data) (Cohen et al. 2007; Flick 2009). It is a very systematic and rule-governed approach and therefore also verifiable (Cohen et al. 2007). There are different techniques in the literature to conduct the data reduction, which involve several steps to summarise and reduce the data and structure the codes and categories (Cohen et al. 2007; Flick 2009).

Although content analysis is a method of qualitative analysis, quantitative elements are often included in the method. This can be done by counting occurrences of codes in order to find out the importance of certain topics in the data (Cohen et al. 2007; Gläser and Laudel 2008). Myers (2009, p. 172) even concludes that content analysis is "in effect, a quantitative method of analysing the content of qualitative data".

Academics criticise that the analysis is based upon a pre-determined set of categories and is therefore very rigid (Silverman 2011). Furthermore, there might be bias because the information is isolated from its contextual meaning during the analysis (Myers 2009).

Grounded analysis is based on Grounded Theory, which was developed by Glaser and Strauss (1967). It is an inductive approach that develops the codes completely from the data. Due to different opinions in the academic discussion about how exactly coding is to be done in a grounded analysis approach, there are several versions of the method. The version by Strauss and Corbin (1990) involves the following three steps: First, *open coding* is used to attach codes and categories to individual parts of a text. In the second step, called *axial coding*, links between the categories are identified with the help of a paradigm model. In the third step, *selective coding*, the coding is taking to a higher level of abstraction. Glaser criticises the procedure of axial coding because it forces a predetermined structure on the data. He suggests an alternative version that uses *theoretical coding* instead, which suggests a list of basic codes grouped as coding families that can be used as a basis for defining codes (Myers 2009; Flick 2009).

In the literature, the approach is criticised because it relies more on the researcher's intuition than the more systematic content analysis (Easterby-Smith et al. 2008). As Flick (2009, p. 317) puts it, "the distinction between method and art becomes hazy." On the other hand, the approach allows more room for a deeper understanding of the text beyond paraphrasing and summarising it (Flick 2009).

6.1.3 Quality of Qualitative Research

Evaluated with traditional criteria such as reliability and validity, the quality of qualitative research has often been doubted (Miles and Huberman 1994). However, there is an ongoing discussion as to how the quality of qualitative research should be assessed. There is debate about whether the same **criteria** as in quantitative research are applicable at all, whether they should be reformulated or whether completely new criteria should be developed (Denzin and Lincoln 2009; Flick 2009). In this section, the traditional evaluation criteria of research and their implications in the context of qualitative research are briefly discussed. Moreover, the measures taken to enhance the quality of the qualitative research for this thesis are identified.

According to Silverman (2011, p. 360), **reliability** "deals with replicability, the question whether or not some future researchers could repeat the research project and come up with the same results, interpretations and claims". In order to enhance the reliability of qualitative research, the following suggestions are made in the literature (Silverman 2011; Flick 2009): First, a high quality of the recording, notes and data documentation should be ensured. In this research, the interviews were audio recorded and subsequently transcribed. However, no verbatim transcripts were made, as discussed in Sect. 6.2.2. Second, it is suggested to provide a detailed documentation of the research process and methods applied. A detailed discussion of the processes and methods applied in this research can be found in Sect. 6.2.

The concept of **validity** seems to be more difficult to grasp in qualitative research. Flick (2009 p. 387) provides the following definition: "The question of validity can be summarized as a question of whether the researchers see what they think they see." There have been various attempts to reformulate the concept of validity for qualitative research, which also depends on underlying philosophical assumptions. For discussion of this issue, the reader is referred to the relevant literature (Hesse-Biber and Leavy 2011; Silverman 2011; Ahrens and Chapman 2008; Flick 2009). One suggestion to enhance validity that can be found in the literature (Flick 2009) is the idea of *communicative validation*, meaning that a second meeting with the interviewees is arranged after the transcription in order to clarify what the candidate had meant with certain statements. However, this idea is quite controversial (Silverman 2011) and also not possible to implement in this research in view of the difficulty in being granted appointments with the interviewees. Instead, efforts were made to validate the meaning of the candidates' statements directly in the interviews. Another suggestion from the literature is the *constant comparative method* (Silverman 2011), which means that during the research, provisional hypotheses should always tested through another case. This was done in the present study by including issues that had come up in previous interviews into the subsequent interviews. Furthermore, *using appropriate tabulations* can enhance the validity of the research (Silverman 2011) because quantification can help the researcher to obtain a sense of variance in the data and furthermore give an indication of the prevalence of a phenomenon. This was also done in the analysis of the data (see Sect. 6.2.7).

The issue of **generalizability** that is often discussed (Flick 2009; Silverman 2011) is not considered relevant in this research because the qualitative findings are corroborated with the help of a quantitative survey.

6.2 Research Design

6.2.1 General Approach

In the literature, a variety of different interview types is described and there are different ways of classifying the approaches. Often, the distinction is made based on the extent to which the interview and the questions and answer possibilities are determined and standardised in advance (Cassell 2011). Completely standardised interviews in which the answer possibilities are also pre-determined are used in *quantitative* social research. In contrast, less standardised forms of interviews are used in *qualitative* research (Cassell 2011; Gläser and Laudel 2008).

Table 6.1 Qualitative interview types

Level of structure	Patton (2002)	Gläser and Laudel (2008)
High	Standardized open-ended interview	Guideline interview
Medium	General interview guide approach	Open interviews
Low	Informal conversational interview	Narrative interviews

Also among the qualitative interviews, there are more and less structured interview types. Table 6.1 outlines two different classifications of interviews as distinguished by Patton (2002) and Gläser and Laudel (2008).

For the purpose of this thesis, a semi-structured interview approach such as the *general interview guide approach* is considered the most suitable interview type. A semi-structured interview approach involves elaborating an interview guide before conducting the interviews that outlines a set of issues or topical areas that are to be investigated during the interview (Flick 2009; Patton 2002). However, in contrast to more standardized interviews where the same sequence and wording of questions is used in each interview, the interviewer is more flexible in asking questions. Compared to unstructured interviews, semi-structured interviews can have a similar conversational style, but are more focused (Patton 2002).

In terms of the objectives of this thesis, this type of interview is especially suitable because it combines two characteristics: On the one hand, it ensures a systematic and comprehensive approach to all key issues to be explored (Patton 2002). This is important for this thesis, because the qualitative interviews are guided by the preliminary model developed and presented in Sect. 3.5.4 and the findings from the literature review. On the other hand, semi-structured interviews provide flexibility in asking questions. First, they allow the incorporation of new aspects that arise in the course of the interview (Saunders et al. 2009). This characteristic is needed for this thesis because the expert interviews also have an exploratory and inductive element in order to refine the preliminary model by including further factors that are identified from the interviews. Second, the flexibility allows interviews to be tailored to the individual perspectives and experiences of the participants (Patton 2002). This is important because the topic of this thesis is very complex and specific and requires that the participants have certain technical expert knowledge. Semi-structured interviews provide the flexibility to focus on the issues about which the interviewee has specialist knowledge.

Moreover, an advantage over unstructured and too openly designed interviews is that the limited time that is available in an interview situation can be used efficiently (Patton 2002). This is especially relevant for this thesis because many of the interviewees are in management positions and are under great time pressure during their working day. On the other hand, it is not too standardized either, which has the advantage that the interviewees are more likely to express their viewpoint in a more open situation (Flick 2009).

Table 6.2 Advantages and disadvantages of telephone interviews

Advantages	Disadvantages
Time savings	No personal contact
Cost savings	Loss of non-verbal signals
Flexibility for candidates	

6.2.2 Data Collection and Documentation

All interviews were conducted by the researcher personally. Depending on the availability and geographical location of the interviewees, the interviews were conducted on a **face-to-face basis** or by **telephone**.

In the literature, different advantages and disadvantages of conducting interviews by telephone are pointed, out as summarised in Table 6.2 and described below.

The key advantages of telephone interviews are easier access and lower cost, because they reduce travelling. This also includes time savings, i.e. telephone interviews are generally more convenient than face-to-face interviews (Gläser and Laudel 2008; Saunders et al. 2009). Moreover, telephone interviews offer greater flexibility because they are easier to reschedule. Therefore, candidates—especially managers—often prefer telephone interviews (Gläser and Laudel 2008). This was also experienced during the interviews for this thesis and was the main reason why some of the interviews were conducted by telephone. Especially in the case of managers from consulting firms, it is difficult to arrange meetings at a fixed date and location, since they travel a lot and are often forced to change their plans at short notice.

Saunders et al. (2009) emphasise the importance of establishing personal contact in order that the participants are willing to engage in the exploratory discussion. They argue that participants may even refuse to take part in telephone interviews because not enough personal contact can be established. Moreover, they state that there is no ability to observe non-verbal behaviour in telephone interviews. While it is true that the possibility to observe non-verbal behaviour is limited, in the interviews for this study, no differences in willingness to participate could be perceived.

Taking these factors into account, efforts were made to arrange face-to-face interviews where possible and economically feasible. However, this aspect is not considered crucial, since it is arguable whether telephone interviews are really a disadvantage. Several studies, as cited by Cassell (2011), could not show any differences in data quality between the modes of data collection. For this thesis, nine interviews (75 %) were conducted face-to-face, while three interviews (25 %) were conducted via telephone.

The interviews were conducted in German. Where the interviewee had agreed, the interviews were **audio recorded**. The audio recording was then translated to English in the transcription process. Patton (2002) strongly recommends audio recording because of higher accuracy of the data collection. First, there is no

6.2 Research Design

conscious or unconscious interpretation of the data during note-taking, since the data is recorded as it naturally occurs. Second, audio recording allows the interviewer to be more attentive to the interviewee, since he or she is not focused on taking notes. However, Flick (2009) is more critical about audio recording and recommends limiting recording to what is absolutely necessary, since it may influence the participants' statements. Also Gläser and Laudel (2008) state that interviewees might withhold information or deliver more socially desirable answers due to the recording. In this study, ten interviews (83 %) were recorded.

For this thesis, the decision was made to apply audio recording but at the same time attempt to reduce the negative effects. This was done via two measures: First, participants were given the opportunity to make statements 'off the record', i.e. to indicate when they wanted to make a statement that would not be recorded. Second, for the audio recording in face-to-face interviews, a mobile phone was used instead of a device with a visible microphone so that the participants were not constantly reminded of the recording during the interview and could talk more naturally.

Technically, the face-to-face interviews were recorded with the help of an Apple iPhone 4S with an app called *AudioMemos*. The telephone interviews were conducted via the internet telephony software *Skype* in order to be able to record the calls with software called *Call Graph*. The participants did not have to use Skype, since it is possible to call regular landline or mobile phones via Skype.

As a next step before the interpretation of the data, the records were **transcribed**. There are different systems for transcription and there is a large amount of specific literature on the topic, as reviewed by Davidson (2009). However, Flick (2009, pp. 299–300) warns that "the formulation of rules for transcription may tempt one into some kind of fetishism that no longer bears any reasonable relation to the question and the products of the research". Therefore, he recommends limiting the transcription to the extent and exactness that is required by the research question. He argues that high exactness is only necessary in exceptional cases, for instance in linguistic research projects that focus on the organisation of language.

Following Flick's argumentation, it was decided that no verbatim transcripts were necessary for this thesis, since there is a strong focus on factual information and the contents of the participants' answers, rather than on linguistic phenomena or other factors such as non-verbal or emotional factors that could be derived from an exact verbatim transcription. Also, an elaborate system of transcription and data management, as discussed by McLellan et al. (2003), was not considered to be necessary taking into account the number of interviews that were conducted.

Flick (2009) recommends using **documentation sheets** in which the context of the interviews that were conducted is recorded. This can include, for instance, the data and place of an interview as well as characteristics of the interviewee, such as gender or age. For this thesis, this information was recorded in a spreadsheet containing the following data for each interview:

- Number of the candidate
- Name of the candidate
- Company

- Type of candidate (consulting or industry professional)
- Position of the candidate
- Academic qualification of the candidate
- Professional experience of the candidate in years
- Date of the interview
- Mode of the interview (face-to-face vs. telephone)
- Location of the interview (if applicable)
- Duration of the interview

The information recorded in the documentation sheet was used to track the status of the data collection and select further interviewees. Moreover, the information was used to provide certain statistics about the interviews in this thesis (see Sect. 6.2.4).

6.2.3 Sampling Approach

There are two main categories of sampling: probability sampling and non-probability sampling. *Probability sampling* is used where it is necessary to make statistical inferences from a representative sample about the characteristics of the population. In contrast, *non-probability sampling* includes subjective judgment in the selection of a sample and cannot be used to make generalisations based on statistics (Saunders et al. 2009).

Qualitative research approaches are generally associated with non-probability sampling strategies. As Flick (2009, p. 117) points out, in qualitative research, there is often no "one-shot drawing of a sample" with a sample size that is defined in advance as in probability sampling. Instead, an approach of **gradual sampling** is used, where decisions about the composition and size of the sample are made in the process of data collection and interpretation. According to Flick, this general principle goes back to the concept of theoretical sampling as developed by Glaser and Strauss (1967). Although the research approach in this study is different from Glaser and Strauss's Grounded Theory, the general idea of sampling in this study is similar to the idea of theoretical sampling as described by Flick (2009, p. 121):

> The basic principle of theoretical sampling is to select cases or case groups according to concrete criteria concerning their content instead of using abstract methodological criteria. Sampling proceeds according to the relevance of cases instead of their representativeness.

In the qualitative stage of this study, the following requirements needed to be fulfilled in terms of the sample:

- the possible factors of the model that explain the cost of capital practices are supposed to be identified, i.e. the characteristics of the cases in the sample should be different in order to identify all important determinants.
- the sample does not have to be statistically representative, as the model will be tested with a quantitative approach in a second stage.

6.2 Research Design

The requirements named above are in line with the idea of gradual sampling. Therefore, a gradual non-probability sampling strategy is considered appropriate for this stage of the research. More specifically, **purposive sampling** has been chosen. As described by Patton (2002) who uses the term purpose*ful* sampling as a synonym, the idea of purposive sampling is to selection information-rich cases which are studied in depth.

For the qualitative stage of this study, **two types of candidate** were interviewed: consultants as external experts and Finance and Accounting professionals from industrial companies. From both groups, efforts were made to identify information-rich cases. However, the criteria for selection and the concrete sampling strategy were slightly different.

(1) Consultants

There are several reasons why consultants are a very suitable type of interview partner. First of all, experienced consultants gain insights into a large number of industrial companies during their careers, since they usually have several clients and also change their clients over time when conducting different projects. Flick (2009, p. 165) describes this idea behind interviewing experts as follows: "*In contrast to biographical interviews, here the interviewees are of less interest as a (whole) person than their capacities as expert for a certain field of activity. They are integrated into the study not as a single case but as representing a group.*" The overview of several companies that consultants possess is seen as a particular advantage in identifying determinants of organisational behaviour concerning cost-of-capital. The consultants can help to identify differences and similarities between companies with different characteristics. Second, they have expert knowledge and also a relatively good theoretical background in their field of specialisation. Third, their views might be more objective compared to professionals from industrial companies, as they are not so much influenced by the cultures and routines of an individual company.

The consultants who were interviewed were selected from several German offices of one of the so-called global "Big Four" financial auditing and advisory firms. They were selected with the help of a **snowball or chain sampling** strategy. Snowball sampling involves asking interviewees to suggest other potential interviewees (Patton 2002; Saunders et al. 2009). The snowball sampling strategy was helpful in the identification of relevant consultants because due to the specialised nature of the research topic, it is hard to identify and gain access to relevant experts. Also, due to the time pressure that experts in senior positions face every day, they are rather reluctant to participate in interviews. Therefore, it was very helpful to be able to tell them that a colleague whom they knew had recommended them as an expert and thus establish personal contact. According to Saunders et al. (2009), the main problem with a snowball sampling strategy is to find the initial contact in the chain. In the case of this study, the initial contact was a person from the professional network of the author of this thesis.

In the snowball process, the following minimum **criteria**, which were determined beforehand, had to be fulfilled for a candidate to be accepted as an interviewee:

- *Hierarchical level*: The interviewee needs to be at least at the level of "Manager" which means that he or she has at least 5 years of professional experience and experience in leading projects.
- *Field of specialisation*: The interviewee needs to possess knowledge or experience that is relevant to the research question.
- *Experience in relevant industry*: Since the consulting firm from which the interviewees were selected is very active in the financial services (i.e. banking and insurance) industry, it was necessary to ensure that the interviewees have experience in industries relevant for this study, too.

There is potential bias in snowball sampling, since a person who is recommended by another person is likely to be similar to the other person (Zikmund and Carr 2012). In the case of this study, this especially means that the consultants all work for the same consulting firm. However, as pointed out previously, an overview of a wide range of companies could be achieved due to the high number of clients with whom experienced consultants have worked during their career. Therefore—in contrast to the sampling strategy for the Finance and Accounting professionals in industrial companies—there was no such strong need to draw a heterogeneous sample. Additionally, the firm from which the consultants were selected has several thousands employees in Germany and covers all types of companies as clients. Moreover, there are no evident differences between the firm that the interviewees work for and the other three "Big Four" firms.

(2) Industry Professionals

For the industry professionals, the sampling strategy was different because they do not act in an oversight role over several companies. Instead, they are seen as individual cases representing their respective company. Therefore, in order to identify all relevant information, the companies for which the candidates work should have different characteristics. Of the 15 purposive sampling strategies that Patton (2002) describes in his book, the one that best serves the purposes of this study is **maximum variation (heterogeneity) sampling**. In heterogeneity sampling, cases are selected that differ in certain criteria or characteristics so that differences and common patterns in the cases can be identified. For the selection of the industry professionals, the following heterogeneity criteria were defined:

- The companies should have different *sizes*.
- The companies should have different *investor structures*, i.e. for instance family-ownership, stock market listing etc.

In part, these criteria were defined in the course of conducting the interviews as suggested by the idea of gradual sampling: The investor structure criterion was named by several of the consultants who were interviewed, so that it was integrated into the selection of the industry professionals.

6.2 Research Design

Apart from the heterogeneity criteria for the companies, the individual candidates had to fulfil certain prerequisites to be eligible to participate. For the industry professionals, no minimum hierarchical level was set, since in Finance and Accounting departments, there are often highly specialised employees who have no management position but a high level of knowledge that is relevant for this study. However, a relevant position such as financial controller or subsidiary controller was assumed in order to ensure that the candidates had relevant knowledge at their disposal. The interviewees were identified from the researcher's personal, academic and business network. That means that some of the interviewees were direct contacts of the researcher, while others were contacts of colleagues or friends.

Concerning **sample size**, it is generally recognised that in purposive sampling and qualitative research in general, very small samples are often sufficient (Saunders et al. 2009; Patton 2002). However, in this study, no sample size was determined in advance. Instead, following the idea of gradual sampling, additional cases were included in the sample until saturation was reached, i.e. until no new data was found with the inclusion of additional cases (Silverman 2011; Flick 2009). The final sample size was 12 experts.

The overall sampling strategy for the qualitative part of this study is summarised in Fig. 6.1.

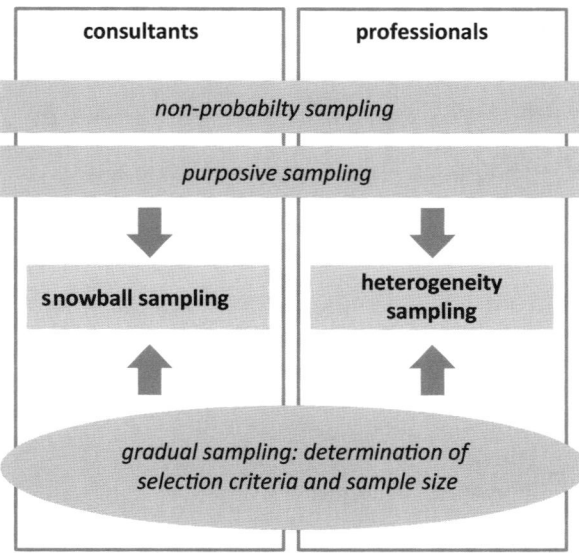

Fig. 6.1 Sampling strategy

6.2.4 Candidates

In total, 12 candidates were interviewed between November 2011 and July 2012, of whom 5 were consultants and 7 were industry professionals. Table 6.3 discloses details about the experts in chronological order of the interviews.

With the help of the experts, insights could be gained into a broad range of different companies.

- With the help of the consultants, information about major *listed* German companies could be obtained. In contrast, five of the seven industry professionals were from *non-listed* companies.
- In terms of *company size*, the industry professionals were from companies with revenues ranging from approximately 25 *million* EUR to 20 *billion* EUR.
- Because of the consultants and some industry professionals who had recently changed their jobs, it was possible to gain insights into a larger number of companies than the number of interview candidates.

6.2.5 Interview Process

All interviews were conducted according to a standardised process, as shown in Fig. 6.2, in order to increase the comparability and reliability of the interviews. However, in order to satisfy the needs of the interviewees, a different sequence of steps was sometimes used. In particular, stages (1) and (2) before the actual interview were sometimes mixed. For instance, one interviewee asked for more information on the background of the researcher and the university before the

Table 6.3 Candidates for expert interviews

No.	Type	Current position	Experience (years)	Academic qualification
1	Consulting	Manager Finance Advisory	8	Master
2	Consulting	Senior Manager Valuation Services	11	Master
3	Consulting	Manager Corporate Finance Advisory	5	Doctorate
4	Industry	Subsidiary controller	5	Master
5	Industry	Financial controller	4	Master
6	Industry	Group controller	7	Bachelor
7	Industry	Subsidiary controller	6	Master
8	Industry	Member of the board	40	Doctorate
9	Consulting	Partner Finance Advisory	10	Master
10	Industry	Subsidiary head of controlling and accounting	7	Bachelor
11	Industry	Investment controller	7	Bachelor
12	Consulting	Manager Finance Advisory	6	Master

6.2 Research Design

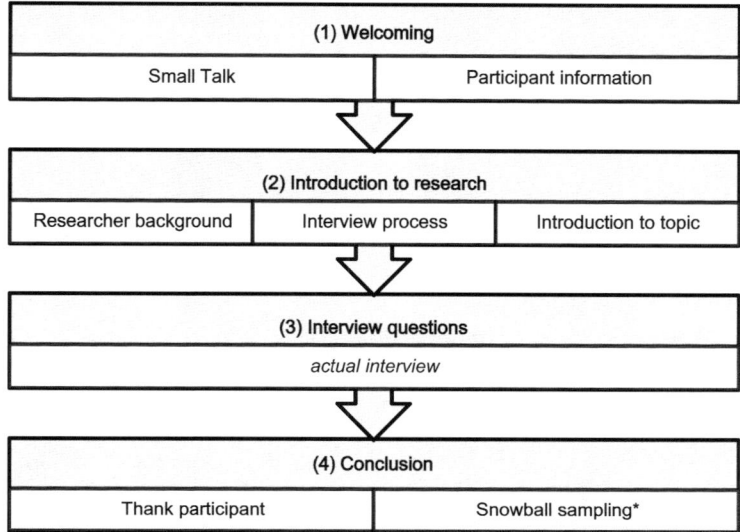

Fig. 6.2 Interview process. *Asterisk*: only in the case of consultants

interview. Another candidate wanted to know details on confidentiality issues at the very beginning.

(1) Welcoming
Each interview was started by making small talk with the interviewee and also asking him or her about his current position and past experiences. The first stage fulfilled two purposes: First, building rapport and a personal relationship, which is considered as crucial for a successful interview (McPhee and Terry 2007; Saunders et al. 2009). Second, gaining more information on the position and specialisation of the participant in order to take into account this contextual information in the formulation of questions and the interpretation of the data collected.

(2) Introduction to Research
In the second stage, the background of the researcher and the university was explained. Moreover, the interview process was discussed which included information on confidentiality and other ethical issues (as discussed in Sect. 4.2.2) as well as the consent to audio recording. Furthermore, due to the complex nature of the topic, a short introduction to the research area was given in order to ensure a common understanding of the discussion and avoid misunderstandings.

(3) Interview Questions
In this stage, the actual discussion of the interview questions was done. Details concerning the questions are provided in Sect. 6.2.6.

(4) Conclusion
In the last stage of the interview the participant was thanked for the participation. Furthermore, in the case of the consultants, candidates were asked whether they

knew a colleague who might be interested in participating in the interview (snowball sampling).

In this study, the average duration of the interviews was approximately 40 min. The duration of the shortest interview was 25 min; the longest interview took 60 min.

6.2.6 Topics and Questions

For conducting the interviews, an interview guide that consisted of a list of topics to be discussed in bullet-point style was used. Every topic was discussed in each interview. However, this was not necessarily done in the sequence of the questions on the list, because efforts were made to create a natural conversational atmosphere instead of an interrogating the candidates. For example, an issue that the candidate had mentioned about his job at the beginning of the conversation was always used as a starting point for the questions.

The selection of topics and questions asked in the expert interviews was guided by the research propositions that were formulated in Sect. 3.5.3. Consequently, two broad categories of questions were asked: First, questions concerning the **cost-of-capital practices** of companies were asked (derived from P1: *There is a theory-practice gap in cost-of-capital methods*). This was done in order to gain an exploratory insight into the cost-of-capital practices of companies. The industry professionals were asked how the topics are dealt with in their respective companies, whereas the consultants were asked about their experience with multiple clients. The following topics were included in the discussion (see Table 6.4):

The second category of questions concerns **influencing factors** for the cost-of-capital practices (derived from P2: *There are systematic differences between companies that explain differences in cost-of-capital practices*). This category of

Table 6.4 Questions concerning cost-of-capital practices

1	**Determination of company cost-of-capital**
	Is it calculated at all?
	Methods/techniques that are used
2	**Differentiated cost-of-capital rates**
	Determination for business units, regions, projects…
	Methods/techniques that are used
3	**Fields of application**
	Fields for which cost-of-capital is used
	Performance management/reporting, capital budgeting, value-based management, IFRS, company valuation
	Group vs. differentiated rates
	Techniques depending on field

6.2 Research Design

Table 6.5 Questions concerning influencing factors

1	**Possible determinants**
	Open question
2	**Company characteristics**
	Size
	Industry
	Culture
	Strategy
	Organisation/decentralisation
	Skills
3	**Reasons against using cost-of-capital**
	Open question
4	**Reasons for using cost-of-capital/benefits and value**
	Open question
5	**Personal opinion of interviewee**

questions attempted to find out reasons for the cost-of-capital practices of the companies in order to be able to build a theory for the construction of the final model of cost-of-capital practices (see Table 6.5).

In the discussion with the experts, different types of questions were asked: First, *open questions* were asked concerning the topics from the list in order to reduce bias and give the candidates the opportunity to come up with their own ideas. In a second step, if the interviewee could not come up with his or her own ideas or had not mentioned all the issues from the interview guide or previous interviews, *theory-driven, hypotheses-directed questions* as discussed by Flick (2009) were asked. These types of question are based on issues identified from literature or previous interviews and can be used to make the interviewee's implicit knowledge, that he or she does not have immediately at hand, more explicit. The following example illustrates the types of question: First, interviewees were asked *"What do you think could be possible influencing factors for this behaviour?"* If the interviewee could not come up with determinants, in the next step, he or she was asked *"Do you think the size of a company could be a possible factor?"* This gave the interviewer the opportunity to discuss the point with the candidate, even though it might not have come to his mind immediately.

6.2.7 Data Analysis Approach

The exploratory findings about the **cost-of-capital practices** based in the question derived from P1 are verbally described, structured by fields of application, in Sect. 6.4.1. For this discussion, no formal data analysis has been conducted.

In order to find out the **influencing factors** on the cost-of-capital practices, which are described in the findings section, the author developed an analysis approach consisting of three steps, which is based on ideas from both grounded theory and content analysis, as discussed in Sect. 6.1.2. That means that in the

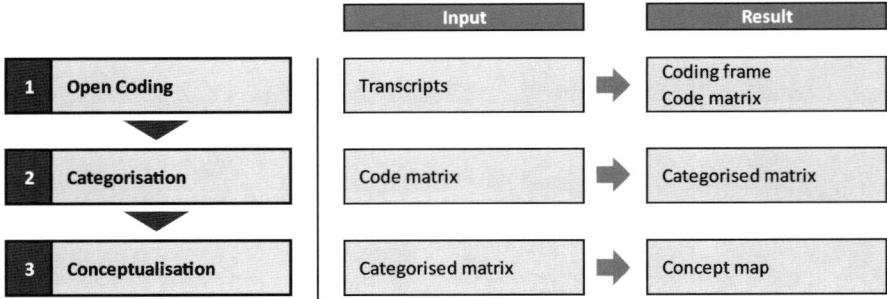

Fig. 6.3 Procedure for qualitative data analysis

analysis, both an inductive and a deductive approach are included. According to Easterby-Smith et al. (2008, p. 173), it is common in research practice to mix the two approaches: "Although we have characterized these two positions as competing alternatives, between them lies a raft of practice and in many ways the choices that researchers face lie on a continuum between content analysis (...) and grounded analysis." Also Myers (2009) argues that it is acceptable to use only some of the ideas of grounded theory in a research project, e.g. to use the approach solely as a coding technique.

The procedure that has been developed analyses the data from the expert interviews in three steps, as outlined in Fig. 6.3. On the left side of the figure, the three steps are shown. On the right side, the documents and tools that are used are mentioned.

(1) Open Coding

In the first step, a procedure similar to open coding from grounded analysis was employed. That means that in each transcript, codes were attached to certain statements from the interviewees. Such a procedure, where in the first step the data is coded on a detailed level without further analysis, is recommended in the literature (Rapley 2011). This approach helps the researcher to avoid including too many presuppositions in the first round of analysis.

In this study, the following procedure was applied in order to make sure that no information was omitted and avoid bias: The statements that involved influencing factors or reasons for cost-of-capital practices were coded. Those parts of the transcripts that describe the cost-of-capital practices were not coded but were marked in red. Biographical information about the interviewees or general company information was marked in blue. Thus, each line (or bullet point) in the transcripts should either be coded or marked in red or blue.

The approach represents an inductive procedure, as no codes were determined before the data analysis. However, as the questions that led to the candidates' answers were derived from the literature review and theoretical considerations, there is a certain deductive character in the whole methodology. Such a procedure is also recommended by Saunders et al. (2009, p. 490), who make the following statement: "Even though you may incorporate an inductive approach in your research, commencing your work from a theoretical perspective may have certain advantages. It will link your research into the existing body of knowledge in your subject area, help you to get started and provide you with an initial analytical framework".

The codes that were determined in the open coding process were recorded in the rows of a matrix together with a description of the codes. In the columns of the matrix, the occurrence of the codes in the individual cases (i.e. interviews) is displayed. This introduces a slightly quantitative element in the analysis, as it is often done in content analysis (see Sect. 6.1.2).

(2) Categorisation

After the codes from the transcripts were recorded in the matrix, they were summarised to categories in the next step. This is a data reduction step that takes the codes to a higher level of abstraction and reduces the number of codes (Rapley 2011).

In this stage of the analysis, the inductive character remains. Also, the quantitative element as described in the previous step is maintained. Thus, the absolute frequency, i.e. the number of times the categories occur in the interviews, can be used as an indication of whether or not the factor could be important.

(3) Conceptualisation

In the third step, no further reduction of the number of categories was made, so that at this stage no detailed information was lost. Instead, the focus of this step was to identify relationships between the categories. This was done by elaborating a network diagram or concept map that shows links between the categories. Based on the links that were identified, some of the categories were grouped.

The development of a concept map requires both inductive and deductive procedures, as explained by Flick (2009, p. 311) in the context of axial coding: "The researcher moves continuously back and forth between inductive thinking (developing concepts, categories and relations from the text) and deductive thinking (testing the concepts, categories and relations against the text)."

The groups of categories that were inductively identified in the conceptualisation phase are regarded as possible influencing factors on cost-of-capital practices in the further course of this thesis. They are used to refine the preliminary model that was developed after the literature review. The refined preliminary model is presented in Sect. 6.5.2.

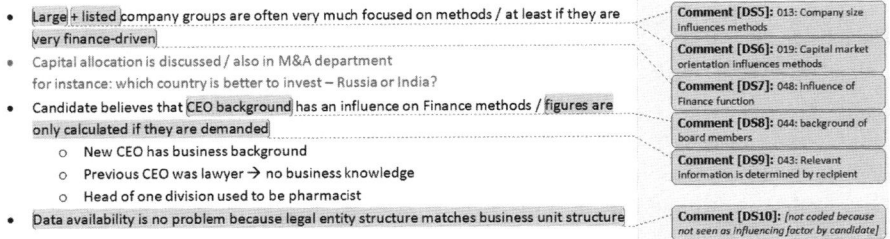

Fig. 6.4 Coding in Microsoft Word

6.3 Data Analysis

6.3.1 Step 1: Open Coding

The transcripts were coded in Microsoft Word with the help of the comment function (see Fig. 6.4). The codes that were identified inductively were numbered and recorded in a spreadsheet matrix in Microsoft Excel.

Fifty-one codes were identified as shown in Fig. 6.5 on page 164. If the code appeared in an interview, it was marked in the respective column of the candidate (cell shaded in grey). Thus, the frequency of occurrence of the code across the cases can be counted. However, no within-case counting was applied because in highly fact-driven interviews with professionals, it is questionable whether the repetition of a statement is an indication of the importance of the point.

There is no order in the matrix in terms of topics. The codes were recorded in the sequence in which they were identified in the analysis. As the analysis was done in the sequence of the interviews, the pattern appears that earlier candidates have more codes with lower numbers. This way, it can also be seen how data saturation increases with the interviews: In the first four cases, many new codes are recorded. In the following cases, only a few new codes are needed. In the last three cases, no new codes appear.

At this point, no interpretation of the data was done. Therefore no discussion in terms of content is included in this section. A complete list of codes and their meaning can be found in Sect. 9.1.

6.3.2 Step 2: Categorisation

In the second step, codes with similar content or meaning were grouped into categories of codes, as shown in the screenshot below (Fig. 6.6). A counting system with colour coding similar to the one in the open coding was applied. However, in the categorisation stage, there is a colour scale indicating how many of the underlying codes of the categories occur within the case.

6.3 Data Analysis

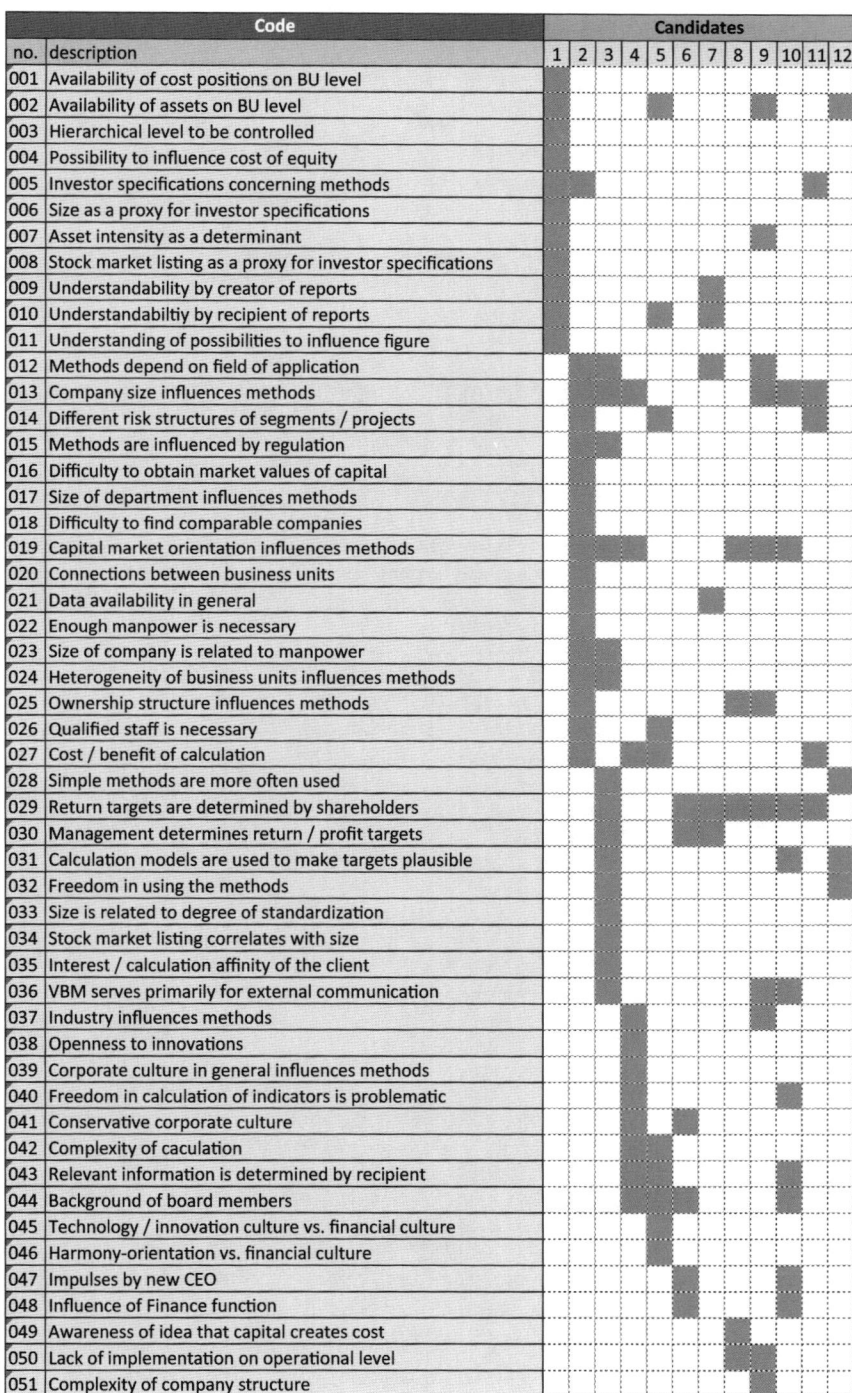

Fig. 6.5 Code matrix in open coding

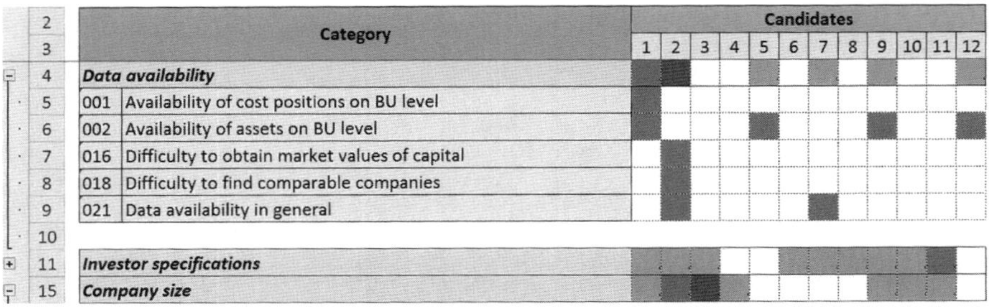

		Category	Candidates											
	2													
	3		1	2	3	4	5	6	7	8	9	10	11	12
	4	**Data availability**												
	5	001 Availability of cost positions on BU level												
	6	002 Availability of assets on BU level												
	7	016 Difficulty to obtain market values of capital												
	8	018 Difficulty to find comparable companies												
	9	021 Data availability in general												
	10													
	11	**Investor specifications**												
	15	**Company size**												

Fig. 6.6 Aggregation of codes to categories

Category	Candidates
	1 2 3 4 5 6 7 8 9 10 11 12
Data availability	
Investor specifications	
Company size	
Staff Resources	
Industry	
Fields of application	
Company structure	
Ownership structure	
Cost / benefit of calculation	
Corporate culture	
Capital market orientation	
Subject complexity	
Scope for creativity in methods	
Management	
Purposes of applying methods	
Regulation	

Colour Key: ■ three underlying codes
■ two underlying codes
■ one underlying code

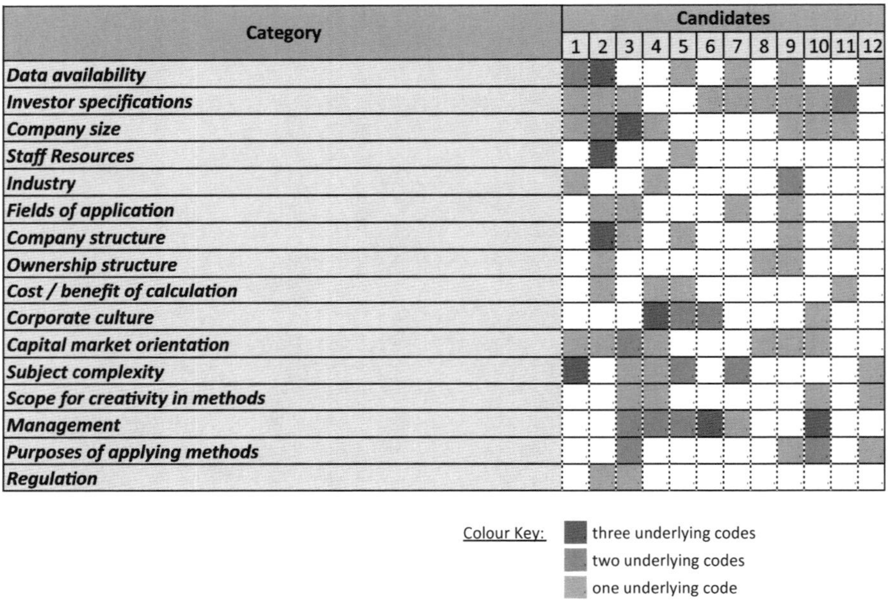

Fig. 6.7 Categorised code matrix

From the 51 codes, 16 categories resulted, which are shown in Fig. 6.7. The allocation of codes to categories can be seen in Sect. 9.2. Four codes were not assigned to any category because they were considered to be less relevant during the analysis in terms of their content and frequency of occurrence (they only occurred in one or two cases).

It can be seen that due to the re-sorting of the codes, there is no longer a pattern resulting from the sequence in which the interviews were analysed as in the initial matrix. Furthermore, from the matrix, it can also be seen that after the categorisation, there are issues that were raised more often, as indicated by the presence of more coloured cells and darker colours, which give an indication of the importance of the factor.

6.3 Data Analysis

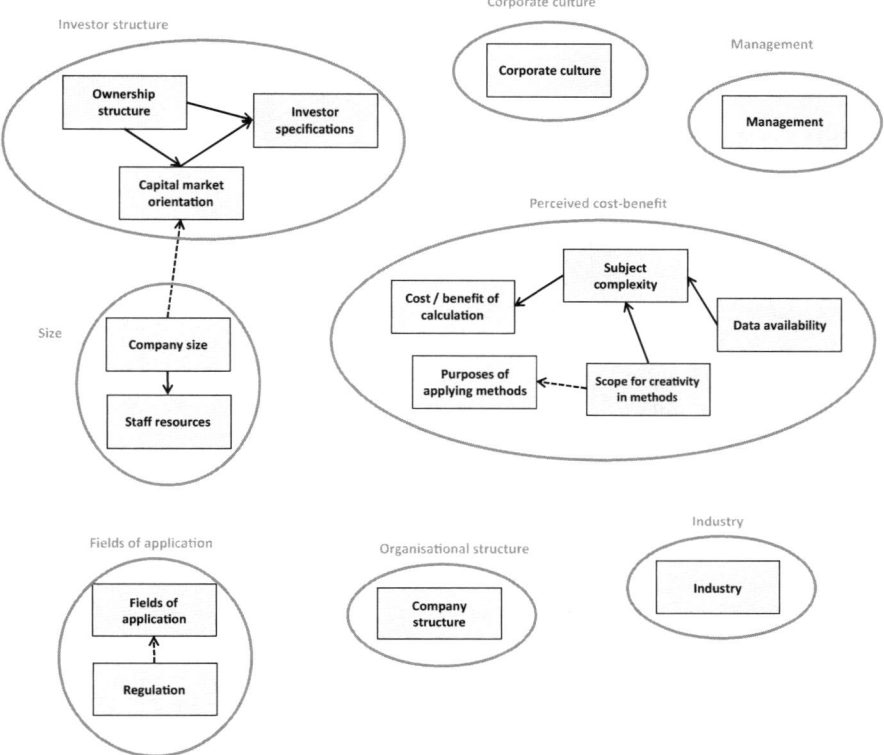

Fig. 6.8 Concept map

Also in this step, no interpretation of the results was done. The resulting categories were adopted in the next step.

6.3.3 Step 3: Conceptualisation

In the third step, the relationship between the categories was analysed, resulting in the concept map that is shown in Fig. 6.8. The arrows indicate a link between the categories, which does not necessarily have to be a causal relationship. The categories were then taken to a higher level of abstraction by grouping them again. The grouping was done by reflecting on the contents of the categories and at the same time taking into account the relationships between them, as indicated by the arrows.

The groups of categories of this concept map serve as the foundation for the refined preliminary model that is presented in Sect. 6.5.2. However, for the presentation of the model, minor changes in the grouping of the categories are made in order to ensure a consistent level of abstractness of the influencing factors in the model.

6.4 Findings

6.4.1 Cost-of-Capital Practices

In this section, findings from the interviews concerning how companies deal with cost-of-capital in practice are presented. One of the main findings from the qualitative research is that there are great differences depending on the field of application of cost-of-capital. This confirms that a focused investigation of the topic, as done in this thesis, is important.

Although the focus of this thesis is Managerial Finance purposes, some findings about fields of accounting and company valuation are briefly summarised below.

(1) Accounting and Company Valuation
For accounting and company valuation purposes—which are not the focus of this thesis—sophisticated techniques as discussed in the literature review are regularly applied to determine cost-of-capital.

In accounting, cost-of-capital is calculated as Weighted Average Cost of Capital (WACC) and cost of equity is determined with the help of the Capital Asset Pricing Model (CAPM) on a group level. Also on a subordinate level, objective methods are applied in order to determine cost-of-capital of CGUs. This is a fact that was mentioned consistently by several of the interviewees—both consultants and industry professionals. One of the interviewees (candidate 3) stressed that these methods are only applied because it is mandatory to use the methods in impairment tests (see Sect. 2.2.2.1) and not because the practitioners see any benefit in applying them.

Also for company valuation purposes, WACC and CAPM are regularly used. On the level of business units and for non-listed companies, comparable company approaches are usually applied. Analytical approaches and practitioner approaches, such as scoring models, as discussed in the literature review, do not play any role in practice. This was stated by one of the interviewed consultants, who regularly conducts company valuations for clients, and also by two of the industry professionals who have been involved in merger and acquisition activities during their careers.

(2) Performance Measurement and Value-Based Management
In performance measurement, where cost-of-capital is used as a return target for company groups, business units or regions, there seem to be larger differences between the companies.

However, in general, it can be said that the *explicit calculation of cost-of-capital* for managerial purposes does not seem to be common practice. Only three of the industry professionals reported that their companies calculate cost-of-capital with the help of WACC; also the consultants estimated that most of the companies did not use cost-of-capital for managerial purposes. Only one of the industry professionals stated that the cost of equity was calculated with the help of the CAPM by the company itself, while in the other case, the cost of equity was specified by the family office of the owners.

However, one consultant stated that it is likely that most of the companies listed in the DAX or MDAX index—i.e. the largest German listed companies—do calculate *value-based performance measures* such as the Economic Value Added (EVA). This was confirmed by one of the candidates from a MDAX listed company. Also a financial controller from a private company (revenue 250 million EUR) stated that their company calculated such figures on a group level while the other industry professionals from non-listed companies said that in their companies, no value-based measures were calculated.

The statement that most of the listed companies calculate value-based measures somehow contradicts the statement that the companies do not calculate cost-of-capital for managerial purposes, because value-based measures are calculated with the help of cost-of-capital rates. However, there seems to be the tendency that the measures are only calculated for external reporting to shareholders and not really used for internal management. This was mentioned by two consultants and also one industry professional from a listed company, who is cited below.

> **Candidate 10 (Country Head of Controlling and International Accounting)**
> "With the EVA it is worked less... we only calculate it for the annual report and to explain it to the attendants of the shareholders' meeting."

However, although it is not often implemented, the topic of cost-of-capital and value-based management seems to attract some attention also in non-listed companies. Two of the industry professionals said that there had been projects in their companies to develop a concept. But in both cases, the project was terminated or the concept was not implemented after it had been written.

In the interviews, participants were also asked whether the companies were managed with the help of *capital return measures* such as Return on Capital Employed (ROCE) or Return on Equity (ROE), which would indicate that there is a certain awareness of cost-of-capital. According to the interviews, larger companies seem to calculate return measures and determine target returns for their whole company in most cases. However, fewer companies determine specific minimum returns for individual business units or regions. The return targets are sometimes derived from competitor returns or cost-of-capital. In many cases, they are also determined by owners, investors or analysts or by the company's top management.

Also the amount of *capital invested* in the company and its segments influences the cost-of-capital in absolute terms. Therefore, respondents were also asked whether capital figures were reported internally. It turned out that in general, there seems to be quite thorough tracking of working capital, while fixed assets are less frequently regarded. One reason for that might be that—as stated by two consultants and one industry professional—it is often difficult to determine the assets that are invested in business units because the financial data is only available for legal entities and one legal entity might be part of more than one business unit.

(3) Capital Allocation and Capital Budgeting

For capital allocation, professional *capital budgeting methods* seem to be commonly used in larger companies. One consultant assumed that generally Net Present Value (NPV) techniques such as the Discounted Cash Flow (DCF) method or the Internal Rate of Return (IRR) are applied. This was also confirmed by an industry professional from a listed company. Static methods such as cost comparison of payback period are used to make the results plausible. However, smaller and non-listed companies might also use static methods exclusively.

An interesting question in this context is how the hurdle rates for investment projects are determined and whether different hurdle rates are used for different projects. Interestingly, it is more common among the interviewed companies to have explicit hurdle rates for investments than to have target returns for the whole company. Two companies reported that they have hurdle rates defined by the owners of the company that are the same for all investment projects. One candidate reported that in his company, the country cost-of-capital rates were also used for investment evaluation. Another candidate said that in their company, specific rates for business units and activities were used.

6.4.2 Influencing Factors of Cost-of-Capital Practices

In this section, details concerning the factors that were identified in the qualitative data analysis from the interview data are discussed. As discussed in the previous section, cost-of-capital practices are different for different disciplines (e.g. Financial Accounting). This is not considered as an influencing factor in this thesis. Instead, for each discipline, its own influencing factors have to be examined; the scope of this thesis is Managerial Finance only.

(1) Size

A commonly mentioned factor is the size of the company (seven candidates, 58 %). It is assumed that larger companies are more likely to calculate their cost-of-capital with more objective methods and in a more sophisticated way. Attempts were made to find out why this is the case. The candidates mentioned the following reasons:

First of all, larger companies have more resources, i.e. more staff in the Finance departments to engage with cost-of-capital considerations (candidates 2 and 3). In large companies, it can be assumed that the knowledge is available, as the quote from one consultant below shows.

6.4 Findings

> **Candidate 2 (Consultant and Valuation Specialist)**
> "I assume that all our clients would be capable of calculating cost-of-capital, as in the large companies, often former colleagues of ours from auditing or advisory or former investment bankers work in the accounting and finance departments."

Second, the size of a company might also influence the investor structure (candidate 1) and thus the information requirements. Larger companies are more likely to be capital market oriented and to have larger investors or interest groups that demand certain figures to be reported. Moreover, larger companies have more standardised and formal processes (candidate 3).

(2) Investor Structure

The way a company is financed and the type of its investors can have an influence on how companies deal with cost-of-capital. Investors include equity providers, i.e. owners or shareholders, as well as debt providers such as banks. The reason is that investors often have specific information requirements and also have the power to enforce that the respective figures are calculated and reported. Indeed, nine candidates (75 %) state that investors often either influence methods, e.g. which figures have to be reported, or set targets for returns or earnings (see category 'investor specifications').

Concerning investors, it could be especially relevant whether a company is *capital market oriented*. This means that it either has emitted equity securities (i.e. is stock market listed) or debt instruments at the capital markets. In this case, often more information requirements have to be fulfilled. This was mentioned by seven of the interviewees (58 %).

Moreover, the type of equity investor, i.e. the *ownership structure*, could have an influence. For instance, if the majority shareholder or owner of the company is a family, the information requirements might be different from a company that is held by a private equity investor.

> **Candidate 2 (Consultant and Valuation Specialist)**
> "The ownership structure makes a difference, e.g. whether the company is still owned by the founder who does not want to question his lifework by asking if it is profitable or whether it is owned by a financial investor that is less passionate and more number-driven. He wants to know, 'how can I maximise my return?'"

From the interviews, it could not be clearly elicited whether a certain type of investor is associated with a certain behaviour concerning cost-of-capital or if the requirements depend more on the individual investor. However, several of the experts believe that capital market oriented companies are more likely to have more sophisticated cost-of-capital practices.

> **Candidate 1 (Consultant and Reporting Specialist)**
> "Especially for the listed companies (...) there might be a large investor involved who simply says which figures he wants to see."

(3) Perceived Cost-benefit

This factor includes several related categories. The main idea behind this factor is that the calculation of cost-of-capital and related figures such as value-based measures is associated with costs. These costs include especially labour costs, but also costs for consultants or information providers. Therefore, the figures are only calculated and reported if the perceived benefits are higher than the costs.

The main driver of the costs is the *complexity* of the subject. Six of the candidates (50 %) stated that understandability of methods is important or that simple methods are preferred over complex ones. The complexity of cost-of-capital calculations is often increased due to problems with *data availability*.

The benefit of cost-of-capital practices is also related to the *purpose of applying the methods*. Three of the candidates (25 %) stated that value-based measures are often only calculated for external communication but not really used internally. Moreover, determination techniques for cost-of-capital are often only used to make targets plausible that have been specified subjectively (stated by three candidates, 25 %). This is possible because of the *scope for creativity* of the methods. In the calculation models, there are certain flexibilities (e.g. the selection of a peer group or time period of capital market data) that can be used to influence the result. On the other hand, this creates additional complexity.

(4) Management

Besides investors, the top management of a company also has a large influence on methods and return targets. Six interviewees (50 %) reported that top management regularly either sets return or earnings targets (code 030) or requires certain measures to be calculated (code 043). Two candidates additionally stated that a new CEO in their company had recently changed Finance methods.

Four candidates (33 %) believed that the background of top management might have an influence on cost-of-capital practices. It is assumed, for instance, that in a company with a CEO from a Finance background, more sophisticated Finance methods are applied. One candidate who works in a company with a CEO from a Marketing background is cited below.

> **Candidate 5 (Financial Controller)**
> "From the point of view of finance... if I suggest to management for instance to implement value-based management... if they don't know the concept themselves, they do not want to introduce it."

However, this point is controversial. A partner from a consultancy firm who was interviewed stated that the factor might also work in the other direction, because CEOs from a non-Business background might be more likely to hire Finance consultants as advisors and therefore introduce more recent methods (candidate 9).

(5) Corporate Culture
The corporate culture of a company could also have an influence on methods applied in Finance. Issues related with corporate culture were mentioned by four of the interviewees (33 %).

One aspect of culture is whether a company is conservative or innovation-friendly, which was mentioned by two candidates. In more conservative companies, new sophisticated methods might be introduced only reluctantly, as the citation below illustrates.

> **Candidate 4 (Subsidiary Controller)**
> "In our company, people are not so innovation-friendly. There are entrenched habits and it is difficult to implement new ideas."

Another aspect is whether a company is very Finance-driven or whether other factors such as technological innovativeness or harmony are more important. This is also related to the question of how influential the Finance and Accounting function is within the company.

> **Candidate 5 (Financial Controller)**
> "Our corporate culture is focused on harmony: for instance, people are not laid off if financial results are bad. Moreover, we are particularly concerned about being *technically* innovative."

(6) Industry
Industry as an influencing factor was mentioned by three interviewees (25 %). In terms of cost-of-capital, an important difference between industries is that they have different degrees of asset intensity, i.e. larger amounts of capital are needed for some industries than for others.

(7) Organisational Structure
This factor refers particularly to the organisational structure of a company in terms of business units. For companies with several business units that are heterogeneous in terms of their business and risk structure, there is a greater need to use differentiated cost-of-capital rates for the business units. Therefore, it could be the case that companies with such a structure have more sophisticated cost-of-capital practices.

On the other hand, one consultant (candidate 9) mentioned that a more complex organisational structure makes it more difficult to apply, for instance, value-based management on a below-group level. This means that although such a concept would make more sense from a theoretical point of view, it might also decrease the likelihood of actual implementation.

The points were mostly brought up by consultants from a more theoretical point of view, and it will have to be confirmed in the quantitative survey whether this factor really influences cost-of-capital practices.

6.5 Conclusion

6.5.1 Summary of Findings

In this chapter, the research design and findings of the qualitative, semi-structured interviews were presented. Twelve interviews were conducted and analysed with the help of an approach that includes both inductive and deductive elements.

The aim of this chapter was to gain insights into companies' cost-of-capital practices and identify factors that influence these practices. One of the main results from the qualitative analysis is that both the cost-of-capital practices and the importance of the individual influencing factors are different depending on the field of application (see Sect. 6.4.2). Therefore, further analyses have to be conducted depending on the field of application. In this thesis, Managerial Finance purposes, as opposed to Financial Accounting or company valuation purposes, are examined.

6.5.2 Refined Preliminary Model

The preliminary model presented after the literature review in Sect. 3.5.4 is based on the idea that cost-of-capital practices are influenced by systematic differences between companies, which was formulated as proposition P2.

This notion is supported by the results of the expert interviews. Hence, the general structure is maintained after the new findings. At this point, the model is refined by including the influencing factors that were identified in the research, as shown in Fig. 6.9. The model is based on the concept map as discussed in Sect. 6.3.3.

6.5.3 Fulfilment of Objectives

As an interim conclusion, it can be stated that the objectives formulated for the expert interviews were fulfilled. Table 6.6 summarises the results of the chapter.

6.5 Conclusion

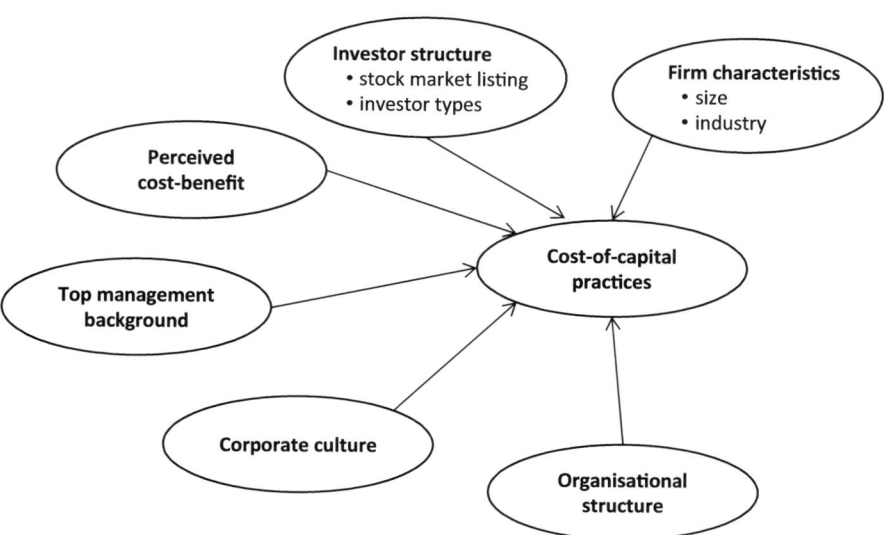

Fig. 6.9 Refined preliminary model

Table 6.6 Objectives and results of the expert interviews

Research aim	Research objectives	Contribution of expert interviews	Result from expert interviews
Examine and explain cost-of-capital practices	(1) To investigate how companies use and determine cost-of-capital	Gain first exploratory results for focus population	An overview of status quo of cost-of-capital practices was gained (see Sect. 6.4.1)

	(2) To develop a model that explains cost-of-capital practices of companies	Identify possible determinants of cost-of-capital practices and relationships between factors	The following possible determinants were identified and integrated in the refined preliminary model (see Sect. 6.5.2):
			• Firm characteristics
			  – Size
			  – Industry
			• Investor Structure
			  – Stock market listing
			  – Investor types
			• Perceived cost-benefit
			• Top management background
			• Corporate culture
			• Organisational structure

	(3) To develop a theory that explains the cost-of-capital practices of companies	Identify reasons for cost-of-capital practices	For each of the possible determinants that were identified, a deeper explanation, underlying reasons or theoretical considerations were discussed in Sect. 6.4.2

References

Ahrens T, Chapman CS (2008) Doing qualitative field research in management accounting: positioning data to contribute to theory. In: Chapman CS (ed) Handbook of management accounting research. Elsevier, Amsterdam, pp 319–342

Bazeley P (2004) Issues in mixing qualitative and quantitative approaches to research. In: Buber R, Gadner J, Richards L (eds) Applying qualitative methods to marketing management research. Palgrave Macmillan, Basingstoke, pp 141–156

Cassell C (2011) Interviews in organizational research. In: Bryman A, Buchanan DA (eds) The SAGE handbook of organizational research methods. Sage, London, pp 500–515

Cohen L, Manion L, Morrison K (2007) Research methods in education. Routledge, London

David M, Sutton CD (2011) Social research. An introduction. Sage, Los Angeles, CA

Davidson C (2009) Transcription: imperatives for qualitative research. Int J Qual Methods 8(2):36–52

Denzin NK, Lincoln YS (2009) Introduction. In: Denzin NK, Lincoln YS (eds) The Sage handbook of qualitative research. Sage, Thousand Oaks, CA, pp 1–32

Easterby-Smith M, Thorpe R, Jackson PR (2008) Management research, 3rd edn. Sage, Los Angeles, CA

Flick U (2009) An introduction to qualitative research. Sage, Los Angeles, CA

Gläser J, Laudel G (2008) Experteninterviews und qualitative Inhaltsanalyse. Als Instrumente rekonstruierender Untersuchungen. VS Verlag für Sozialwissenschaften, Wiesbaden

Glaser BG, Strauss AL (1967) The discovery of grounded theory. Strategies for qualitative research. Aldine, Chicago, NY

Hesse-Biber SN, Leavy P (2011) The practice of qualitative research. Sage, Los Angeles, CA

McLellan E, Macqueen KM, Neidig JL (2003) Beyond the qualitative interview: data preparation and transcription. Field Methods 15(1):63–84

McPhee N, Terry R (2007) The hidden art of interviewing people. How to get them to tell you the truth. Wiley, Chichester

Miles MB, Huberman AM (1994) Qualitative data analysis. An expanded sourcebook. Sage, Thousand Oaks, CA

Myers MD (2009) Qualitative research in business and management. Sage, London

Patton MQ (2002) Qualitative research and evaluation methods. Sage, London

Rapley T (2011) Some pragmatics of data analysis. In: Silverman D (ed) Qualitative research. Issues of theory, method and practice. Sage, Los Angeles, CA, pp 273–290

Saunders M, Lewis P, Thornhill A (2009) Research methods for business students. Financial Times Prentice Hall, Harlow

Silverman D (2011) Interpreting qualitative data. A guide to the principals of qualitative research. Sage, London

Strauss A, Corbin J (1990) Basics of qualitative research. Grounded theory procedures and techniques. Sage, London

Zikmund WG, Carr JC (2012) Business research methods. South-Western, Mason, OH

Chapter 7
Primary Research: Company Survey

In this chapter, the research design and findings of the company survey are presented. The main objectives of this chapter are to gain quantitative results of cost-of-capital practices for the focus population and to quantitatively test the influencing factors that were identified in the previous chapter.

First of all, in Sect. 7.1, research hypotheses for the company survey are formulated based on the findings of the expert interviews and the refined preliminary model that was constructed in the previous chapter. Next, the research design of the company survey is discussed in detail (Sect. 7.2). The data analysis and findings are presented in several stages in Sects. 7.3–7.6. The chapter closes with a brief conclusion.

7.1 Research Hypotheses

After the literature review, research propositions were formulated and a preliminary model was constructed. The propositions and the preliminary model provided a guideline for the development of a research design for the expert interviews. Based on the findings of the expert interviews and the refined preliminary model that was presented in the previous chapter, testable research hypotheses were formulated.

Based on proposition P1 (*There is a theory-practice gap in cost-of-capital methods*), the expert interviews revealed that there is indeed a theory-practice gap. This proposition is now to be tested in the company survey in the form of the following hypothesis.

H1: There is a theory-practice gap in cost-of-capital methods

Moreover, the expert interviews revealed a number of influencing factors of cost-of-capital practices. The results are based on proposition P2 (*There are systematic differences between companies that explain differences in cost-of-capital practices*) that can now be expressed in several testable hypotheses.

H2: The size of a company influences its cost-of-capital practices

H3: The industry sector of a company influences its cost-of-capital practices
H4: Stock market listing influences cost-of-capital practices
H5: The investor types of a company influence its cost-of-capital practices
H6: Perceived cost-benefit of the methods influences cost-of-capital practices
H7: Top management's background influences cost-of-capital practices
H8: Corporate culture influences cost-of-capital practices
H9: The organisational structure influences cost-of-capital practices

7.2 Research Design

7.2.1 Total Survey Design Perspective

When designing a survey, a number of decisions have to be made that affect the quality of the data that is collected. As Fowler (2009, p. 7) states, "in the past, researchers have focused on one or two features of the survey, such as sample size or response rate". However, in order to achieve good quality data, all design features of a survey have to be taken into account in an approach that Fowler refers to as "total survey design perspective".

One aspect in the overall survey design is to optimise the use of available resources (Fowler 2009). As resources are limited, compromises are necessary, for instance to accept a certain amount of sampling error (Stopher 2012). Following Fowler's idea of total survey design perspective, in this survey it was attempted to balance the available time and resources between the design features in order to achieve an appropriate data quality. In the following sections, the design of the various components is discussed in detail. Table 7.1 gives an overview of the design features and methods.

Table 7.1 Design features of the survey

Design feature	Approach of this survey	Section
Sampling		7.2.2
Target population	German real economy companies	7.2.2.1
Sample frame	Multiple frame design	7.2.2.2
Sampling approach	Multiple approaches	7.2.2.3
Sample size	96 companies	7.2.2.4
Response rate	Listed companies: 9.5 % Non-listed companies: N/A	7.2.2.4
Survey instrument	Questionnaire	7.2.3
Mode and process of data collection		7.2.4
Mode of data collection	Self-administered online questionnaire	7.2.4.1
Process of data collection	Listed companies: email enquiries Non-listed companies: various	7.2.4.2

Apart from the design features, in Sect. 7.2.6 the *data analysis approach* of this survey will be discussed. Moreover, possible *error and bias* in the survey as well as measures taken to reduce these effects are discussed in Sect. 7.2.5.

7.2.2 Sampling

7.2.2.1 Target Population

As a first step, the **target population** of this survey has to be defined. In the literature, target population is defined as the "group of elements for which the survey investigator wants to make inferences using the sample statistics" (Groves et al. 2009, p. 69). The target population of this survey is defined as all companies with the following characteristics:

- *Operating in the real economy sector.* The following definition of the sector was used: The real economy sector is engaged in the "circulation and exchange of goods and services amongst the members of society" (Empel 2008, p. 5) as opposed to the financial services sector, which includes, for instance, banks, stock exchanges, asset management firms and insurances (Fasnacht 2009). Hence, the target population includes manufacturing companies as well as service and wholesale/retail companies.
- *Headquartered in Germany.*

For this survey, the target population was defined relatively broadly. First of all, the *industry sector* to be considered was defined very broadly. This is common practice in comparable company surveys in the Finance discipline (see Sect. 3.1.1). One reason why no particular industry was chosen as a target population was the possibility of cross-sectional comparison between production and service companies, which was identified as a possible influencing factor of cost-of-capital practices in the qualitative interviews. Moreover, in the case of company surveys, there is a trade-off between a focused view on a particular industry and obtaining a reasonable sample size (see Sect. 7.2.2.3) due to the limited number of companies in a national economy. It was decided that in the case of a Finance survey, a higher sample size is more valuable, since focused market segmentation is of less relevance than, for instance, in Marketing research. Secondly, no restriction was made concerning the *company size*. Also, in the case of company size, one objective was to explore whether this factor has an influence on the cost-of-capital practices. Therefore, both large companies and SMEs were included in the target population.

7.2.2.2 Sample Frame

After the target population has been defined, the next step in a survey is to determine the sample frame, i.e. "lists or procedures intended to identify all element of a target population" (Fowler 2009, p. 70). In concrete terms, this means that a list has to be compiled or procedures have to be implemented to be able to contact the companies from the target population. From this definition of a sample frame, it can already be derived that an important point concerning the sample frame is its comprehensiveness, i.e. it should not omit any particular groups (Fowler 2009). That means that as many companies as possible that are defined as belonging to the target population should have a chance to be selected for the survey.

The challenge in this survey was that no list of addresses of the companies in the target population was available. Therefore, the sample frame had to be compiled from different sources. In order to maximise the number of companies in the sample frame and to reduce undercoverage (see Sect. 7.2.5.2), a **multiple frame design** as discussed by Groves et al. (2009) was applied. When using multiple frames, there is a danger of overlapping frames, i.e. companies might be represented in more than one frame. However, only one questionnaire per company should be considered in the survey. It is particularly important to address this issue in research dealing with organisations. The reason is that organisations consist of several departments and people that might potentially receive the survey from different sources (i.e. different sampling frames) and might fill out the questionnaire without knowing that another person from the organisation has already submitted it.

Before it is explained how this risk was minimised in this research, the different sample frames that were used are discussed. First of all, two categories of companies were formed, which were dealt with differently in terms of sampling: stock market listed companies and non-listed companies.[1]

In Fig. 7.1, the sampling frames that were used are illustrated as circles. For the *listed companies*, it can be seen that only one sample frame was used. The sample frame was developed based on a list of all companies listed at the **Frankfurt Stock Exchange**, which is the main stock exchange in Germany. From this list, the companies from the financial services sector were excluded. Moreover, all companies were excluded that are listed at the Frankfurt Stock Exchange but headquartered outside of Germany, as well as all companies that are still listed but have filed for bankruptcy. This adjusted list consisted of approximately 500 companies for which contact data was manually retrieved from the companies' websites. The strategy used to contact the listed companies was to send an enquiry to the Investor Relations (IR) department with the request to forward the mail to the Management Accounting department.[2] The IR department was chosen because the email addresses and contact persons are regularly available on the company website and in most companies this department is related to the Finance and Accounting

---

[1] Often, the terminology "public" and "private" companies is used to denote whether a company's shares are publicly dealt (see for instance Atrill and McLaney 2009; Miller and Jentz 2010). In this thesis, the terms "listed" and "non-listed" are preferred in order to avoid confusion with the public sector in the sense of companies being held by the government (Miller and Jentz 2010).

[2] This thesis is written from the perspective of the Managerial Finance discipline. However, in German companies, the Management Accounting department is typically responsible for respective topics in practice.

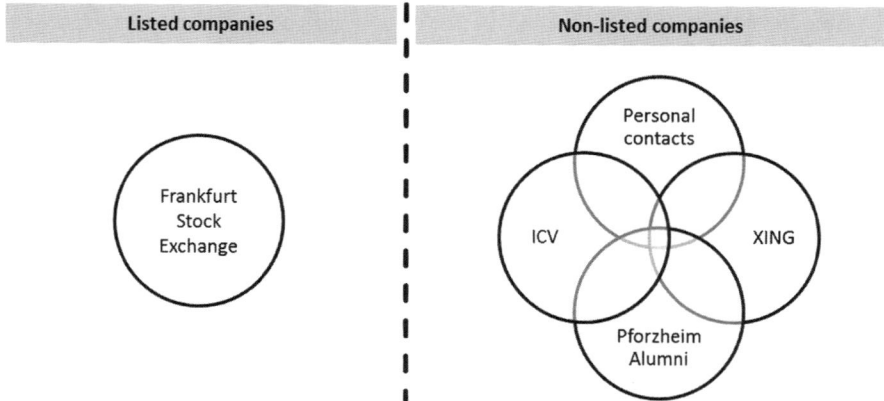

Fig. 7.1 Multiple sample frames of this study

department. If no IR contacts were available, a general email address that could be found on the website (such as info@...) was used. Overall, after deducting undeliverable mails and companies for which no contact information was found, 441 companies were contacted.

It can be summarised that for the listed companies, it was possible to compile an almost comprehensive sample frame which allowed companies to be contacted individually. For the non-listed companies, no such comprehensive list could be generated. Instead, several channels were used in parallel to collect as many responses as possible and to minimize undercoverage. The following procedures were used to collect data:

First, Finance and Accounting professionals from the researcher's **personal contacts** were asked to fill out the questionnaire on behalf of their employers. The personal contacts included especially former fellow students and former co-workers who work in relevant fields and companies. Moreover, clients of the consulting firm for which the researcher works were asked to take part. Additionally, second level contacts, i.e. contacts of co-workers and friends of the researcher, were used. The advantage of this sample frame was the higher trust in someone the participants knew—as opposed to a request to fill out a survey by a complete stranger. Furthermore, there is greater willingness to invest time and support the research of someone whom one knows personally. Therefore, this sample frame was quite successful in terms of the number of responses collected (see Sect. 7.2.2.3). Another advantage was that although the responses were recorded anonymously, it was possible for the researcher to control the quality of the responses, since it could be ensured that the individual persons who responded for the companies had the necessary background and knowledge.

A second sample frame that was aimed at collecting responses from non-listed companies is the **Internationaler Controller Verein (ICV)**[3] which is an

---

[3] Translation: International Association of Management Accountants. Website (in German): http://www.controllerverein.com

association of Management Accountants from Germany, Austria and Switzerland. The ICV kindly agreed to include the survey link into its newsletter "Controller's E-News". Against expectations, the number of responses obtained from this sample frame was very low. Considering that the ICV has approximately 6,000 members, more responses were expected (although it is not known how many of the members have subscribed to the newsletter).

Moreover, the survey link was distributed via the **alumni** platform of Pforzheim University, Germany. Additionally, the link was sent to alumni from the Finance and Accounting study programmes. This was done as a non-personalised mass mailing.

Finally, the German social network **XING** was used, which is a business network comparable to the internationally known platform LinkedIn. As XING's market share in Germany in terms of members and visitors is substantially higher than LinkedIn's (Zachrau 2013), it was chosen to use XING only. The platform was used in two ways: First, the survey link was posted in relevant expert groups (forums). These posts were also 'shared', i.e. further distributed, by supporters in order to increase the reach. Second, with the help of the advanced member search function, relevant members in terms of position (especially positions such as Head of Finance or Head of Accounting) and company were identified and contacted individually.

As pointed out previously, when using multiple sample frames, it is important to take into account **overlaps between the sample frames** in order to avoid double participation of companies. The following theoretical overlap possibilities have to be dealt with:

(1) Listed Companies Are Contacted via Sample Frames Intended for Non-listed Companies

Previously, it was stated that listed and non-listed companies were dealt with separately. Looking at the four sample frames which were used for non-listed companies, it could be possible that with these sample frames, answers were collected from listed companies. Therefore, questionnaires from listed companies which turned up from the other sample frames were either checked for redundancy—if it was known which particular company responded—or not considered.[4] This ensured that none of the listed companies were counted twice.

(2) Double Consideration of Non-listed Companies

A second case of redundancy that could theoretically occur is that one non-listed company is contacted via several of the sample frames and the questionnaire is filled out several times. This risk cannot be completely excluded. However, this is considered to be very unlikely for the following reasons:

- There is quite good transparency over the companies which have responded because a large number of the responses are from individual requests via personal contacts or XING. It is ensured that within this group of responses,

---

[4] The listed companies could be filtered out, since stock market listing was a question in the questionnaire.

there are no overlaps. The absolute number of cases which could be subject to duplicate responses is limited.
- Non-listed companies are regularly substantially smaller than listed companies (with exceptions). Therefore, the number of people that could potentially get in touch with the questionnaire is limited.
- Additionally, due to the limited number of Accounting or Finance professionals in these firms, it is likely that it would be recognized if several people received the questionnaire.
- Due to the low percentage of people who actually respond to the questionnaire if they receive it through one of the channels, it is unlikely that two people from one company would fill out the questionnaire—even if it was received several times within one organization.

In summary, it can be said that with the help of the multiple sample frame approach, it was intended to maximise both the number of absolute responses, i.e. the sample size, and the coverage of the target population.

7.2.2.3 Sampling Approach

Due to the limited size of the target population, the absence of a complete list of addresses for the whole population and the expectation of relatively low response rates, the decision was made not to apply a random sampling approach. Instead, the focus was to maximise the absolute number of responses and use every response that could be obtained. Therefore, a discussion of different statistical sampling strategies which can be found in the literature (for example Fuller 2009) is not part of this thesis.

Nevertheless, in this section, it is intended to classify the sampling approach for each sample frame that was applied in this research. The implications of this classification for the question of representativeness and error/bias will be discussed in Sect. 7.2.5.

Frankfurt Stock Exchange (listed companies) In the case of the listed companies, a request was sent to all companies in the sampling frame. This could be classified as an attempt at a census, which is defined as "gathering information about every individual in a population" (Fowler 2009, p. 4). However, due to the significant amount of non-response, the sampling approach could rather be classified as a *self-selected sample*, which is a sample in which the units themselves decide whether or not they participate in the survey (Sterba and Foster 2008).

Personal Contacts The use of personal contacts as participants can be classified as convenience sampling, which is defined as using "the most convenient group available" (Utts and Heckard 2012, p. 165). However, only appropriate contacts with the required background and characteristics were used, so that the characteristics of the respondents are likely to be similar to the ones in the other sample frames.

XING, Pforzheim Alumni and ICV The sampling approach that was applied for these three sample frames can also be labelled as a self-selected sample. The survey link was made available to the potential participants. However, the decision as to who actually responded was made by the participants.

7.2.2.4 Sample Size and Response Rate

In this study, no explicit target **sample size** was determined. Instead, all possible effort was taken to maximize the identification of suitable respondents for this research. Additionally, one goal was to ensure an adequate representation of different sub-groups in the sample, such as listed vs. non-listed companies as well as companies of different sizes. The final sample consists of 96 companies. In Fig. 7.2, the composition of the sample in terms of sample frame can be seen.

In Fig. 7.3, a comparison of this study's sample size with previous studies is made. It can be seen that the sample size for this study corresponds to the median sample size of previous studies. There are some studies with substantially higher sample sizes. However, it must be emphasised that the studies with the largest sample sizes are based on larger populations such as the U.S. (Block 2003, 2005; Graham and Harvey 2001) or several countries (Brounen et al. 2004). Although the size of the population does not influence the necessary sample size for large populations from a statistical point of view (Stopher 2012), a larger population enables the researchers to achieve larger absolute sample sizes. Another reason why some studies have larger sample sizes could be that they have higher response rates because they cooperate with renowned organisations such as the Financial Executives Institute (FEI) (Graham and Harvey 2001). Overall, a sample size of 96 companies is considered to be appropriate for this study.

Due to the multiple frames sampling approach that is pursued in this study, a total **response rate** cannot be calculated. This is only possible for the Frankfurt Stock Exchange (FSE) sample frame. In this sample frame, a response rate of 9.5 % eligible responses was achieved. This is considered satisfactory taking into account

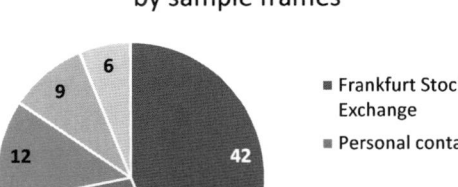

Fig. 7.2 Sample composition in terms of sample frames

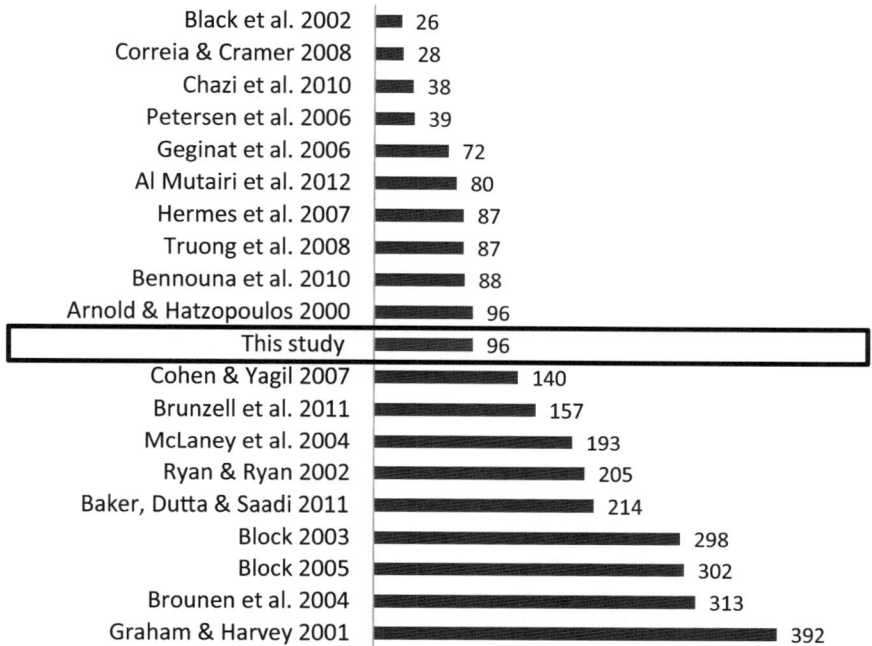

Fig. 7.3 Sample size of comparable studies

the fact that only completely filled out questionnaires were counted and that the complete sample frame was contacted, which means that 9.5 % of *all* listed companies in Germany are considered in the sample.

Sending reminder mails had a positive effect on the response rate. 29 (69 %) of the eligible responses from the FSE companies were received after the first request. By sending a reminder, another 13 answers (31 % of the eligible responses) were obtained from this sample frame.

Figure 7.4 shows an analysis of the companies' responses from the FSE sample frame. As can be seen, in addition to the eligible responses, another 5 % of the companies started filling out the questionnaire but did not finish it. These incomplete responses were not considered in the sample. A further 13 % of the companies replied to the email request announcing that they would not take part in the survey. Overall, taking into account incomplete responses and explicit refusals, 28 % of the listed companies in Germany have responded to the request in some way.

The companies that explicitly refused to take part stated different reasons for their non-participation: Many companies reported scarce staff resources or employees' high workload. Moreover, many companies stated that they received numerous requests to participate in studies. Less commonly mentioned reasons were exceptional situations that the companies were in (e.g. a severe crisis or a

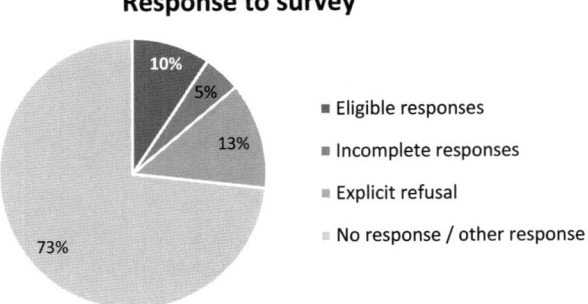

Fig. 7.4 Responses to survey from FSE sample frame

takeover), confidentiality of the information requested or that they operate according to the principles of lean administration, focusing on their core tasks.

7.2.3 Survey Instrument

7.2.3.1 Structure and Questions

The survey instrument for this study was developed based on the hypotheses formulated in Sect. 7.1. As explained in Sect. 5.2, the two methods that are used in this research—expert interviews and a company survey—form part of an integrated concept. Since the results from the qualitative have been used as a basis to develop the hypotheses, they are triangulated and quantitatively tested with the help of this survey instrument.

Table 7.2 gives a high-level overview of the structure of the questionnaire and for each section shows the hypotheses to which it is related. The complete questionnaire can be found in Sect. 9.5.[5] It can be seen that the questionnaire starts with questions concerning country and sector/industry. These questions are used to make sure that the scope of the target population is maintained and additionally to measure the sector/industry factor. Next, several questions concerning the cost-of-capital practices are asked. These sections include many aspects of cost-of-capital practices—for instance concerning the determination of WACC and CAPM and the use of cost-of-capital rates in investment evaluation. Finally, questions are asked concerning influencing factors such as company characteristics as well as characteristics of the participant.

---

[5] The data was collected using a questionnaire in German; the questionnaire in the appendix is a translated version.

7.2 Research Design

Table 7.2 Structure of the questionnaire

Section of questionnaire		Purpose/hypothesis
1	**Country, sector/industry**	
	Country	*Delimitation of scope*
	Sector/Industry	*Delimitation of scope*, H3
2	**Cost-of-capital practices**	
2.1	Determination of cost-of-capital	*Cost-of-capital practices*, H1
2.2	Performance management and cost-of-capital	*Cost-of-capital practices*, H1
2.3	Investments and cost-of-capital	*Cost-of-capital practices*, H1
3	**Influencing factors**	
3.1	Cost and benefit of cost-of-capital practices	H6
3.2	Company data: Size and investors	H2, H4, H5
3.3	Company data: Organisational structure	H9
3.4	Company data: Management and corporate culture	H7, H8
3.5	Further data	*Participant information*

7.2.3.2 Level of Measurement

Most questions in the questionnaire of this survey use nominal or ordinal measurement scales, with a few exceptions. In general, it can be said that the following logic was applied in terms of scales:

For the questions about **cost-of-capital practices**, the following principle was applied: Each theme starts with a general question about whether this practice is relevant at all. For example, the questionnaire asks whether a company determines its cost of equity *at all*. This is done using a dichotomous (yes/no) scale. For the next level of detail, i.e. which particular methods or models are used to determine the cost of equity, an ordinal rating scale is used. The different methods or models are rated in terms of how relevant they are on a scale ranging from "not relevant" to "relevant". A rating scale is used in order not only to establish whether a method is applied at all, but also to be able to compare the importance of different methods.

For questions about **objectively measurable company characteristics**, nominal scales are used. This includes, for instance, the question of whether a company is stock market listed, the ownership structure or the department of the respondent. An exception is the company size, which is measured by the revenues and number of employees as a numerical value (ratio scale).

For questions about **'soft' influencing factors**, ordinal rating scales are used. On the one hand, these factors include characteristics of the company which are not objective facts. An example is the degree of centralisation, which is rated on a five-point scale from "low" to "high". On the other hand, this includes, for example, the cost/benefit factor, which is measured with the help of statements and a five-point Likert-type scale ranging from "strongly disagree" to "strongly agree".

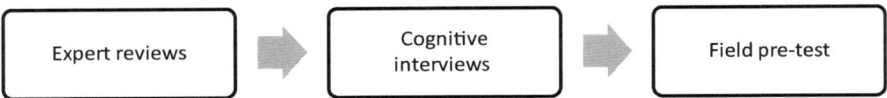

Fig. 7.5 Survey instrument evaluation

7.2.3.3 Review and Testing

Testing and evaluation of questions before the actual data collection is recommended in the literature (Fowler 2009)—especially for self-administered questionnaires where no interviewer is present to solve any problems that occur. The aim of such evaluations is to decrease measurement error. In order to evaluate and improve the survey instrument for this research, three evaluation methods were applied sequentially, as illustrated in Fig. 7.5.

As a first step, **expert reviews** were conducted. In the literature, it is recommended to have the questionnaire reviewed by both subject matter experts and questionnaire design experts (Groves et al. 2009). This recommendation was followed in this research. The questionnaire was reviewed by two management consultants who work in the field and one academic subject matter expert. Some minor changes concerning wording of questions and response alternatives were recommended by the subject matter experts. Furthermore, one person who has worked in a market research institution for several years was consulted as an expert for questionnaire design. The discussion with this expert especially focused on technical issues of the questionnaire such as measurement scales, length and order of questions.

As a second step, **cognitive interviews** with members of the target population were conducted. In total, three cognitive interviews with professionals working in Finance or Accounting departments were conducted. According to Groves (2009), the term "cognitive interviewing" refers to several cognitively inspired procedures. In this research, a procedure that is referred to as "concurrent think-alouds" has been used. That means that the interviewees were handed a paper version of the questionnaire and asked to fill it out and to describe their thoughts while doing so. In the cognitive interviews, the emphasis was to check how well the questions were understood by the target population in order to increase validity. The outcomes of the cognitive interviews were some minor wording changes in the survey instrument.

As a last step in the development and evaluation of the survey instrument, a **field pre-test** with a limited number of companies from the target population was performed. The field pre-test was conducted with both non-listed and listed companies. As the number of listed companies that can be contacted is limited, only approximately 100 requests to listed companies were sent out in order that not too many companies from the sample frame were 'used up'. Additionally, personal contacts were used to collect responses. In total, the final sample size of the pre-test was approximately 30. The intention of the pre-test was not only to test the survey instrument but also the data collection process and the response rate. This way, it would have been possible to change for instance the cover letter in the final data collection. Concerning the survey instrument, it was checked whether the respondents that did not complete the entire questionnaire had always cancelled at a certain point in the questionnaire. Statistically, the data was only analysed descriptively in Microsoft Excel to get a first impression of the results and variances in the answers. As no problems in the survey instrument or data collection process were identified in the field pre-test, it was decided not to make any more changes to the survey instrument. A positive side effect of this decision was that the data collected in the field pre-test could also be used for the final sample.

7.2.4 Mode and Process of Data Collection

7.2.4.1 Mode of Data Collection

Given today's technical possibilities, there is a large variety of methods for the collection of survey data, ranging from face-to-face or telephone interviewing, through mail surveys to web-based surveys. However, the choice should be made thoroughly under consideration of the implications on the survey quality (Groves et al. 2009). The mode of data collection can have an effect not only on the cost of data collection, but also on survey error (Groves et al. 2009). For example, measurement quality can depend on the mode of data collection (Groves et al. 2009). Moreover, the methods used for data collection can have an effect on coverage, i.e. how well the sample describes the target population (Fowler 2009).

For this survey, the decision was made to use a self-administered online questionnaire as a data collection tool. The hyperlink to the survey tool was distributed in a systematic process that is described in Sect. 7.2.4.2. In the remaining part of this section, the choice of this mode of data collection is discussed, taking into account the implications on cost, coverage, measurement quality and non-response.

In terms of *cost*, it can be said that online surveys are relatively cheap (Bethlehem and Biffignandi 2012; Iacobucci and Churchill 2010). Although the fee-based tool SurveyMonkey was used in this survey, the cost is still substantially lower than for a paper-based survey. Given the limited financial resources of a PhD project, this was one aspect in the decision concerning the mode of data collection.

In the literature (Iacobucci and Churchill 2010; Groves et al. 2009; Fowler 2009), it is often stated that the *coverage* of web surveys is problematic because not all households have Internet access. In the case of this survey, this is not an issue, since all companies have Internet access and thus can be contacted via email and use the online tool.

One possible disadvantage of web surveys is the higher rate of *non-response* compared to paper-based surveys that is generally assumed in the literature (Groves et al. 2009). Fowler (2009) furthermore states that in self-administered surveys it is more likely that participants will not complete the questionnaire after they have started filling it out, since there is no interviewer involved. However, when reading the survey methods literature, one has to be aware that the literature is generally assuming the case of consumer surveys. In the case of this research, where companies are surveyed, there are other mechanisms that have to be taken into account where web-based surveys offer substantial advantages. First of all, for the topic of this research, direct contact details for the relevant people in the organisations are not publicly available. Therefore, it is necessary that the questionnaire can be easily forwarded within the organisation. With the setup used in this research—i.e. survey links sent by email that can be easily forwarded—it is more likely that the questionnaire will actually reach the relevant people in the organisation than in the case of paper-based questionnaires. Moreover, as Iacobucci and Churchill (2010) state, a web-based questionnaire is flexible and convenient for the respondents, because they can access it virtually anytime. This is especially helpful for executives in the organisations, who have a very tight schedule and are very difficult to contact by telephone.

Last but not least, an issue that should be considered in the choice of a mode of data collection is *measurement quality*. On the one hand, a disadvantage of self-administered questionnaires for complex topics like the one in this research is that there is no interviewer present who could explain the questions if necessary. However, as all participants are professionals in this field and the questionnaire was pre-tested (see Sect. 7.2.3.3), this is not expected to be an issue. On the other hand, a self-administered online questionnaire gives the respondents the chance to consult with their colleagues or check in their files if they do not know the answers to a question (Fowler 2009). Additionally, the bias toward "textbook answers" or "politically correct" answers which is assumed in the literature (Bancel and Mittoo 2011; Serita 2008) might be weakened if there is no interviewer listening and the answers are recorded anonymously.

In conclusion, it can be said that a self-administered online questionnaire is considered the most appropriate mode of data collection for this survey. The main reasons for this decision are cost advantages, the expectation of a higher measurement quality and the expectation of a higher response rate due to a convenient process for the respondents.

7.2.4.2 Process of Data Collection

The survey instrument was technically implemented with the help of a fee-based account for the commercial online tool SurveyMonkey.[6] Besides its easy-to-use functionality, this tool was particularly selected because of the following features:

- The possibility to customize hyperlinks and use variables in the URL, which provided the opportunity to generate individual links for each participant in order to be able to track whether the questionnaire had been filled out (see below).

---

[6] http://www.surveymonkey.com

- The possibility to export the survey data in an Excel and SPSS format. This feature reduces manual effort and increases data quality, since no errors can be made when entering or converting the data

The link to the survey was distributed using a systematic procedure, which is discussed below separately for listed companies and non-listed companies, since a different procedure was used depending on the sample frame.

As previously explained, for the **listed companies** a list of email addresses was compiled from the companies' websites. Each of the companies was sent an individual link to the online survey by email. The URL of the hyperlink contained a four-digit numerical code that was used to track whether or not the companies had already filled out the survey. Since response rate was considered to be a critical issue, particular attention was dedicated to the question of how it could be increased. To do so, recommendations from the literature (Groves et al. 2009) concerning design features of the survey and mailing were followed. Moreover, the issue was discussed with peer researchers and the researcher's supervisors. The following measures were taken:

- High emphasis was placed on the *cover letter* (i.e. the email text). First of all, if an individual email address and the name of the recipient were known, a personal form of address was used (i.e. 'Dear Mr. Smith' instead of 'Dear Sir or Madam'). This way, the impression of a mass mailing was avoided. Moreover, the approximate completion time for the questionnaire was indicated. Furthermore, at the bottom of the letter, the email addresses of the researcher and the supervisors were mentioned, as well as a landline telephone number for the researcher, in order to emphasise that the mail was a serious request.
- In the letter, recipients were assured that the data would be analysed on an *anonymous* basis and the answers would be treated *confidentially*.
- As an *incentive* to participation, participants were offered a summary of the study's results free of charge. This was considered to be a higher incentive than a material incentive, since business organisations are often interested in gaining the possibility to benchmark their methods and processes against other companies. Moreover, a material prize might have created legal problems in a business context due to German tax laws. Additionally, very high attention has recently been paid to so-called 'compliance' issues after several bribery scandals in large German company groups in the last few years.
- Three weeks after the initial request, a friendly *reminder* was sent to those companies that had not yet answered the request. This helped to increase the response rate. Initially, it was planned to call all companies by telephone as a last step in addition to the email reminders. This was attempted with some of the companies. However, after some days of effort, it turned out that this strategy did not result in any further responses, since it was not possible to reach persons in the organisations who were in a position to fill out the questionnaire. On the one hand, often it was not possible to be redirected to the relevant department. On the other hand, even if it was possible to talk to someone in a relevant department, it was often said that only the head of the department was allowed to answer such

external requests and it was very hard to reach this person by telephone. Some of the people offered to forward the survey internally; however, this did not result in any further responses. Therefore, no further telephone reminders were made.

In order to be able to manage the process of data collection, which included sending requests to approximately 450 companies, a database was set up in Microsoft Excel. For each company, a four-digit code, the email address and the name of the contact person (if applicable) were stored. Moreover, it was recorded when the requests and reminders were send out and whether the respective company had replied or filled out the questionnaire. In order to reduce the manual effort associated with the data collection, a self-programmed Visual Basic macro was used. The macro allowed the automatic generation of individualised emails in Microsoft Outlook with a personal form of address and an individual link to the survey for each of the companies.

For the sample frames of the **non-listed companies**, a less standardised procedure was applied:

- The *personal contacts* were all contacted individually depending on the relationship and contact possibilities, e.g. by telephone, in person or by email.
- In the social network *XING*, the posts and mails were all sent manually. For the individual mails, the same cover letter as in the case of the listed companies was used.
- Alumni from *Pforzheim University* as well as the members of the *ICV* were contacted via standardised mass mails.

Overall, the data collection took approximately 8 months. The literature (Fowler 2009) recommends using a long data collection period in order to make more persons aware of the survey request. Indeed, it turned out that a high level of patience was required to collect the answers. Another reason for the long duration of the data collection period was the high workload associated with collecting the answers.[7]

7.2.5 Error and Bias

7.2.5.1 Types of Error

As Fowler (2009, p. 4) states, "like all measures in all sciences, social survey measurement is not error free". Thus, it has to be accepted that error cannot be completely avoided. However, it is important to be aware of the possible sources of error and to attempt to minimise this error. In the following sections, the author will discuss possible sources of error that can be found in the literature and identify

---

[7] It has to be mentioned that the long data collection period is not expected to produce any error or bias, since the cost-of-capital practices that are examined are stable over a long period of time.

which of them might be relevant for this survey. Based on this discussion, the measures that have been taken in the survey design in order to reduce error will be explained.

First of all, some definitional issues are clarified. In this thesis, the following terminology is used, which can be found in the literature: In general, two types of error exist: random error and systematic error (Fowler 2009; Stopher 2012). Systematic error is usually termed bias (Stopher 2012). That means that the general term 'error' includes both random error and systematic error (bias).

Error can occur in two inference steps, as shown in Fig. 7.6: in the first inference step, there can be error associated with the answers that are given, i.e. error in measurement. This type of error is discussed in Sect. 7.2.5.2. In the second inference step, there can be error associated with who answers, because regularly only part of the population, i.e. a sample, is surveyed. As Stopher (2012, p. 72) states, "error exists in all sample surveys by the nature of a sample survey. They exist because a sample can never be a complete representation of the population from which it is drawn". This type of error will be discussed in Sect. 7.2.5.3.

7.2.5.2 Measurement Error

In this thesis, the term 'measurement error' is used for any error associated with answers and their measurement. In order to avoid measurement error, it is necessary to design the measurement as carefully as possible (Stopher 2012). In this section, the particular considerations that have been made concerning validity and reliability of the measurement are discussed.

According to Groves et al. (2009, p. 50), **validity** is the "extent to which the measure is related to the underlying construct". It could be argued that validity is especially an issue in other disciplines such as psychometrics that deal with more subjective constructs that are not easily measurable. However, bias can also occur in research that has a strong focus on objective facts, particularly due to three issues that are discussed below.

First, the participants might *have problems understanding the question* (Fowler 2009). On the one hand, this might be an issue in this survey because the topic is very specific and complex. On the other hand, the people who fill out the questionnaire are professionals, and are thus familiar with the technical terminology that is used. Additionally, the questionnaire was evaluated and tested in several steps (see Sect. 7.2.3.3), so the author feels that enough care has been taken concerning this issue.

Second, the respective person answering the question *might not have the necessary knowledge* (Fowler 2009). This problem is also mentioned in the specialised literature about survey research in Finance (Frank 2007; Serita 2008), as in large organisations it is often difficult to gain access to executives at a senior level. It is recognised that it is difficult to access certain people in organisations. However, for the quality of the data and the necessary knowledge, it is not the hierarchical level of the person that is decisive but his or her subject-specific knowledge. In this

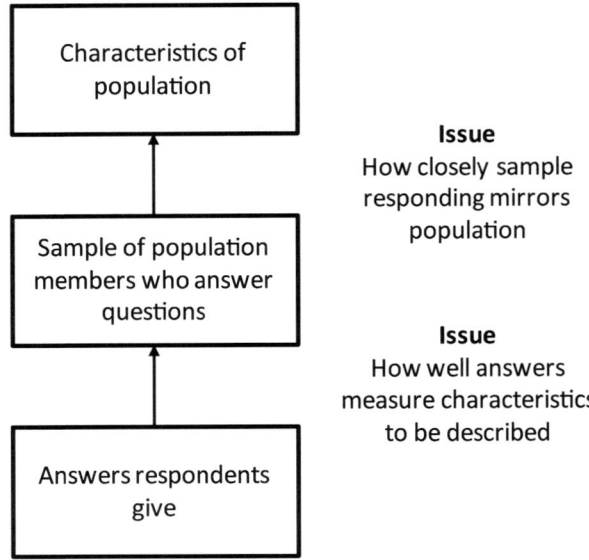

Fig. 7.6 Inference in survey research (reproduced from Fowler 2009)

survey, it is assumed that this knowledge is available because the survey's covering letter asked the recipient to forward the survey to a relevant department. Moreover, the advantage of an online survey is that it can be easily forwarded within the organisation until an appropriate respondent is found. There are cases where this actually happened, which could be seen because the author received a copy of the internal email communication from several companies.

Third, the topic referred to in the literature as *social desirability* (Fowler 2009) might be an issue. Social desirability is the "tendency for individuals to portray themselves in a generally favourable fashion" (Craighead and Weiner 2010, p. 1628). Although this definition from the literature refers to individual persons, companies might also distort answers in order to look good (Bancel and Mittoo 2011). This might apply to organisations as a whole or to individual departments that are presented in a favourable way by their heads. One reason for the decision to conduct this survey on an anonymous and confidential basis was to mitigate this problem. Another point that might make the problem less severe is that the questionnaire is self-administered so that no social desirability effect towards an interviewer occurs. Therefore, social desirability bias is not expected to have a strong influence on the survey results.

Reliability of a survey instrument refers to whether a questionnaire is able to obtain consistent results each time it is used in a comparable situation (Miller et al. 2011). In general, it can be said that standardised survey instruments that use closed questions, like the questionnaire used in this research, have fewer reliability problems (Fowler 2009). Still, effort was taken to improve the reliability. Specifically, every effort was made to use wording and technical terminology that is as precise as possible. This was ensured in the development by conducting expert reviews and cognitive interviews with member of the target population (see

Sect. 7.2.3.3). Moreover, as recommended in the literature (Fowler 2009), a "don't know" or "N/A" option was introduced for some of the questions in order to avoid respondents ticking a random box if they did not know the answer. However, no formal statistical tests of the survey instrument's reliability were made, such as test-retest or split-half reliability, which are discussed in the literature (Miller et al. 2011). The reason is that all cases of the target population that could be contacted and were willing to participate in the survey were required for the actual sample.

7.2.5.3 Sampling or Representation Error

Sampling or representation error occurs in surveys that use a sample, i.e. surveys that do not collect data from every single unit in the population. Such data collections are based on the premise that with the help of the characteristics of the sample, the population can be described (Fowler 2009). Also within this category of error, it is possible to distinguish between random error and systematic error (bias). Random sampling error is a random variation of the sample characteristics from the true characteristics of the population as a whole. In contrast, sampling bias is based on some systematic deviation between the sample characteristics and the population (Fowler 2009). Stopher (2012) points out that effort should be taken especially to reduce bias, as it is not possible to reduce bias by increasing the size of the sample. In the following paragraphs, possible sources of sampling bias are identified and measures that have been taken by the author to reduce bias are explained.

In this research, there was no complete sample frame in terms of a list that includes all companies from the target population. Therefore, as a proxy, several sample frames in terms of data collection procedures were used. In such a procedure, there might be the problem that the frame population deviates from the target population, as illustrated by Groves et al. (2009) in Fig. 7.7. This results in two **coverage problems**: First, it could be the case that there are companies in the population that are not covered by the sample frame (undercoverage). Second, it could be the case that the sample frame covers units which are not part of the target population (ineligible units).

Because of the absence of a single complete sample frame that matches the target population, the risk of *undercoverage* cannot be completely excluded from this survey. However, by using a multiple frame design, effort was made to cover as many companies as possible via different channels. Therefore, it is assumed that there is no major undercoverage problem in this research.

Obviously, the sampling strategy that was followed in this research can lead to the effect that data from *ineligible units* is collected. In the case of this research, ineligible units are companies from the financial services sector and companies that are not headquartered in Germany. In order to avoid these units becoming part of the sample, the survey instrument includes questions about the location of the headquarters and the sector in which the company works. This way, cases that do

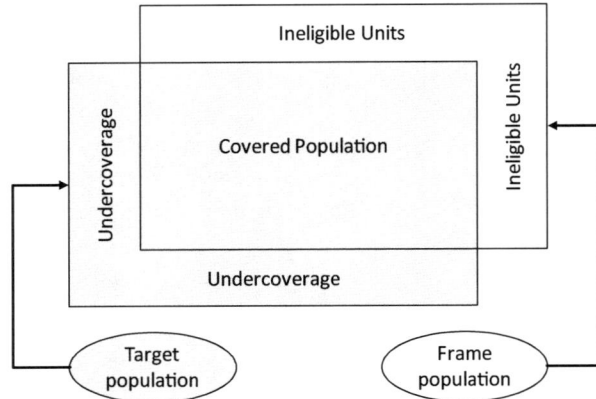

Fig. 7.7 Coverage of a target population by a frame (reproduced from Groves et al. 2009)

not match the target population can be filtered out. Therefore, the risk of ineligible cases in the sample is very low.

Furthermore, bias could occur in the process of selecting units from the sample frame, i.e. in the **sampling approach**. From a statistical point of view, a random sample should be drawn from the sample frame in order that the sample is representative of the population. In this research, non-probability sampling approaches were used. That means that there might be bias in the sampling, which could be referred to as *non-response bias* or *self-selection bias*. Regardless of the term which is used to describe the bias, there might be a systematic deviation between the characteristics of the sample and the population if no strict random sample is drawn. One possible reason for that in a self-selected sample could be that people who have a strong opinion about the subject are more likely to respond (Utts and Heckard 2012).

In the literature (Groves et al. 2009; Utts and Heckard 2012), it is generally assumed that with a sampling approach like the one in this thesis, there is no statistical basis to infer the results beyond the sample. As there was no possibility to use a strict random sample given the restrictions of this research in terms of the availability of participants, it has to be accepted that in the interpretation of the results, one has to be aware that they might only be applicable to the sample from a strictly statistical point of view.

However, looking at the distribution of companies in the sample, e.g. in terms of size and investor structure (see Sect. 7.3.2), it could be argued that a good representation of all relevant subsets of the population has been achieved (although this is not based on strict statistical grounds).

7.2.6 Data Analysis Approach

7.2.6.1 Recoding and Adjustment of Data

The data was already available from SurveyMonkey in a format that could be used for the data analysis. Only the following data was recoded:

- For some aspects of the data analysis, the ordinal scale of dependent variables (cost-of-capital practices) was recoded to a nominal scale, interpreting the two highest points as "relevant". This is a common procedure that is also applied in previous studies (e.g. Al Mutairi et al. 2012; Baker et al. 2011; Graham and Harvey 2001).
- The size variable (revenues and number of employees) was recoded from a ratio scale to an ordinal scale. The reason is that it was the only ratio variable in the data and the size effects could be analysed more easily with descriptive statistics using an ordinal scale.
- Some variables were technically recoded using 1-0 for yes-no questions instead of 1-2 as in the original SurveyMonkey coding.

Some researchers make adjustments to the data in order to cope with item non-response, i.e. missing responses to single questions (Groves et al. 2009). In the literature (Fowler 2009), the possibility of building models to predict the value of missing items is discussed. In this research, the decision was made to make no adjustment to the data based on statistical predictions and instead to reduce the number of cases for questions with missing responses. As incomplete questionnaires were not included in the data analysis anyway, this effect is very small and only concerns a few questions.

The only exception where manual adjustments of the data were made is the company size in cases where it was obviously not filled out correctly, e.g. turnover of 1. If the company was known, the correct size was entered. Otherwise, the field was cleared.

7.2.6.2 Statistical Analysis Methods

The data analysis for this company survey was conducted with IBM SPSS version 20. The charts and tables for this thesis were mainly built with the help of Microsoft Excel (based on the SPSS analyses).

For the data analysis, several statistical analyses and procedures were conducted in several stages, as shown in Table 7.3. Details are discussed below the table and in the respective sections indicated in the table.

(1) Sample Characteristics
Many statistical procedures assume data to be normally distributed: i.e. if the data is not normally distributed, these procedures should not be used (Thode 2002). Therefore, as a first step, the distribution of the data is examined in order to

Table 7.3 Overview of statistical methods used

Stage	Methods	Section
1. Sample characteristics	• Test for normality • Histogram plotting • Measures of central tendency (mean/median) • Measures of distribution (skewness/kurtosis) • Absolute frequencies • Relative frequencies	7.3
2. Descriptive statistics of cost-of-capital practices	• Absolute frequencies • Relative frequencies	7.4
3. Bivariate analysis between influencing factors and cost-of-capital practices	• Cross tabulation • Spearman correlation • Mann–Whitney U-test • Kruskal-Wallis test • Chi-squared test	7.5
4. Multivariate analysis taking into account relationships among influencing factors	• Test for multicollinearity • Sample stratification • Partial rank correlation	7.6

determine which type of statistical procedures can be used. This will be done in Sect. 7.2.6 using descriptive statistical plots and measures. It is revealed that the data is not normally distributed, so that non-parametric methods must be used.

Moreover, characteristics of the companies in the sample, e.g. size and investor structure, as well as respondent characteristics, e.g. department, were analysed descriptively using absolute and relative frequencies.

(2) Descriptive Statistics of Cost-of-Capital Practices

As a first simple analysis of the companies' answers, the cost-of-capital practices are analysed descriptively in terms of absolute and relative frequencies of particular cost-of-capital methods.

(3) Bivariate Analysis

One objective of the company survey is to test quantitatively whether the influencing factors that were identified in the expert interviews show statistically significant relationships with cost-of-capital practices. Therefore, in a first step, bivariate measures of association are calculated between the influencing factors and cost-of-capital practices. In doing so, a large number of combinations of variables is tested pair-wise, since there are multiple variables for both influencing factors and cost-of-capital practices.

For non-normally distributed data, non-parametric statistical methods have to be used that do not assume a particular distribution of the data. Additionally, non-parametric methods are more robust to outliers (Moore and McCabe 2006). Non-parametric statistical tests are based on ranking the data (Field 2013). As shown in Table 7.4, depending on the level of measurement of the variables,

Table 7.4 Measures of association used for bivariate analysis

	Dichotomous	Ordinal
Dichotomous	Chi-Squared/Phi	Mann–Whitney U-test
Nominal	Chi-Squared/Cramer's V	Kruskal-Wallis test
Ordinal	Mann–Whitney U-test	Spearman's Rho

Source: Based on Hain (2013), David and Sutton (2011), Craighead and Weiner (2010) and Moore and McCabe (2006)

different measures of association have to be used. The table only takes into account combinations of scales that are relevant for this thesis.

(4) Multivariate Analysis

All but one (Brunzell et al. 2011) of the previous studies discussed in Chap. 3 (see Table in Sect. 3.1.1) confine themselves to univariate or bivariate analysis of the survey data. However, the development of an explanatory model based on bivariate analysis is problematic because spurious relationships might distort the findings. While the bivariate analysis is able to test the relationship between individual influencing factors and cost-of-capital practices, it does not take into account the relationship among different determinants. Therefore, in this thesis, multicollinearity of explanatory variables is tested and controlled for using sample stratification and partial rank correlation.

7.3 Analysis 1: Sample Characteristics

7.3.1 Test for Normality

As discussed in Sect. 7.2.6.2, the question of whether the data is normally distributed influences the choice of statistical analysis procedures. In the statistics literature, there are a large number of different methods that can be used to test data for normality (Thode 2002). In this section, the most common procedures are briefly discussed and applied to the data of this survey.

As a first step, the use of **graphical plots** is generally recommended to check the distribution of the data visually and evaluate its normality subjectively. In the literature, the use of histograms as well as P-P plots is suggested (Field 2013; Thode 2002). In this thesis, histograms were used to visualise the distribution of all ordinal variables and compare it to a normally distributed bell curve. In the charts, it could already be seen visually that most of the variables seemed to be non-normally distributed.

In a second step, the distribution can be examined using descriptive statistical measures. In a symmetrical distribution, the **measures of central tendency** mean, median and mode are identical (Frankfort-Nachmias and Leon-Guerrero 2011). These measures were calculated for all ordinal variables; the results can be found in Sect. 9.4. It can clearly be seen that for important cost-of-capital practices (e.g. WACC on a group level), the distribution is negatively skewed, i.e. the mode is higher than the median; and the median is higher than the mean. This makes sense because the scale measures the importance of the cost-of-capital method, i.e. a negatively skewed distribution indicates a higher relevance of the method. Although not all variables show such a clear deviation of the measures of central tendency, it can be said that most of the variables are not normally distributed.

As a further step, **skewness and kurtosis** of the distribution can be calculated in SPSS. These measures can also be found in the table in Sect. 9.4. The way skewness is calculated in SPSS, zero means that the data is symmetrically distributed (Field 2013). Kline (2009) states that values higher than 3 indicate an extremely skewed distribution. In this thesis, values higher than 1 are considered as a clearly skewed distribution. Concerning kurtosis, zero also indicates a normal distribution. Positive values indicate a pointed distribution, while negative values indicate a flat distribution (Field 2013). Also for kurtosis, it can be seen in the data that the values are generally different from zero, which indicates non-normally distributed data.

Besides these simple methods using descriptive statistics, there are **advanced tests for normality** suggested in the literature (Field 2013; Reinard 2006), such as the *Lilliefors modification of the Kolmogorov-Smirnov one-sample test* or the *Shapiro-Wilk test*. Such procedures test, for instance, whether the skewness and kurtosis are significantly different from zero. Since the simple tests above have already shown that the data in this research are obviously not normally distributed, further statistical tests of the distribution are not conducted. Furthermore, such significance tests are problematic because they lack power to detect distribution problems in small samples and might show significant deviations from the normal distribution in large samples even if the effect is very small (Field 2013).

Overall, the **conclusion** can be drawn that the data is not normally distributed. This is not surprising, since normally distributed data for measures of the relevance of cost-of-capital practices would mean that all methods are equally relevant. This result would be contrary to prior studies and the findings from the qualitative expert interviews. However, some explanatory variables—in particular company size, measured on a (recoded) ordinal scale—appear nearly normally distributed. The result from this section, that most of the variables are not normally distributed, has consequences for the statistical procedures that are used in this thesis: for statistical tests, non-parametric methods will be used, which do not assume a particular statistical distribution of the data.

7.3.2 Company Characteristics

This section briefly describes the characteristics of the companies in the sample. In terms of revenues p.a., the sample includes companies ranging from comparably small companies with revenue of 1.2 million EUR to some of the largest companies

7.3 Analysis 1: Sample Characteristics

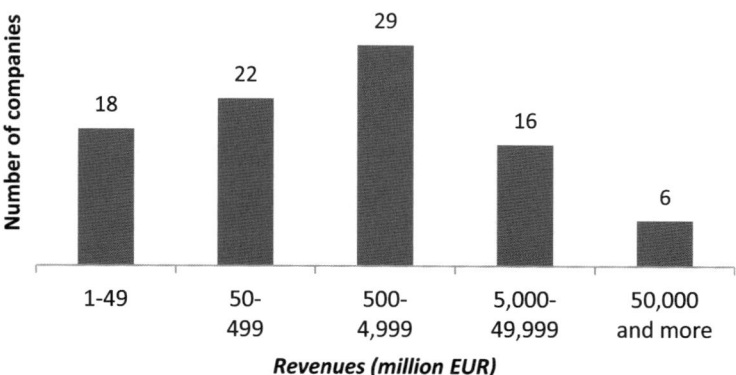

Fig. 7.8 Size of companies in sample

in Germany with revenue of 50 billion EUR and more.[8] As can be seen in Fig. 7.8, companies from all size groups are represented adequately. The median revenue of the participating companies is 750 million EUR; the mean revenue is 9.8 billion EUR.[9] In terms of number of employees, the companies range from 17 employees to 100,000 and more, with a median of 3.050 and a mean of 37.041.

Concerning the investor structure of the companies in the sample, it can be said that all investor types are represented in the sample, as can be seen in Fig. 7.9. However, the importance or role of the investor groups varies. While individual private investors and families are often in a majority shareholder role, other groups, such as management owners, are more often restricted to a small share in the companies. In terms of stock market listing of the companies (not in chart), 58 of the companies (60 %) are listed and 38 are non-listed (40 %).

With regard to the industry sector, 65 production companies, 22 companies from the wholesale, retail or services sector and 9 other companies (mainly telecommunications) took part in the survey. Among the production companies, producers of machinery and equipment are the largest group (24 responses), followed by the automotive industry and the electrical industry (9 responses each).

7.3.3 Respondent Characteristics

In order to give an indication of the quality of the answers and to evaluate whether there might be measurement error, because respondents do not understand the question or might not have the necessary knowledge (see Sect. 7.2.5.2), information about the respondents is presented below.

---

[8] In order to protect the privacy of the companies, the exact revenues of the largest participants are not mentioned.

[9] Calculated based on original metric scale data.

Fig. 7.9 Investor types in sample companies

	\multicolumn{6}{c}{Share in company}
	0-10%	11-25%	26-50%	51-75%	>75%	Total
Individual private investors / families	17	2	9	10	28	66
Institutional investors (e.g. banks)	23	7	6	2	4	42
Financial investors (e.g. Private Equity)	22	6	2	3	2	35
Corporate / strategic investors	18	6	1	2	6	33
Management ownership	33	3	1	1	4	42
Free float	14	12	12	5	8	51

As can be seen in Fig. 7.10, the majority of respondents have a managerial position. In terms of the department (not in chart), 82 of the respondents (85 %) are from different Finance or Accounting departments such as Management Accounting or Treasury, 8 respondents (8 %) are employed in management-related departments and five respondents (5 %) in the Investor Relations department.

Given this structure of respondents, it can be assumed that the respondents generally have the necessary knowledge to ensure good data quality.

7.4 Analysis 2: Cost-of-Capital Practices (Univariate Analysis)

7.4.1 Company Cost-of-Capital

As a first cost-of-capital question, the companies were asked whether they explicitly determined **cost-of-capital** on the company group level. A high number (65) of the companies (68 %) reported that they do so. As can be seen in Fig. 7.11, for 52 of the companies (54 %), the WACC is a relevant method to calculate their company cost-of-capital, as suggested by Finance theory.[10]

---

[10] Based on recoded variables interpreting 4 and 5 of ordinal scale as "relevant": see Sect. 7.2.6.1.

7.4 Analysis 2: Cost-of-Capital Practices (Univariate Analysis) 173

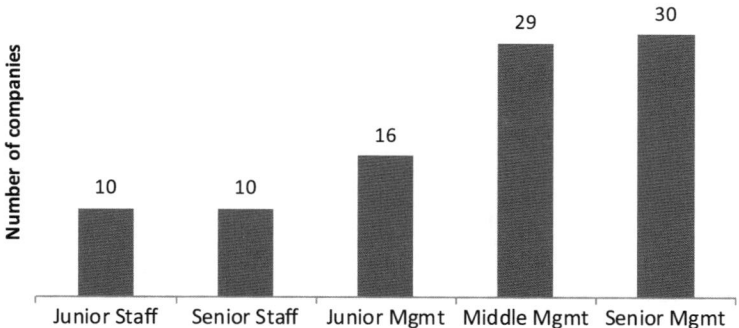

Fig. 7.10 Position of respondents

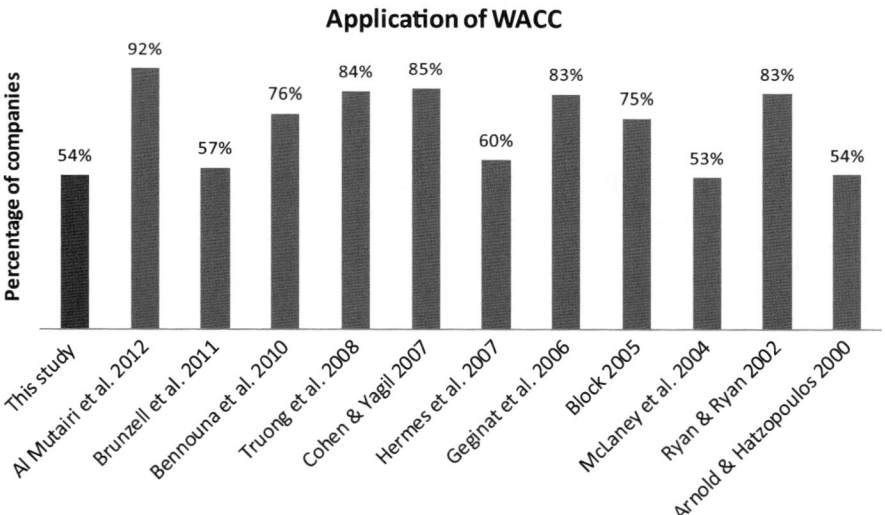

Fig. 7.11 Application of WACC compared to previous studies

Compared to previous studies, this is a relatively low percentage. The differences from other studies can partly be explained by taking into account the influencing factors that were identified in this research (see Sect. 7.5). For instance, Al Mutairi et al. (2012) only include listed companies in their survey, which generally apply more sophisticated methods. Compared to studies with comparable sample structures in terms of company size (Arnold and Hatzopoulos 2000; McLaney et al. 2004), the level of sophistication of cost-of-capital practices appears comparable to other Western countries.

Of all participating companies in this study, 58 companies (60 %) reported to explicitly calculate their **cost of equity**.

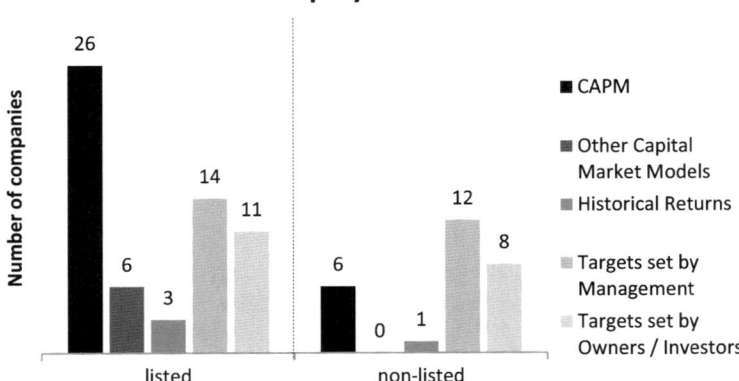

Fig. 7.12 Application of cost of equity methods

Those companies that do explicitly determine their cost of equity were also asked *how* they determine it. As shown in Fig. 7.12, it turns out that the Capital Asset Pricing Model (CAPM) as suggested by theory is the most relevant method.[11] Thirty-two companies consider the CAPM as relevant, which corresponds to 55 % of those companies that do explicitly determine their cost of equity.

Other capital market models that are discussed by academics (e.g. Arbitrage Pricing Theory: see Sect. 2.1.2.2) appear less relevant, as well as using historical returns on the company's stock. This confirms the common assumption in the literature (Subrahmanyam 2013; Smith and Walsh 2013) that the CAPM remains the standard theoretical model for the determination of cost of equity due to a lack of a workable alternative.

Besides the CAPM, many companies rely on subjective methods, i.e. targets set by management or investors, to determine their cost of equity, which provides support for the hypothesis of a theory-practice gap.

However, it can be seen that there are large differences in terms of the importance of the methods between listed and non-listed companies, as shown in Fig. 7.12.[12] In the listed companies, the CAPM is the most important method, while in the non-listed companies, subjective methods are dominant.[13]

---

[11] Based on recoded variables interpreting 4 and 5 of ordinal scale as "relevant": see Sect. 7.2.6.1. Figures do not add up to 58 due to multiple selection possibilty and recoding/different measurement levels.

[12] Please note that based on the values in Fig. 7.12, no meaningful comparison of listed and non-listed companies by absolute values is possible because the number of listed and non-listed companies in the sample is not equal. However, the relative importance of the individual methods per category of company can be compared.

[13] In the figure, it can be seen that some non-listed companies also apply the CAPM. Although there is no stock market data available, they can use proxy methods to estimate the beta factor, as discussed in Chap. 2, Sect. 2.5.

7.4 Analysis 2: Cost-of-Capital Practices (Univariate Analysis)

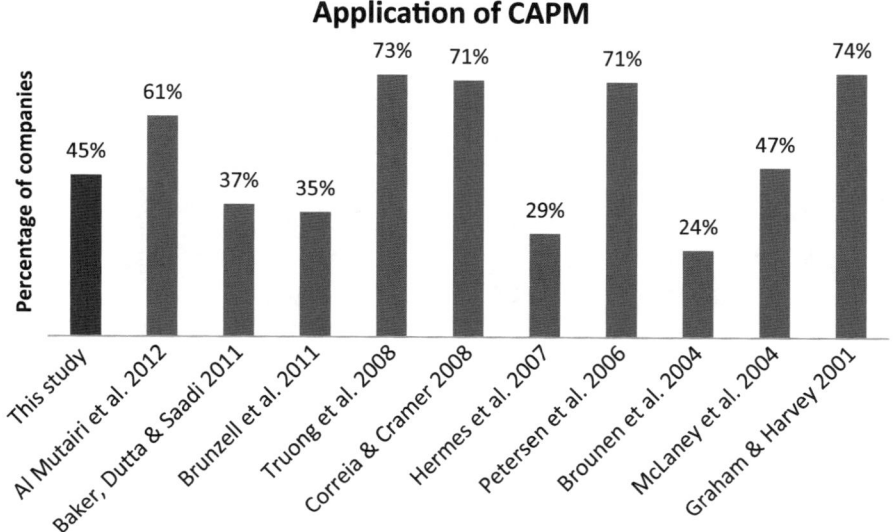

Fig. 7.13 Application of CAPM compared to previous studies

Compared to previous results on CAPM usage, the results of this study are in the midrange, with 45 % of the listed companies using the CAPM, as shown in Fig. 7.13.[14] On the one hand, some studies report significantly higher percentages of companies using the CAPM (Truong et al. 2008; Graham and Harvey 2001). On the other hand, the theory-practice gap appears much larger in other previous studies (Brunzell et al. 2011; Hermes et al. 2007; Brounen et al. 2004).

As in the case of the WACC, a possible explanation for this could be differences in the structure of the population. A possible interpretation why the variance of the CAPM results is greater than that of the WACC results could be the higher sophistication of the model, as discussed in the subsequent section.

Due to the greater variance of the CAPM results among different studies, the analysis of influencing factors (see Sect. 7.5) might be particularly interesting for the interpretation of the CAPM results.

7.4.2 Cost-of-Capital on the Level of Business Units

The next set of questions in the survey dealt with cost-of-capital on the level of subsidiaries, business units, segments, product lines, projects or regions.[15]

---

[14] In order to increase the comparability with previous studies, the percentage of companies using CAPM is related to listed companies only.

[15] Subsequently referred to as business unit (BU) only.

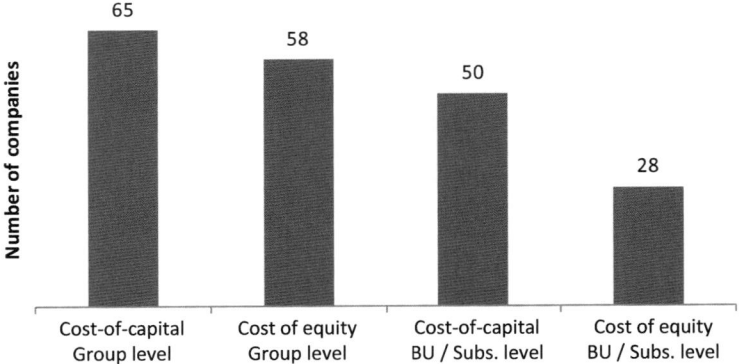

Fig. 7.14 Explicit determination of cost-of-capital

In the literature review (see Sect. 2.3.1.3), it was pointed out that it is important to use different cost-of-capital rates for BUs depending on the respective risk in order to avoid misallocation of capital. From a theoretical standpoint, this would require calculating cost-of-capital rates for the BUs and the company group.

As illustrated in Fig. 7.14, fewer respondents report that their companies explicitly determine cost-of-capital on a BU level than on a group level. This could be interpreted as a growing theory-practice gap with an increasing sophistication or level of detail of the methods. This would also explain why fewer companies explicitly determine cost of equity than overall cost-of-capital, both on a group and a BU level. The highest level of sophistication, i.e. an explicit calculation of cost of equity on a BU level, is only pursued by 28 companies (29 %).

As can be seen in Fig. 7.15, also on a BU level, WACC is the most prominent model to determine cost-of-capital, applied by 29 companies (30 %). However, there are many companies that rely on subjective estimation methods on a BU level.[16]

Analysing WACC usage further, it can be said that 29 of the 50 companies that do explicitly calculate cost-of-capital on a BU level use the WACC (58 %), as opposed to 80 % (52 out of 65) on a group level. This also confirms that on a BU level, companies tend to use less sophisticated methods.

Concerning techniques to determine cost of equity on BU level, the theory-practice gap seems to be even larger, as shown in Fig. 7.16.[17]

Only 13 companies (14 % of all companies) report using the comparable company approach (CCA), which seems to be the most widely advocated approach

---

[16] Based on recoded variables interpreting 4 and 5 on an ordinal scale as "relevant": see Sect. 7.2.6.1.

[17] Based on recoded variables interpreting 4 and 5 of ordinal scale as "relevant": see Sect. 7.2.6.1.

7.4 Analysis 2: Cost-of-Capital Practices (Univariate Analysis)

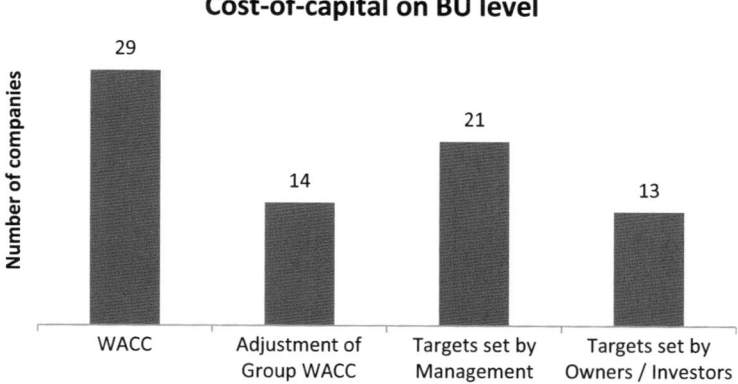

Fig. 7.15 Determination of cost-of-capital on BU level

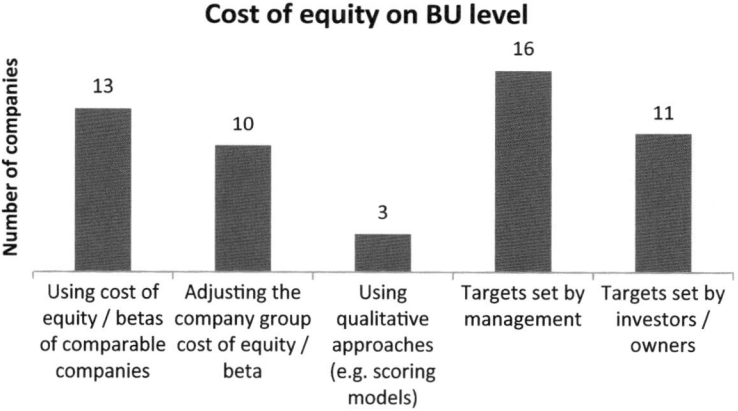

Fig. 7.16 Determination of cost of equity on BU level

in theory. This figure is in line with prior research by Block (2003), who reports that 12 % of all companies use the CCA.[18] Figures for the few other studies that deal with BU cost of equity cannot be directly compared due to a different context (Petersen et al. 2006; Geginat et al. 2006).

In terms of determination techniques for cost-of-capital and cost of equity, the interim conclusion can be drawn that there remains a large theory-practice gap both on company group and BU level.

---

[18] See also Sect. 3.3.1; percentages deviate between the section since Block's figures shown in Sect. 3.3.1 are calculated based on a subset of respondents only while in this section, all respondents are used as a basis.

7.4.3 Performance Measurement and Value-Based Management

As discussed in the literature review (see Sect. 2.2.2.3), performance measures that are related to capital can give an indication of how effectively and efficiently capital is invested and allocated in the company. Thus, they indicate a certain awareness of cost-of-capital in the companies. Therefore, the respondents were also asked which performance measures they use in their company.

In Fig 7.17 the companies uses *capital return measures* on the group level. Also *absolute capital measures* seem to be commonly applied. Although these two measures do not explicitly take into account cost-of-capital, the use of the measures might indicate that many companies have an awareness of the basic idea that capital creates an opportunity cost and should yield an adequate return. This is also confirmed by a different question in the survey. When asked directly whether they participants find it important that an adequate return on the owners' capital is generated, 72 % of the respondents agreed.[19] To the author's best knowledge, this implicit cost-of-capital awareness by companies has not been previously investigated in comparable studies, so no comparison with prior results can be made.

Value-based measures directly include cost-of-capital figures by deducting cost-of-capital from profit (see Sect. 2.2.2.3). In this study, 31 respondents (32 %) reported that they use value-based metrics on a group level and 22 companies (23 %) use the measures on a BU level. As studies on value-based management were not in the scope of the literature review, the reader is referred to Britzelmaier (2013) for an overview of value-based management studies in Europe. Compared to the studies cited by Britzelmaier, value-based management seems to be less frequently applied in the sample of this study. This can again be explained by the composition of the population, as the prior studies are all based on large, listed companies only (the importance of value-based metrics by size groups will be discussed in Sect. 7.5.2).

However, without explicitly deducting cost-of-capital from profit, the idea of value-based management and cost-of-capital can also be considered implicitly by determining hurdle rates for capital return figures. Therefore, this study goes one step further and asks whether and how the companies determine **return targets** for their overall company or for BUs. Forty-seven companies (49 %) reported that they determine explicit capital return targets on group level and 39 companies (41 %) report to do so on BU level (see Fig. 7.18). However, only approximately half of the companies that do determine return targets follow theoretical recommendations and use the calculated cost-of-capital rate as a hurdle rate. The majority of the companies that determine return targets use specifications by management as a hurdle rate.

In terms of performance measurement and value-based management, the interim conclusion can be drawn that the underlying philosophy of cost-of-capital seems to

---

[19] Agree = top two points of Likert type scale.

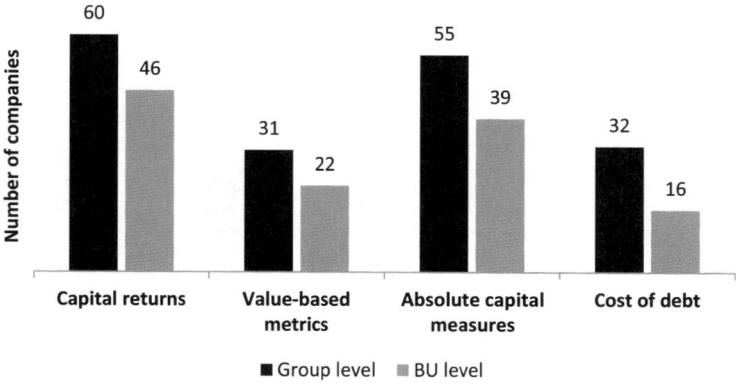

Fig. 7.17 Capital-oriented performance measures

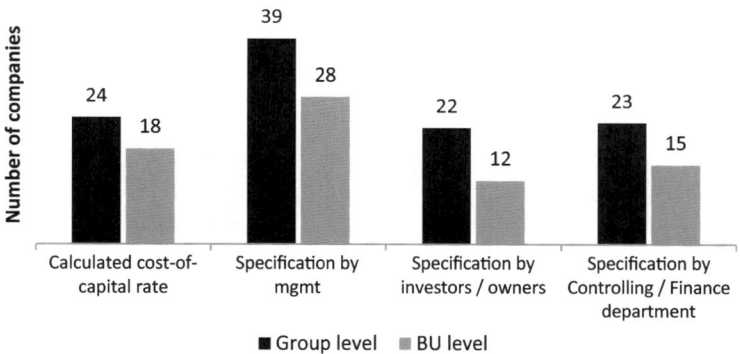

Fig. 7.18 Determination of capital return targets

have arrived in practice somewhat, since many companies monitor invested capital and determine capital return targets. However, fewer companies use value-based measures or calculated cost-of-capital rates in their calculations, so that there is still a substantial theory-practice gap.

7.4.4 Capital Allocation and Capital Budgeting

In capital allocation and capital budgeting, cost-of-capital serves as a hurdle rate for investment decisions (see literature review Sect. 2.2.2.2). In this context, two issues are particularly interesting in terms of a possible theory-practice gap: First, whether the companies use different hurdle rates depending on the risk of the investment,

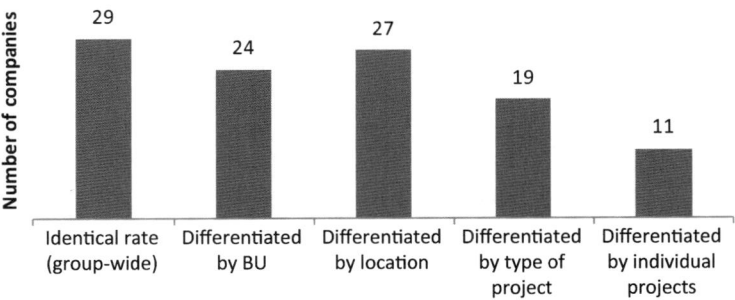

Fig. 7.19 Differentiation of hurdle rates in capital budgeting

and second, whether the companies actually use cost-of-capital calculations as a hurdle rate in investment decisions.

Concerning the first question—**differentiation of hurdle rates**—surprisingly the theory-practice gap is relatively small. The majority of companies seem to differentiate their hurdle rates either by BU, by geographical location, by type of project or even by individual projects (see Fig. 7.19).[20] Only 29 companies (30 %) report using an identical group-wide hurdle rate to be relevant for them.

The results of this study are generally in line with the findings by Brunzell et al. (2011), who report that 29 % of the companies in their study use the overall company hurdle rate for all investment projects. Also Bennouna et al. (2010) find that 63 % of the Canadian companies in their study use differentiated rates. On the other hand, there is also lots of contrasting evidence that reports that a majority of companies primarily use the overall company cost-of-capital regardless of the individual risk of the investment project (Baker et al. 2011; Chazi et al. 2010; Brounen et al. 2004; Graham and Harvey 2001). However, the results are not entirely comparable to this study, since the exact questions as well as the answer possibilities are different in most of the studies.

Concerning the second question of this research—**how the hurdle rates are determined**—the theory-practice gap appears larger, with only 37 companies (39 %) considering the calculated cost-of-capital rate as relevant in investment decisions (see Fig. 7.20).[21] As in the case of return targets in performance measurement, the specification by management seems to be an important method to set the target. However, investors or owners seem to be involved less in investment

---

[20] Based on recoded variables interpreting 4 and 5 of ordinal scale as relevant, see Sect. 7.2.6.1. Figures do not add up to total sample size due to multiple selection possibilty and recoding/different measurement level.

[21] Based on recoded variables interpreting 4 and 5 on the ordinal scale as "relevant": see Sect. 7.2.6.1.

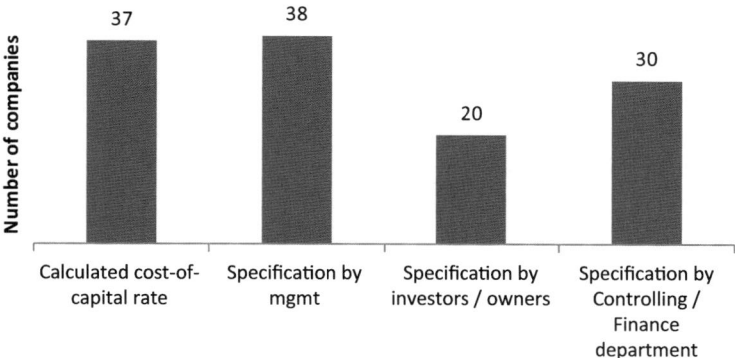

Fig. 7.20 Determination of hurdle rates in capital budgeting

decisions than in performance measurement of the group or BUs. Instead, the Accounting/Finance department plays a more important role in this process.

As an interim conclusion to cost-of-capital practices in the context of capital allocation and capital budgeting, it can be stated that the results concerning differentiated hurdle rates are relatively favourable from a theoretical point of view. However, only a minority of the companies uses the calculated cost-of-capital rate as a hurdle rate in investment decisions.

7.5 Analysis 3: Influencing Factors (Bivariate Analysis)

7.5.1 Overview

In the third stage of data analysis, the relationship between the influencing factors and the cost-of-capital practices is analysed based on bivariate methods. The significance of the relationships is tested using different statistical methods depending on the level of measurement of the respective variables, as discussed in Sect. 7.2.6.2.

In the subsequent Sects. 7.5.2–7.5.9, each influencing factor is analysed separately, as shown in Table 7.5. In doing so, the focus of the discussion is laid on meaningful significant relationships. The significant relationships will be illustrated descriptively and discussed with reference to previous literature.

In this Sect. 7.5.1, transparency over significant associations between all combinations of dependent and independent variables is given. In doing so, the data is first presented in a conventional format using matrices and tables. In a second step, the author developed a new approach to present statistically significant

Table 7.5 Bivariate analysis of influencing factors

Influencing factor	Section
Size	7.5.2
Industry	7.5.3
Stock market listing	7.5.4
Investor types	7.5.5
Perceived cost-benefit	7.5.6
Top management background	7.5.7
Corporate culture	7.5.8
Organisational structure	7.5.9

relationships that is visually more appealing and cognitively less demanding to interpret (subsequently referred to as the *relationship matrix*).

In the subsequent four tables, the significant relationships between the dependent and independent ordinal variables are shown (see Tables 7.6, 7.7, 7.8 and 7.9. Only relationships that are significant at the 0.05 level are included. The independent variables (influencing factors) are shown in the first column, while the dependent variables (cost-of-capital practices) are shown in the second column. The third column is the correlation coefficient (Spearman's rho).

In the preceding tables, it can be seen that there are a high number of significant relationships between the possible determinants and cost-of-capital practices. Moreover, the significant relationships for one influencing factor tend to have the same direction for different cost-of-capital practices. For instance, the significant correlations for individual private investors are always negative for different dependent variables.

For nominally scaled variables, **chi-squared tests** were conducted for all combinations of influencing factor variables and cost-of-capital practices variables. In Table 7.10, the Phi or Cramer's V values are displayed for the significant relationships between dependent and independent variables. As in the preceding Spearman correlation tables, the independent variables (influencing factors) are listed in the first column, whereas the dependent variables (cost-of-capital practices) are listed in the second column.

It can clearly be seen that stock market listing and the question of whether a company has issued debt securities are significantly correlated with most of the nominal dependent variables.

In order to examine relationships between nominal variables and ordinal variables, the **Mann Whitney U-test and the Kruskal-Wallis** test were used in two different ways: First, the dichotomous *dependent* variables (yes-no questions) were used as grouping variables (see Table 7.11). Second, nominal *independent* variables were used as grouping variables (see Table 7.12).

In Tables 7.11 and 7.12, significant group differences are marked with asterisks. It can be seen that also when using tests for group differences, some influencing factors seem to consistently influence different cost-of-capital practices.

However, due to the necessity of using different scales in the questionnaire of this study and the large number of both independent and dependent variables, the

7.5 Analysis 3: Influencing Factors (Bivariate Analysis)

Table 7.6 Significant correlations of ordinal variables (company cost-of-capital)

Variable 1	Variable 2	Rho	Sig.	N
Revenues	Weighted Average Cost of Capital (WACC)	0.503	0.000	68
Revenues	Capital Asset Pricing Model (CAPM)	0.562	0.000	48
Employees	Weighted Average Cost of Capital (WACC)	0.524	0.000	67
Employees	Capital Asset Pricing Model (CAPM)	0.621	0.000	47
Private investors	Weighted Average Cost of Capital (WACC)	−0.355	0.007	57
Private investors	Other capital market models	−0.434	0.008	36
Private investors	Historical returns on the company's stock	−0.385	0.027	33
Institutional investors	Historical returns on the company's stock	0.481	0.008	29
Corporate/strategic investors	Historical returns on the company's stock	0.422	0.032	26
Free float	Other capital market models	0.345	0.037	37
Free float	Historical returns on the company's stock	0.433	0.011	34
Calculation is costly	Targets set by investors/owners	0.356	0.014	47
Cost is higher than benefit	Weighted Average Cost of Capital (WACC)	−0.350	0.003	69
Cost is higher than benefit	Capital Asset Pricing Model (CAPM)	−0.417	0.003	50
Finance knowledge top mgmt	Historical returns on the company's stock	0.403	0.012	38
Finance knowledge top mgmt	Targets set by management	0.298	0.036	50
Finance knowledge top mgmt	Targets set by investors/owners	0.288	0.050	47
Company is open to innovations	Historical returns on the company's stock	0.417	0.009	38
Company is open to innovations	Targets set by investors/owners	0.323	0.027	47
Influence accounting dept.	Weighted Average Cost of Capital (WACC)	0.352	0.003	71
Influence accounting dept.	Capital Asset Pricing Model (CAPM)	0.330	0.018	51
Conservative corporate culture	Historical returns on the company's stock	−0.326	0.046	38
Degree of centralisation	Weighted Average Cost of Capital (WACC)	−0.285	0.017	70
Degree of centralisation	Capital Asset Pricing Model (CAPM)	−0.293	0.039	50
Heterogeneity of local units	Other capital market models	0.323	0.042	40

Table 7.7 Significant correlations of ordinal variables (business unit cost-of-capital)

Variable 1	Variable 2	Rho	Sig.	N
Revenues	Weighted Average Cost of Capital (WACC)	0.580	0.000	44
Revenues	Using cost of equity/betas of comparable companies	0.606	0.001	25
Employees	Weighted Average Cost of Capital (WACC)	0.554	0.000	44
Employees	Using cost of equity/betas of comparable companies	0.648	0.000	25
Employees	Adjusting the company group cost of equity/beta	0.454	0.020	26
Private investors	Weighted Average Cost of Capital (WACC)	−0.407	0.015	35
Calculation is costly	Weighted Average Cost of Capital (WACC)	−0.373	0.011	46
Cost is higher than benefit	Weighted Average Cost of Capital (WACC)	−0.650	0.000	45
Cost is higher than benefit	Using cost of equity/betas of comparable companies	−0.543	0.003	27
Cost is higher than benefit	Adjusting the company group cost of equity/beta	−0.407	0.028	29
Differentiating hurdle rates makes sense	Weighted Average Cost of Capital (WACC)	0.358	0.014	47
Finance knowledge top mgmt	Using cost of equity/betas of comparable companies	0.397	0.037	28
Company is open to innovations	Weighted Average Cost of Capital (WACC)	0.405	0.005	47
Influence accounting dept.	Weighted Average Cost of Capital (WACC)	0.600	0.000	47
Influence accounting dept.	Using cost of equity/betas of comparable companies	0.421	0.026	28
Conservative corporate culture	Weighted Average Cost of Capital (WACC)	−0.332	0.024	46
Conservative corporate culture	Adjusting the company group cost of equity/beta	−0.405	0.026	30
Complexity of organisation	Weighted Average Cost of Capital (WACC)	0.368	0.013	45

conventional tables used above do not offer an intuitive and comprehensive overview of which variables are important influencing factors of cost-of-capital practices. Therefore, the author has developed a **relationship matrix** that integrates the results from all of the different tests of association presented above.

The relationship matrix can be seen in Fig. 7.21. The influencing factors are listed in the rows of the matrix, the individual cost-of-capital practices in the columns. Significant relationships are indicated using a colour scale; the lighter colour represents a significant relationship at the 0.05 level, the darker colour a

7.5 Analysis 3: Influencing Factors (Bivariate Analysis)

Table 7.8 Significant correlations of ordinal variables (performance measurement)

Variable 1	Variable 2	Rho	Sig.	N
Revenues	Using the cost-of-capital rate	0.512	0.005	28
Revenues	Using the calculated cost-of-capital rate	0.366	0.022	39
Employees	Using the cost-of-capital rate	0.496	0.009	27
Employees	Using the calculated cost-of-capital rate	0.383	0.018	38
Financial investors	Specification by management	−0.391	0.040	28
Financial investors	Specification by investors/owners	−0.563	0.002	27
Financial investors	Using the cost-of-capital rate	0.619	0.004	20
Financial investors	Specification by management	−0.447	0.037	22
Determination is complex	Specification by controlling/finance department	−0.457	0.009	32
Cost is higher than benefit	Using the cost-of-capital rate	−0.378	0.036	31
Cost is higher than benefit	Using the calculated cost-of-capital rate	−0.404	0.008	42
Influence accounting dept.	Specification by controlling/Finance department	0.330	0.027	45
Influence accounting dept.	Using the calculated cost-of-capital rate	0.338	0.028	42

relationship at the 0.01 level. For each variable, the level of measurement is indicated. The correlation coefficients as well as the Phi and Cramer's V values are indicated as numerical values. Additionally, the direction of the relationship (i.e. positive or negative) between dichotomous and ordinal variables is indicated, interpreting the "yes" group as the higher value.[22]

The advantage of the relationship matrix is that for each of the influencing factors, an overview of all significant relationships with cost-of-capital practices is given, regardless of the level of measurement. Thus, reading the matrix by rows, influencing factors with more coloured cells can be interpreted as being more important.

7.5.2 Size

The company size factor is measured in the survey with the help of two variables: revenues and number of employees. From the relationship matrix, it can be seen that both variables are significantly related to all of the most important cost-of-capital practices variables, mostly at the 0.01 level. It can also be seen that there are only minor differences between the results for the two variables (as they measure

---

[22] That means that a "+" symbol indicates that the "yes" group has a higher median value of the ordinal variable.

Table 7.9 Significant correlations of ordinal variables (capital budgeting)

Variable 1	Variable 2	Rho	Sig.	N
Revenues	Value-based methods (e.g. EVA)	0.445	0.000	74
Revenues	Identical hurdle rate for all projects (group-wide)	0.370	0.000	85
Revenues	Hurdle rates differentiated by BU	0.471	0.000	80
Revenues	Hurdle rates differentiated by geographical location	0.570	0.000	80
Revenues	Hurdle rates differentiated by type of project	0.366	0.001	80
Revenues	Hurdle rates differentiated by individual projects	0.282	0.013	77
Revenues	Cost-of-capital calculation	0.615	0.000	83
Revenues	Specification by management	0.247	0.026	81
Revenues	Specification by controlling/finance	0.317	0.004	79
Revenues	Different cash flow or earnings estimations	0.261	0.016	85
Revenues	Different hurdle rates	0.475	0.000	84
Employees	Value-based methods (e.g. EVA)	0.344	0.003	74
Employees	Identical hurdle rate for all projects (group-wide)	0.356	0.001	85
Employees	Hurdle rates differentiated by BU	0.390	0.000	80
Employees	Hurdle rates differentiated by geographical location	0.541	0.000	80
Employees	Hurdle rates differentiated by type of project	0.311	0.005	80
Employees	Hurdle rates differentiated by individual projects	0.263	0.021	77
Employees	Cost-of-capital calculation	0.597	0.000	83
Employees	Specification by management	0.308	0.005	81
Employees	Specification by controlling/finance	0.362	0.001	79
Employees	Different cash flow or earnings estimations	0.226	0.038	85
Employees	Different hurdle rates	0.477	0.000	84
Private investors	Value-based methods (e.g. EVA)	0.302	0.012	69
Private investors	Hurdle rates differentiated by BU	−0.321	0.006	72
Private investors	Hurdle rates differentiated by type of project	−0.283	0.016	72
Private investors	Hurdle rates differentiated by individual projects	−0.278	0.020	70
Private investors	Cost-of-capital calculation	−0.267	0.024	72
Private investors	Different cash flow or earnings estimations	−0.246	0.033	75
Private investors	Different hurdle rates	−0.254	0.030	73
Institutional investors	Value-based methods (e.g. EVA)	0.295	0.026	57
Institutional investors	Identical hurdle rate for all projects (group-wide)	0.303	0.018	61

(continued)

7.5 Analysis 3: Influencing Factors (Bivariate Analysis)

Table 7.9 (continued)

Variable 1	Variable 2	Rho	Sig.	N
Institutional investors	Cost-of-capital calculation	0.389	0.002	61
Institutional investors	Specification by controlling/finance	0.259	0.050	58
Institutional investors	Different cash flow or earnings estimations	0.275	0.032	61
Institutional investors	Different hurdle rates	0.368	0.004	61
Corporate/strategic investors	Hurdle rates differentiated by BU	0.315	0.014	60
Corporate/strategic investors	Specification by management	0.302	0.020	59
Corporate/strategic investors	Different cash flow or earnings estimations	0.267	0.033	64
Calculation is costly	Identical hurdle rate for all projects (group-wide)	−0.262	0.014	87
Calculation is costly	Different hurdle rates	−0.286	0.007	87
Cost is higher than benefit	Value-based methods (e.g. EVA)	−0.317	0.005	76
Cost is higher than benefit	Identical hurdle rate for all projects (group-wide)	−0.255	0.017	87
Cost is higher than benefit	Hurdle rates differentiated by geographical location	−0.311	0.004	83
Cost is higher than benefit	Cost-of-capital calculation	−0.413	0.000	86
Cost is higher than benefit	Specification by controlling/finance	−0.300	0.006	83
Cost is higher than benefit	Different cash flow or earnings estimations	−0.255	0.017	88
Cost is higher than benefit	Different hurdle rates	−0.333	0.002	86
Differentiating hurdle rates makes sense	Hurdle rates differentiated by BU	0.321	0.003	83
Differentiating hurdle rates makes sense	Hurdle rates differentiated by geographical location	0.275	0.012	83
Differentiating hurdle rates makes sense	Hurdle rates differentiated by individual projects	0.361	0.001	80
Differentiating hurdle rates makes sense	Cost-of-capital calculation	0.294	0.006	87
Differentiating hurdle rates makes sense	Specification by management	0.284	0.009	84
Differentiating hurdle rates makes sense	Specification by controlling/finance	0.305	0.005	82
Differentiating hurdle rates makes sense	Different hurdle rates	0.345	0.001	88
Finance knowledge top mgmt	Specification by controlling/finance	0.250	0.023	83
Finance knowledge top mgmt	Different cash flow or earnings estimations	0.243	0.022	89
Company is open to innovations	Value-based methods (e.g. EVA)	0.263	0.020	78
Company is open to innovations	Hurdle rates differentiated by individual projects	0.253	0.023	81
Company is number-driven	Value-based methods (e.g. EVA)	0.260	0.022	78
Company is number-driven	Different cash flow or earnings estimations	0.339	0.001	89

(continued)

Table 7.9 (continued)

Variable 1	Variable 2	Rho	Sig.	N
Company is number-driven	Different hurdle rates	0.235	0.027	88
Influence Accounting dept.	Value-based methods (e.g. EVA)	0.261	0.021	78
Influence Accounting dept.	Specification by controlling/finance	0.269	0.014	83
Influence Accounting dept.	Different cash flow or earnings estimations	0.374	0.000	89
Conservative corporate culture	Hurdle rates differentiated by individual projects	−0.227	0.041	81
Degree of centralisation	Hurdle rates differentiated by type of project	0.230	0.036	83
Complexity of organisation	Hurdle rates differentiated by geographical location	0.342	0.002	83
Complexity of organisation	Cost-of-capital calculation	0.247	0.023	85
Complexity of organisation	Different hurdle rates	0.286	0.008	86

Table 7.10 Significant relationships of nominal variables

Variable 1	Variable 2	Phi/Cramer's V	Sig.	N
Listed	Cost-of-capital group	0.352	0.001	96
Listed	Cost of equity group	0.303	0.003	96
Listed	Cost-of-capital BU	0.290	0.005	96
Listed	Cost of equity BU	0.205	0.047	94
Listed	Capital return targets group	0.239	0.019	96
Listed	Capital return targets BU	0.236	0.021	96
Debt securities	Cost-of-capital group	0.417	0.000	92
Debt securities	Cost of equity group	0.339	0.001	92
Debt securities	Cost-of-capital BU	0.420	0.000	92
Debt securities	Cost of equity BU	0.350	0.001	90
Debt securities	Value-based metrics group	0.315	0.003	92
Debt securities	Value-based metrics BU	0.348	0.001	92
Debt securities	Capital return targets group	0.370	0.000	92
Debt securities	Capital return targets BU	0.343	0.001	92
Industry: Machinery	Capital return targets BU	0.299	0.014	96
Industry: Automotive	Value-based metrics group	0.236	0.021	96

the same construct), so that the following discussion is based on revenues only. A size factor has previously been detected for a number of different dependent variables by several studies (e.g. Al Mutairi et al. 2012; Chazi et al. 2010; Block 2003). This study confirms the previous findings and complements them by showing the relationship for specific variables in the field of cost-of-capital.

7.5 Analysis 3: Influencing Factors (Bivariate Analysis)

Table 7.11 Test for group differences (part 1)

		Grouping variables						
		Cost-of-capital group	Cost of equity group	Cost-of-capital BU	Cost of equity BU	Value-based metrics Group	Value-based metrics BU	Capital return targets group	Capital return targets BU
Ordinal varialbes	Size (revenues)	a	a	a	b	a	a	a	a
	Employees (no.)	a	a	a	a	a	a	a	a
	Private investors	b							
	Institutional investors	a	b		b	a	a		b
	PE investors	b							
	Strategic investors								
	Mgmt ownership								
	Free float	a	b						
	Complexity	b							
	Cost	b	b	b					
	Cost higher than benefit	a	a	a	b	b	a		a
	Importance of return								
	Sense of differentiation for investments						b		
	Finance knowledge					b	b		
	Innovations					a	a		
	Number-driven				b	a	a		
	Influence accounting dep.	b	b		b	a	a		b
	Conservative								b
	Centralisation								b
	Heterogeneity								
	Complexity					b	b		b

[a]Significant difference of mean rank at 0.01 level
[b]Significant difference of mean rank at 0.05 level

Table 7.12 Test for group differences (part 2)

Ordinal variables			Grouping variables							
			Listed	Debt securities	Background	Sector	Industry: Machinery	Industry: Electrical	Industry: Automotive	Org. structure reporting
Cost-of-capital determination		WACC	a	a						
		CAPM	b	a						
		Other capital market models	b	b						
		Historical returns	a				b			
		Targets by mgmt								
		Targets by investors								
		WACC	a	a			b			
		Adjust group WACC								
		Targets by mgmt								
		Targets by investors								
		Comparable companies		a						
		Adjust group value								
		Qualitative approach								
		Targets mgmt	b							
		Targets investors					b			
Performance measurement		Cost-of-capital rate	b	a				b		
		Specification by mgmt		b						
		Specification by investors								
		Specification by accounting							b	
		Cost-of-capital rate		a						
		Specification by mgmt								

7.5 Analysis 3: Influencing Factors (Bivariate Analysis)

Capital budgeting	Specification by investors	b	
	Specification by accounting		a
	Value-based measures investments		a
	Group-wide hurdle rates		b
	by business units	a	a
	by geographical location		b
	by type of project		b
	by project	b	b
	Cost-of-capital calculation	a	a
	Specification by mgmt		
	Specification by investors		
	Specification by accounting	b	b
	Different cash flow		
	Different hurdle rate		

[a] Significant difference of mean rank at 0.01 level
[b] Significant difference of mean rank at 0.05 level

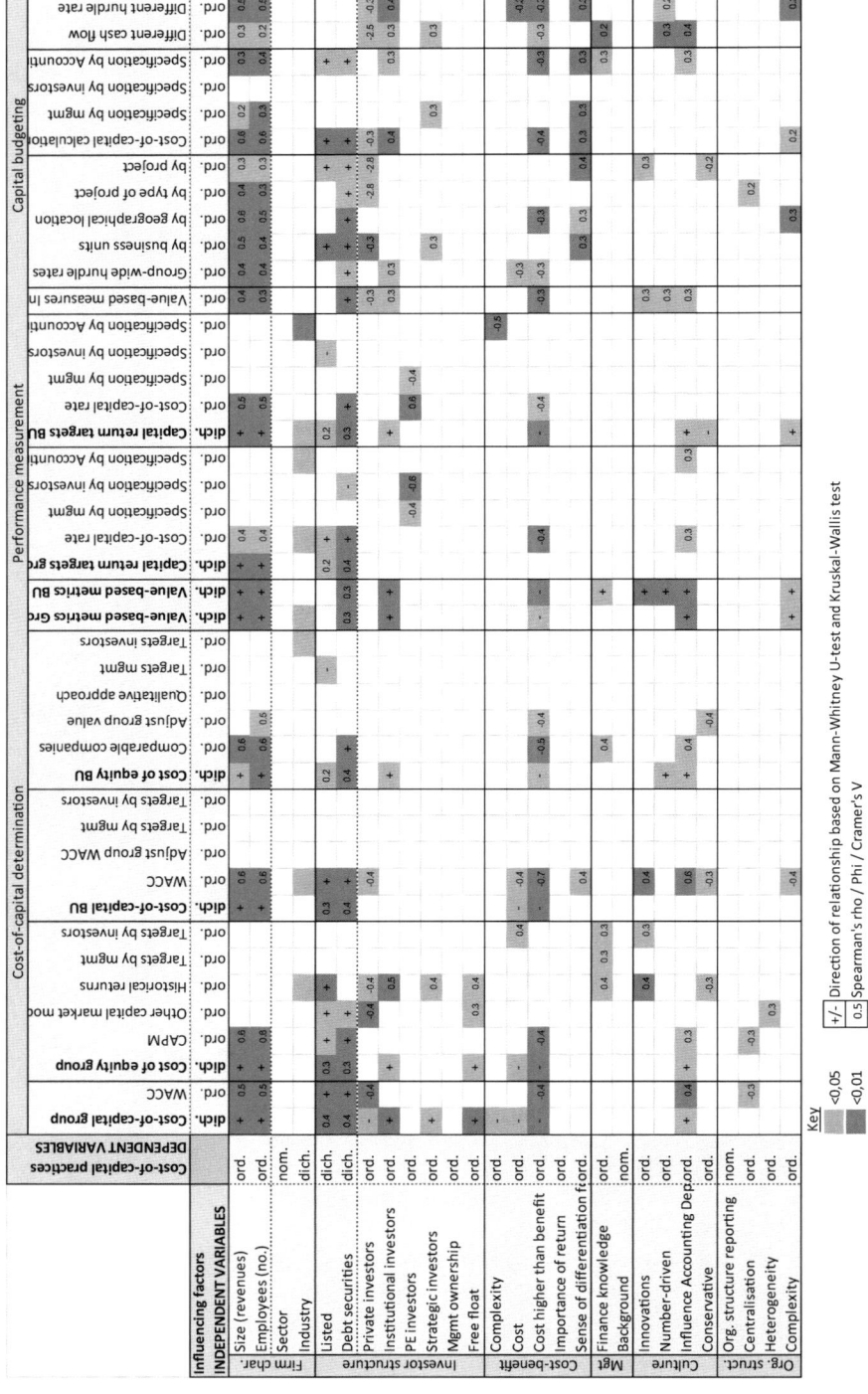

Fig. 7.21 Relationship matrix

7.5 Analysis 3: Influencing Factors (Bivariate Analysis)

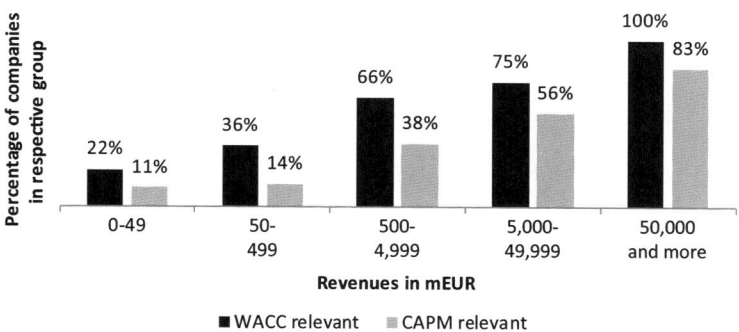

Fig. 7.22 Relevance of WACC and CAPM by size groups

Concerning **determination techniques for the cost-of-capital**, the direction of the relationship is consistently positive, i.e. the larger a company is, the more likely it is to apply more sophisticated methods. In Fig. 7.22, this relationship is illustrated using the most prominent models, WACC and CAPM, as an example.[23] The positive relationship between company size and the use of the two models also helps to interpret this study's relatively low results for WACC and CAPM usage compared to previous studies (see Sect. 7.4.1). If only large companies had been included in the population, as in some other studies, the values would have been higher.

The relationship with CAPM usage has previously been found to be significant by Baker et al. (2011) as well as Graham and Harvey (2001), who distinguish between small and large companies. Also, Al Mutairi et al. (2012), who classify companies as small, medium and large, report a significant relationship.

Furthermore, the question of whether the companies determine their cost-of-capital or cost of equity at all is significantly related to company size (cp. test for group differences in Table 7.11). Only 39 % of the companies of the smallest category determine their cost-of-capital at company level, whereas all of the companies from the largest category report that they do so. On the BU level, the only prior study that has shown this relationship is the one by Block (2003) in the U.S. This study complements his findings by showing that the relationship is also relevant for Germany. Company size is also a significant factor for cost-of-capital practices in the context of **performance measurement and value-based management** in this study.

This effect concerns, for instance, the use of value-based measures, which are more likely to be used in large companies, as illustrated in Fig. 7.23. Moreover,

---

[23] Based on recoded variables interpreting 4 and 5 of ordinal scale as "relevant": see Sect. 7.2.6.1.

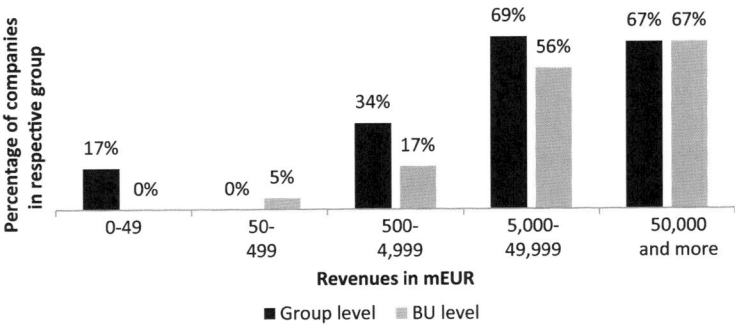

Fig. 7.23 Use of value-based measures by company size

large companies are more likely to determine explicit capital return targets on company group and BU level. Additionally, among those companies that do define explicit return targets, there is again the tendency that larger companies are more likely to use the calculated cost-of-capital rate as a return target.

With regard to **capital allocation and capital budgeting**, the following findings were obtained for the size factor: In the relationship matrix, it can be seen that concerning the differentiation of hurdle rates or discount rates, both the use of group-wide hurdle rates and differentiated hurdle rates are correlated with the size of the company. Although this might seem contradictory at first sight, it can be explained when looking at the data in more detail. For smaller companies, all kinds of hurdle rates seem to be. This means that company size is not a determinant of using differentiated vs. non-differentiated hurdle rates but rather whether a company uses hurdle rates for investment decisions at all. The same paradox occurs in Baker et al.'s (2011) data, where both using the company's overall discount rate and using a divisional discount rate in capital budgeting are significantly less likely for small companies.

A possible explanation for the irrelevance of hurdle rates for small companies could be that they do not use the IRR method in order to evaluate investment possibilities (IRR is typically used in combination with a hurdle rate). Also the NPV method is less relevant for small companies than for large companies. The significance of the size factor to explain the use of the IRR technique confirms previous findings by Baker et al. (2011), whereas Al Mutairi et al. (2012), who also test this relationship, find no significant correlations.

Concerning the determination of hurdle rates, large companies are more likely to use calculated cost-of-capital for hurdle rates in this study. Also hurdle rates specified by management are more likely to be used by large companies. However, taking into account the finding that hurdle rates in general appear less relevant for smaller companies, these results should be interpreted with caution.

At this point, the interim conclusion can be drawn that size is a significant influencing factor of cost-of-capital practices based on a bivariate data analysis.

7.5.3 Industry

For this factor, two items were measured. First, the company's broader sector, classified as "production", "wholesale/retail/services" and "other", was requested. Due to the high importance of production companies in the German economy, for production companies a second question on the concrete industry based on the International Standard Industry Classification (ISIC) by the United Nations was asked.

In this study, no significant influence of the broader sector on cost-of-capital practices can be reported based on the bivariate analysis. Similar results were obtained by Graham and Harvey (2001), who distinguish between manufacturing companies and other companies. In their study, only a few significant correlations were found for capital budgeting questions, while cost-of-capital techniques were independent from the industry.

For the more detailed ISIC classification, only industries with more than five cases were further examined. It was found that the machinery and equipment industry has a significant negative influence on some cost-of-capital practices. The companies are less likely to use historical returns to determine cost-of-capital, to use WACC on BU level and to use targets set by investors for the cost of equity on BU level. Moreover, they are less likely to employ capital return targets on BU level. Companies from the automotive industry are more likely to use value-based measures. Moreover, these companies are more likely to use capital return targets specified by the Finance and Accounting function on group and BU level. In contrast, in the electrical industry, using the calculated cost-of-capital rate as a return target for the group level is more common. A similarly detailed industry classification was used by Al Mutairi et al. (2012) in their study. Their results indicate that the real estate, industry, services and food sectors, in particular, significantly influence cost-of-capital practices.

Overall, the survey results in this study suggest that the detailed industry factor seems to have some influence on cost-of-capital practices, although other factors appear more important in the real economy sector in Germany

7.5.4 Stock Market Listing

The influence of stock market listing on cost-of-capital practices has only been considered by one study that is included in this literature review (Graham and Harvey 2001). The lack of previous findings can partly be explained by the fact that some studies (e.g. Al Mutairi et al. 2012) focus on listed companies in their

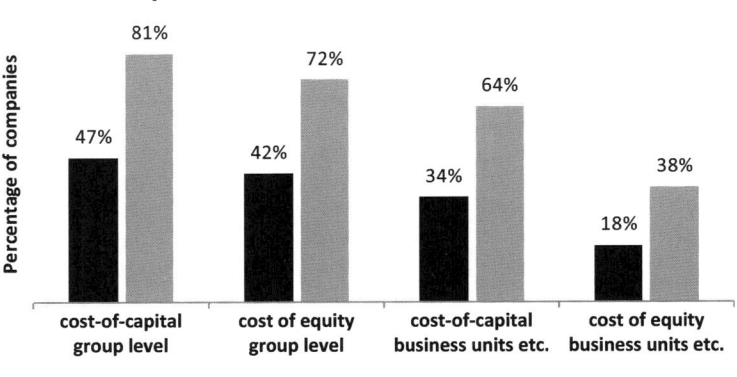

Fig. 7.24 Influence of stock market listing on determination of cost-of-capital

samples. The broad composition of this study's sample provides the opportunity to further investigate this influencing factor.

In this study, it is found that the variable is highly correlated with cost-of-capital practices. First of all, there is a significant relationship between stock market listing and the question of whether cost-of-capital and cost of equity are explicitly determined, as can be seen in Fig. 7.24. Secondly, it can be stated that listed companies are more likely to apply the CAPM, but also other capital market models and historical returns on the company's stock. Also, in the study by Graham and Harvey (2001), the relevance of the CAPM is significantly higher for listed companies. On the one hand, this is plausible, since stock market data is necessary for regular use of these models. On the other hand, this generally confirms that listed companies use more sophisticated methods.

Concerning *performance measurement*, listed companies are more likely to set explicit return targets on both group and BU level and use the cost-of-capital rate as a return target. With regard to *capital budgeting*, listed companies are significantly more likely to use hurdle rates or discount rates differentiated by BU, with a median relevance score of 3 on the five-point ordinal scale compared to 1 for non-listed companies. Also, differentiation by project is significantly correlated with stock market listing—although this also seems to be rather irrelevant for listed companies, with a median score of 2. Furthermore, it can be said that the use of the calculated cost-of-capital rate as a hurdle rate or discount rate in investment appraisal is more relevant for listed companies.

As can be seen in the relationship matrix (Fig. 7.21), similar relationships can be reported not only for a stock market listing of a company's equity, but also if a company has issued debt securities. As there are large overlaps between these factors, the explanations above are based on stock market listing only. The strong relationships between these factors and cost-of-capital practices might be an indication that there is indeed pressure from the capital markets for these companies to

7.5.5 Investor Types

In the previous literature, the influence of certain investor types on cost-of-capital practices has only been analysed in terms of management ownership, which is included in the surveys by Graham and Harvey (2001) and Al Mutairi et al. (2012). Al Mutairi et al. (2012) find that CFO ownership increases the probability of CAPM usage. In contrast, Graham and Harvey (2001) report a negative relationship. In this study, the analysis of investor types is extended by including seven investor types into the analysis. Contrary to the previous studies' results, management ownership is not found to significantly influence cost-of-capital practices in this study. However, there are two types of investors that appear particularly important: First, *individual private investors or families* who are consistently associated with a negative relationship for sophisticated cost-of-capital practices, i.e. the higher the share of this investor type in a company, the less likely the company is to have sophisticated cost-of-capital practices. A significantly negative relationship can be reported for the question of whether the companies explicitly determine their cost-of-capital on group level, the use of WACC and other capital market models. In performance measurement, there is a negative influence on using cost-of-capital as a return target. In capital budgeting, differentiation of hurdle rates by BUs is less likely for companies with a high share of family investors as well as the use of the calculated cost-of-capital as a hurdle or discount rate.

Second, for *institutional investors*, the opposite influence can be reported: the higher the share of institutional investors in a company, the more likely the company is to have sophisticated cost-of-capital practices. The relationship for the determination of cost-of-capital is illustrated in Fig. 7.25. It can be seen that the higher the share of institutional investors, the more likely the companies are to determine their cost-of-capital explicitly. One possible interpretation for this phenomenon could be that institutional investors directly influence cost-of-capital practices of their investments by demanding that certain measures be calculated.

Besides the determination of cost-of-capital, there is a significant positive relationship for institutional investors with the use of value-based measures in performance measurement and explicit capital return targets on a BU level. In the field of capital budgeting, there are significant relations with the use of group-wide hurdle rates and calculated cost-of-capital rates as discount rates.

Overall, based on the bivariate analysis, it can be concluded that institutional investors as well as private or family investors seem to have an influence on cost-of-capital practices, while other investor types are less relevant.

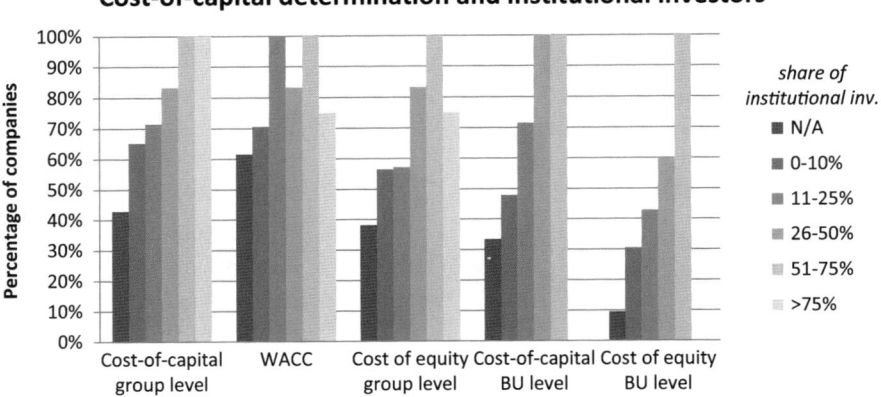

Fig. 7.25 Influence of institutional investors on cost-of-capital practices

7.5.6 Perceived Cost-Benefit

This influencing factor was originally identified in the expert interviews of this study. To the author's best knowledge, there are no corresponding previous results to which the findings could be compared.

In order to measure the cost and benefit of cost-of-capital techniques, several questions were asked (see questionnaire in Sect. 9.5). However, for this analysis, only the item that has shown the most significant relationships with cost-of-capital practices is used. This question asked the respondents to rate the following statement on a five-point Likert type scale from 'strongly disagree' to 'strongly agree': "Overall, the cost to calculate differentiated cost-of-capital is higher than the benefit."

First of all, significant correlations with explicit cost-of-capital determination can be reported, as illustrated in Fig. 7.26. As can be seen, among the respondents who disagree with the statement—i.e. who do *not* think that the cost of applying the methods is higher than the benefit—a high percentage of companies actually do explicitly calculate their cost-of-capital. Similar results can be reported for applying WACC, CAPM and CCA.

In the companies' value-based management practices, a significant correlation with the perceived cost-benefit factor can be reported both on group and BU level, i.e. companies that have a negative cost-benefit attitude toward a differentiated cost-of-capital treatment are also less likely to calculate value-based measures. The same is true for setting capital return targets on BU level. With regard to *capital budgeting*, the use of group-wide hurdle rates, the use of hurdle rates by geographical location and the use of calculated cost-of-capital rates as hurdle rates are negatively correlated, with a high perception of cost compared to benefit.

7.5 Analysis 3: Influencing Factors (Bivariate Analysis)

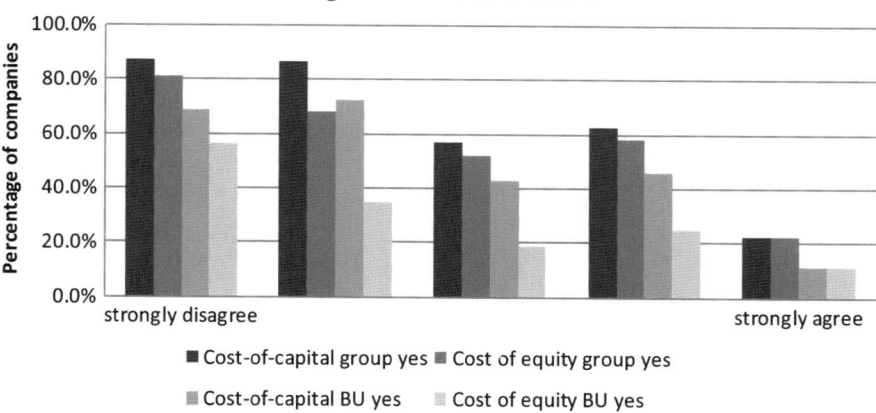

Fig. 7.26 Perceived cost-benefit and cost-of-capital determination

Overall, the results of the bivariate analysis suggest that the cost-benefit ratio perceived by the practitioners has an influence on the actual use of the methods.

7.5.7 Top Management Background

Concerning top management background, two aspects were included in the survey: the CEO's background (Finance, Marketing etc.) and top management's Finance and Accounting knowledge. While previous studies have focused on the question of whether the CEO has an MBA (Baker et al. 2011; Al Mutairi et al. 2012), for this study, familiarity with Finance and Accounting topics is considered more important, based on the expert interviews.

However, no significant relationships were found between CEO background and cost-of-capital practices. In contrast, some significant correlations could be found for the question of whether the top management possesses sufficient knowledge in the area of Finance and Accounting. Surprisingly, if the top management possesses greater knowledge in this area, they are more likely to apply methods for the determination of cost of equity that are not considered as state-of-the-art by Finance theory, such as using historical returns, targets set by management and targets set by investors. Also, in the area of capital budgeting, these companies are more likely to rely on hurdle rates specified by the Accounting or Finance department. A possible interpretation of this effect could be that these managers are aware of the drawbacks of methods like the CAPM and thus prefer to use subjective methods. Another possible interpretation could be that they do not feel that they have to rely on objective measures to protect themselves due to their higher trust in their specialist knowledge. However, in order to determine cost of equity of BUs, companies with greater top management knowledge of the area are more likely to use the CCA, which is somewhat contradictory to the findings for the group cost of equity. Also, they are more likely to use value-based measures on BU level.

Overall, it can be said that there is some evidence that supports the management factor. However, other factors such as size, investor structure or perceived cost-benefit appear more important based on the bivariate analysis.

7.5.8 Corporate Culture

Another factor that has not been previously examined in the context of cost-of-capital practices is corporate culture. The experts who were interviewed in the first stage of this research suggested different dimensions of corporate culture, as illustrated in Table 7.13: *openness to innovations in management, the extent to which an organisation is number-driven, the influence of the Finance and Accounting function and the degree to which an organisation is conservative*. Each of these dimensions was measured with one Likert-type item in the survey.

In general, it can be reported that for each of the dimensions, significant relationships can be found. The first three factors are *positively* correlated with the importance of individual cost-of-capital practices, whereas a conservative corporate culture appears to have a *negative* effect on the use of the cost-of-capital methods.

The question of whether cost-of-capital is determined and which techniques are used seems to be especially contingent on the influence of the Finance and Accounting function in the organisation. As can be seen in Fig. 7.21, the most important questions concerning cost-of-capital determination are positively correlated with this cultural dimension. For the significant relationships, the median score of the culture variables is respectively one point higher for the companies using the respective methods. However, the other cultural variables also seem to have some influence on individual cost-of-capital variables.

With regard to performance measurement and value-based management, the use of value-based performance measures on BU level in particular is influenced by corporate culture, as can be seen in Fig. 7.27. Moreover, the use of capital return targets on BU level is positively related to the influence of the Finance and

Table 7.13 Quantitative support of cultural dimensions

Cultural dimension	Support from quantitative data[a]
Open to innovations in management	Medium
Number-driven	Weak
Influence of finance and accounting function	Strong
Conservative	Medium

[a]Based on number of significant relationships with cost-of-capital practices; see Fig. 7.21

7.5 Analysis 3: Influencing Factors (Bivariate Analysis)

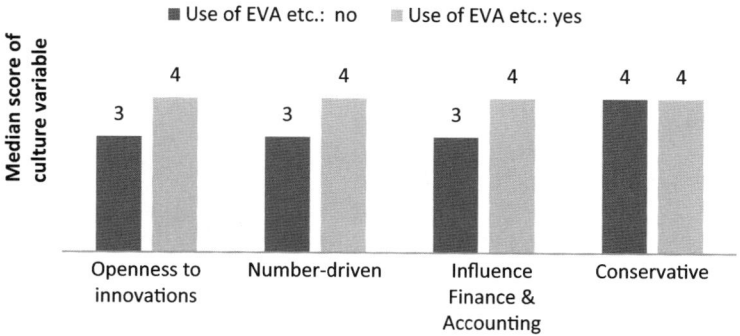

Fig. 7.27 Cultural dimensions and value-based performance measures on BU level

Accounting function and negatively influenced by a conservative corporate culture. In the area of capital budgeting, fewer significant relations can be reported (see Fig. 7.21).

Overall, it can be concluded that the influence of the Finance and Accounting function is a significant cultural dimension, whereas the other variables are only partially supported by the results of the bivariate analysis.

7.5.9 Organisational Structure

Another factor that was identified based on the expert interviews is organisational structure. Several aspects of organisational structure were examined in this survey. First of all, the *primary structure which is used for reporting purposes* was examined, i.e. whether reports are organised by legal entities, by BUs or by regions. This factor did not show any significant relationships with cost-of-capital practices.

Moreover, the *level of centralisation* in the company group was examined. It was found that with a higher level of centralisation, companies are less likely to use WACC or CAPM to determine their cost-of-capital.

As opposed to what Finance theory suggests, the *heterogeneity of business units* does not have a significant effect on whether companies use differentiated cost-of-capital rates. From a theoretical perspective, the benefit of calculating cost-of-capital for individual BUs and using the figure as a capital return target and hurdle rate is higher if the BUs have a different risk (see literature review Sect. 2.3).

Finally, the influence of the organisational structure's complexity on cost-of-capital practices was analysed. The results suggest that there is a significant influence on performance measurement and value-based management as well as on capital budgeting. As shown in Fig. 7.28, the higher the complexity of the

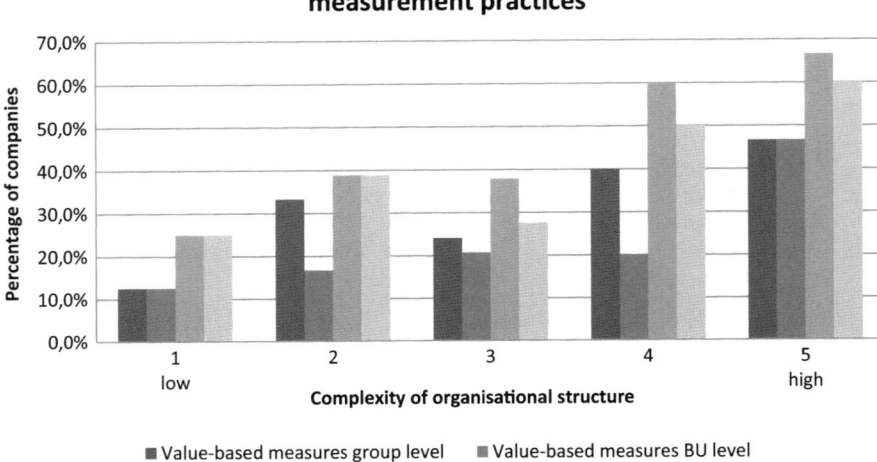

Fig. 7.28 Influence of organisational structure complexity

organisational structure, the more likely a company is to use value-based measures or to set explicit capital return targets. Similar results can be reported in the area of capital budgeting for the use of hurdle rates differentiated by geographical location and the use of the calculated cost-of-capital as a hurdle rate.

It could be interpreted that with an increasing complexity of the organisational structure, there is less transparency for the top management in terms of the BUs or local entities in different regions, so that they tend to rely more on setting return targets and hurdle rates for the divisions.

7.6 Analysis 4: Influencing Factors (Multivariate Analysis)

7.6.1 Analysis of Multicollinearity

7.6.1.1 Definition and Consequences

Multicollinearity means that the explanatory variables are highly correlated with each other (Brooks 2008). While a certain degree of association is always present, a high degree of multicollinearity has consequences for the data analysis, particularly for the suitability of multiple regression methods.

In multiple regression, the occurrence of multicollinearity increases the standard errors of regression coefficients with the consequence of wider confidence intervals and a decreased likelihood of significant coefficients (Berry and Feldman 1985; Siegel 2012). Additionally, multicollinearity leads to the situation that small

7.6 Analysis 4: Influencing Factors (Multivariate Analysis)

changes in the regression, such as adding or removing variables, cause the model to change significantly, i.e. the regression becomes very sensitive (Brooks 2008).

According to Siegel (2012), multicollinearity is less of a problem for predictive models because it is still possible to make reliable forecasts of the dependent variable. However, if the main purpose of the model is to explain rather than to predict, the consequences of multicollinearity are more relevant (Berry and Feldman 1985). The reason is that it is not possible to distinguish between the effects of the different explanatory variables (Siegel 2012).

The purpose of the multivariate analysis in this thesis is to separate the effects of the different influencing factors in order to judge which ones actually influence cost-of-capital practices. Therefore, the presence of strong multicollinearity disqualifies multivariate regression as a suitable method.

7.6.1.2 Test for Multicollinearity

As Siegel (2012, p. 372) states, "there are no tests that provide irrefutable evidence that multicollinearity is or is not a problem". In the statistics literature (Siegel 2012; Brooks 2008), it is recommended to use a simple approach and look at bivariate correlations pair-wise in order to detect multicollinearity.

This recommendation was followed in this thesis. Similar to the procedure in the bivariate analysis of influencing factors (Sect. 7.5), Spearman correlation, Chi-Squared, the Mann–Whitney U-test and the Kruskall Wallis test were used to detect multicollinearity pair-wise.

Although there is no clear definition of high multicollinearity, the pair-wise analysis clearly shows that there are a large number of significant relationships between the influencing factors. The presence of high multicollinearity is also confirmed by an exploratory attempt by the author to calculate multiple regression models. It turned out that the effects discussed in the previous section—an overall good fit of the regression, little significance of individual coefficients and a high sensitivity of the model to small changes in the regression—occur with the data.

7.6.1.3 Conclusion

The presence of multicollinearity in the data for this thesis is not surprising. Indeed, multicollinearity could be anticipated because there are natural relationships between various company characteristics. For instance, it is obvious that large companies tend to be listed while SMEs tend to be non-listed. Another example of a natural relationship between influencing factors is size and investor types. For instance, SMEs are generally less likely to have institutional equity investors involved than large listed companies. Although many influencing factors are highly correlated, they have to be regarded separately from a content perspective and should not be statistically combined with methods such as factor analysis.

As a consequence of the multicollinearity, no regression models will be calculated in this thesis. The reason is that the models would be very sensitive and unreliable and no meaningful interpretation would be possible. Instead, elaboration analyses will be conducted in the subsequent sections in order to control for confounding variables and separate the effects of different influencing factors.

7.6.2 Elaboration Analysis

7.6.2.1 Detecting Spurious and Suppressed Relationships

In view of the high multicollinearity of the explanatory variables that has been detected, there is the danger that the relationships that have been identified in the bivariate analysis of influencing factors in Sect. 7.5 are biased. The reason is that some of the relationships might be influenced by third variables. Therefore, the subsequent sections will test whether the relationships that were detected in the bivariate analysis hold when controlling for third variables.

The main purpose of these analyses is to detect *spurious relationships*. A spurious relationship is the situation when two variables are correlated because they are both affected by a common third factor although there is no causal relationship between the two initial variables (Shannon 2004; de Vaus 2002). For example, in this study, the complexity of the organisational structure is correlated to certain cost-of-capital practices. It might be the case that organisational structure actually influences cost-of-capital practices. However, it could also be possible that the correlation only exists because both organisational structure and cost-of-capital practices are influenced by the size of a company. Moreover, the contrary effect might also occur. There could also be a so-called *suppressor variable* that has the effect of reducing a correlation between two variables. In this case, when controlling for the third variable, the correlation would become larger (Norris 2012).

The literature (Frankfort-Nachmias and Leon-Guerrero 2011; de Vaus 2002) recommends conducting a so-called *elaboration analysis* in order to detect spurious relationships. The focus of this analysis is to regard the initial relationship (i.e. between the influencing factors and cost-of-capital practices) when controlling for a third variable (another influencing factor). If the relationship was spurious, it would disappear when a third variable is introduced (Shannon 2004). This general idea is illustrated in Fig. 7.29.

In a first step, the variables that could potentially confound relationships of other variables and need to be controlled have to be determined. Shannon (2004, p. 1062) states that "theory or logic should specify a third variable that may account for the observed correlation". In this thesis, it was decided to control for two variables: *company size* (*revenues*) and *stock market listing*. The selection of these two variables as potentially confounding variables is based on the following reasons:

7.6 Analysis 4: Influencing Factors (Multivariate Analysis)

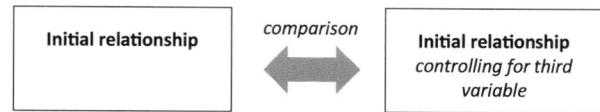

Fig. 7.29 Principle of elaboration analysis

- Company size and stock market listing are among the *strongest influencing factors* identified in the bivariate analysis (see Sect. 7.5.1) and a major distinguishing characteristic of companies.
- The two variables show a high level of correlation with other influencing factors in the analysis of *multicollinearity* (see Sect. 7.6.1).

7.6.2.2 Controlling for Stock Market Listing

According to Vaus (2002), elaboration analysis can be done with the help of summary statistics (partial correlation), by cross-tabulation or with graphs. Due to different levels of measurements that are necessary for the contents of this study, several different methods have to be used to control for third variables. In order to control for stock market listing, it was decided to stratify the sample by stock market listing. That means that the data is filtered by the variable stock market listing and the complete bivariate analysis as discussed in Sect. 7.5 is repeated for the sub-set of listed companies. If the relationships that were found in Sect. 7.5 disappear, then they were spurious.

In order to compare the relationships before and after controlling for stock market listing, the complete relationship matrix (see Sect. 7.5.1) was calculated again only for listed companies. This relationship matrix can be found in Sect. 9.5. Comparing the initial and the recalculated relationship matrix, it can be seen whether the relationships were distorted by the fact whether a company is stock market listed or not.

In Fig. 7.30, a comparison of the initial number of significant relationships with the number of significant relationships controlling for stock market listing is made for each influencing factor.

In the second column, the number of significant relationships identified within the sub-set of listed companies is shown. In the third column, the number of relationships for the respective factor in the initial bivariate analysis is shown. The last column compares how many of the relationships have disappeared (spurious relationships) or emerged (suppressed relationships).[24]

It can be seen that there are a number of spurious relationships in the initial bivariate analysis. First of all, there seems to be some bias in the *size factor*. However, also when controlling for stock market listing, a high number of

---

[24] Statistically, the significance of a relationship is influenced by the sample size (Easterby-Smith et al. 2012). As the sub-set of listed companies has a smaller sample size, this might also influence the number of significant relationships. For the purpose of this elaboration analysis, this effect is neglected.

Influencing factors		Number of significant relationships		
		Controlled listed companies	Initial all companies	Delta
Firm char.	Size (revenues)	16	25	-9
	Employees (no.)	17	26	-9
	Sector	4	0	+4
	Industry (14x)	4	0	+4
Investor structure	Listed			
	Debt securities			
	Private investors	3	12	-9
	Institutional investors	2	13	-11
	PE investors	4	4	+0
	Strategic investors	2	5	-3
	Mgmt ownership	3	0	+3
	Free float	1	4	-3
Cost-benefit	Complexity	1	2	-1
	Cost	5	7	-2
	Cost higher than benefit	13	21	-8
	Importance of return	5	0	+5
	Sense of differentiation for investments	9	8	+1
Mgt	Finance knowledge	3	7	-4
	Background	1	0	+1
Culture	Innovations	1	6	-5
	Number-driven	4	5	-1
	Influence Accounting Dep.	6	15	-9
	Conservative	4	5	-1
Org. struct.	Org. structure reporting	0	0	+0
	Centralisation	5	3	+2
	Heterogeneity	0	1	-1
	Complexity	4	7	-3

Fig. 7.30 Elaboration analysis controlling for stock market listing

significant relationships remain for the size factor. In contrast, most of the significant relationships for the *type of investor* seem to be spurious. Controlling for stock market listing, only two or three significant relationships remain for private investors and institutional investors, which appeared relatively important in the initial bivariate analysis. The *perceived cost-benefit* factor also seems to contain some spurious relationships but remains on a high level. Concerning *corporate culture*, the influence of the Finance and Accounting department appears less relevant when controlling for stock market listing.

7.6.2.3 Controlling for Company Size

In contrast to stock market listing, which is a dichotomous variable, the company size factor is measured on a five-point ordinal scale. Given the sample size of this thesis, a stratification of the sample by company size is not possible because the size

7.6 Analysis 4: Influencing Factors (Multivariate Analysis)

of the sample subsets would be too small to conduct a meaningful analysis within the size groups. Therefore, in order to control for company size, an approach is pursued that is different from the one used to control for stock market listing.

In order to control for company size in the relationship between variables on an ordinal scale, partial correlation can be used. As Norris et al. (2012, p. 278) explain, "partial correlation is a statistically precise way of calculating what the relationship between two variables would be if one could take away the influence of one (or more) additional variables". As previously discussed, in this thesis non-parametric measures of association are used. Therefore, partial *rank* correlation is applied to control for company size.[25]

For the relationship among nominal variables, the chi-squared analysis can be complemented with so-called layers in order to control for a third variable. This means that a combination of three variables is cross-tabulated. One requirement of the chi-squared test is that the expected frequencies are not too small. According to Newcomer and Wirtz (2004), a common rule is that the expected frequency in each cell should be at least five. Due to this restriction, a combination of three variables in a chi-squared test is not possible with the sample size of this study. Therefore, the elaboration analysis is made based on the ordinal variables using partial rank correlation only.

As in the previous section, also controlling for company size, the complete relationship matrix is calculated again and compared to the initial relationship matrix. The relationship matrix controlling for company size can be found in Sect. 9.6. As in the previous section, Fig. 7.31 shows the effect of controlling for company size on the number of significant relationships for the influencing factors.[26]

In the figure, it can be seen that the relationship of *investor structure* and cost-of-capital practices is not only influenced by stock market listing, but also by company size. Furthermore, the *perceived cost-benefit* factor partly seems to be based on a spurious relationship. The relationships between *corporate culture* and cost-of-capital practices remain robust on a medium level. In terms of *organisational structure*, several suppressed relationships appear, so that the level of centralisation is more important than initially assumed.

---

[25] The SPSS graphical user interface does not offer non-parametric partial correlation (partial rank correlation). In order to use partial rank correlation, the syntax has to be entered manually. The relevant commands can be found on the IBM website: http://www-01.ibm.com/support/docview.wss?uid=swg21474822

[26] Please note that the number of significant relationships in the chart refers to correlations between ordinal variables only.

	Influencing factors	Number of significant relationships (ordinal variables only)		
		Controlled partial correlation	Initial correlation	Delta
Firm char.	Size (revenues)			
	Employees (no.)			
	Sector			
	Industry (14x)			
Investor structure	Listed			
	Debt securities			
	Private investors	3	11	-8
	Institutional investors	1	7	-6
	PE investors	4	4	+0
	Strategic investors	1	4	-3
	Mgmt ownership	1	0	+1
	Free float	2	2	+0
Cost-benefit	Complexity	2	1	+1
	Cost	4	4	+0
	Cost higher than benefit	3	14	-11
	Importance of return	0	0	+0
	Sense of differentiation for investments	8	8	+0
Mgt	Finance knowledge	5	6	-1
	Background			
Culture	Innovations	7	5	+2
	Number-driven	1	3	-2
	Influence Accounting Dep.	6	9	-3
	Conservative	1	4	-3
Org. struct.	Org. structure reporting			
	Centralisation	5	3	+2
	Heterogeneity	0	1	-1
	Complexity	2	4	-2

Fig. 7.31 Elaboration analysis controlling for company size

7.7 Conclusion

7.7.1 Summary of Findings

In this chapter, results of the company survey based on a sample of 96 German companies were presented. One of the main purposes of this chapter was to quantitatively test the expert interviews that were presented in the previous chapter.

The survey results show that there is a theory-practice gap, although in certain areas companies already apply sophisticated techniques, as suggested by theory. The quantitative analysis shows that most of the influencing factors identified in the expert interviews are significantly correlated with cost-of-capital practices, although an elaboration analysis shows that some of them are spurious correlations influenced by company size and stock market listing.

7.7.2 Support and Rejection of Hypotheses

In this section, the hypotheses formulated at the beginning of the chapter are discussed. A final discussion of the influencing factors, taking into account the results from the expert interviews and previous studies, can be found in Chap. 8.

The quantitative results fully support some of the hypotheses that were derived from the research propositions and the results from the expert interviews. However, other hypotheses are only supported partially or have to be rejected.

H1: There is a theory-practice gap in cost-of-capital methods

Especially large companies do follow recommendation by theory and apply sophisticated cost-of-capital methods (see Sect. 7.5.1). However, overall, there remains a large theory-practice gap, with only 54 % of the companies in the sample using WACC and only a minority of companies using objective methods to determine their cost of equity on company group level (see Sect. 7.4.1). On BU level, the theory-practice gap is even larger (Sect. 7.4.2). Overall, *H1 is supported* by the survey results.

Hypotheses H2–H9 are all concerned with the role of different influencing factors. In order to follow a clearly defined and transparent approach in the evaluation of the hypotheses, the following conditions are formulated in order that a hypothesis is considered to be supported by the survey results (see Table 7.14): If there are at least ten significant relationships between an influencing factor variable and different cost-of-capital practices, the factor is considered to be supported. This condition has to be met in the initial bivariate analysis as well as in the elaboration analysis. This means that ten or more cells in one row of the relationship matrices (see Sects. 7.5.1, 9.5, and 9.6) have to be marked. For five to nine significant relationships, the influencing factor is considered to be partially supported.

H2: The size of a company influences its cost-of-capital practices

The size factor measured by revenues and number of employees is significantly related with all major cost-of-capital variables. Although some correlations disappear when controlling for stock market listing, the size factor remains the most

Table 7.14 Conditions for hypothesis evaluation concerning influencing factors

Hypothesis outcome	Condition
Supported	Ten or more significant relationships with cost-of-capital practices variables for one of the factor items (has to be fulfilled also controlling for third variables)[a]
Partially supported	Five to nine significant relationships as defined above
Rejected	None of the above

[a]As the number of significant relationships controlling for company size is based on ordinal variables only, this condition is formulated rather conservatively

significant explanatory variable for cost-of-capital practices. Thus, hypothesis *H2 is clearly supported*.

H3: The industry sector of a company influences its cost-of-capital practices
In this study, no substantial influence of the broader sector or a specific industry can be reported. Consequently, hypothesis *H3 is rejected*.

H4: Stock market listing influences cost-of-capital practices
In the quantitative analysis, stock market listing showed a high number of significant relationships with cost-of-capital practices. Therefore, *hypothesis H4 is supported* by the survey results.[27]

H5: The investor types of a company influence its cost-of-capital practices
In terms of types of investors, the initial bivariate analysis showed a significant influence of institutional investors as well as private/family investors. However, controlling for size and stock market listing, most of the correlations disappeared, so it is assumed that the relationships were spurious. Consequently, *hypothesis H5 is rejected*.

H6: Perceived cost-benefit of the methods influences cost-of-capital practices
In order to test this hypothesis, five survey items that asked about cost- and benefit-related issues were examined. One item that asks about the overall cost-benefit perception of the participants showed a very high number of significant relationships in the initial analysis. Many of these relationships were caused by the influence of the controlled third variables. However, overall the perceived cost-benefit factor is *partially supported* due to relationships of other factor items with cost-of-capital practices.

H7: Top management's background influences cost-of-capital practices
Concerning management, two issues were examined: an estimation of top management's Finance and Accounting knowledge as well as the CEO's background. However, the hypothesis that the management factor influences cost-of-capital practices has to be *rejected*.

H8: Corporate culture influences cost-of-capital practices
Regarding corporate culture, four aspects were examined. The one that showed most significant relationships with cost-of-capital practices is the influence of the Finance and Accounting function. Although some of these correlations were apparently caused by the statistical influence of stock market listing, the variable remains significant, so that hypothesis H8 is *partially supported*.

H9: The organisational structure influences cost-of-capital practices
In terms of organisational structure, the influence of centralisation, heterogeneity and complexity on cost-of-capital practices was examined, as well as the primary organisational structure used in reporting. Overall, this factor appears to have a

---

[27] For the statistical reasons discussed in Sect. 7.6.2.3, the stock market listing factor could not be controlled for company size.

Table 7.15 Objectives and results of the company survey

Research aim	Research objectives	Contribution of company survey	Results from company survey
Examine and explain cost-of-capital practices	(1) To investigate how companies use and determine cost-of-capital	Gain quantitative results for focus population	Detailed descriptive data analysis presented (Sect. 7.4).
	(2) To develop a model that explains the cost-of-capital practices of companies	Test factors quantitatively	Influencing factors analysed quantitatively using bivariate analysis (Sect. 7.5) as well as multivariate analysis (Sect. 7.6). Five influencing factors were supported by the quantitative results.
	(3) To develop a theory that explains the cost-of-capital practices of companies		

rather weak influence. However, due to suppressed relationships of the level of centralisation of the organisational structure that emerged when controlling for stock market listing and company size, hypothesis *H9 is partially supported*.

7.7.3 Fulfilment of Objectives

As an interim conclusion, it can be stated that the objectives formulated for the company survey were fulfilled. Table 7.15 summarises the results of the chapter.

References

Al Mutairi M, Tian G, Hasan H, Tan A (2012) Corporate governance and corporate finance practices in a Kuwait stock exchange market listed firm: a survey to confront theory with practice. Corp Gov 12(5):595–615

Arnold G, Hatzopoulos PD (2000) The theory-practice gap in capital budgeting: evidence from the United Kingdom. J Bus Finance Account 27(5/6):603–626

Atrill P, McLaney EJ (2009) Management accounting for decision makers. Financial Times Prentice Hall, Harlow

Baker HK, Dutta S, Saadi S (2011) Corporate finance practices in Canada: where do we stand? Multinatl Finance J 15(3/4):157–192

Bancel F, Mittoo UR (2011) Survey evidence on financing decisions and cost of capital. In: Baker HK, Martin GS (eds) Capital structure & corporate financing decisions. Theory, evidence, and practice. Essential perspectives. Wiley, Hoboken, NJ, pp 229–248

Bennouna K, Meredith GG, Marchant T (2010) Improved capital budgeting decision making: evidence from Canada. Manag Decis 48(2):225–247

Berry WD, Feldman S (1985) Multiple regression in practice. Sage, Beverly Hills, CA

Bethlehem JG, Biffignandi S (2012) Handbook of web surveys. Wiley, Hoboken, NJ

Black C, Parry J, Anderson H, Bennett JA (2002) Are New Zealand chief financial officers the 'country cousins' of their American counterparts? Univ Auck Bus Rev 4(1):1–11

Block S (2003) Divisional cost of capital: a study of its use by major U.S. firms. Eng Econ 48 (4):345–362

Block S (2005) Are there differences in capital budgeting procedures between industries? An empirical study. Eng Econ 50(1):55–67

Britzelmaier B (2013) Controlling. Grundlagen—Praxis—Umsetzung. Pearson, Munich

Brooks C (2008) Introductory econometrics for finance. Cambridge University Press, Cambridge

Brounen D, de Jong A, Koedijk K (2004) Corporate finance in Europe: confronting theory with practice. Financ Manag 33(4):71–101

Brunzell T, Liljeblom E, Vaihekoski M (2011) Determinants of capital budgeting methods and hurdle rates in Nordic firms. Account Finance 53(1):85–110

Chazi A, Terra PRS, Zanella FC (2010) Theory versus practice: perspectives of Middle Eastern financial managers. Eur Bus Rev 22(2):195–221

Cohen G, Yagil J (2007) A multinational survey of corporate financial policies. J Appl Finance 17 (1):57–69

Correia C, Cramer P (2008) An analysis of cost of capital, capital structure and capital budgeting practices: a survey of South African listed companies. Meditari Account Res 16(2):31–52

Craighead WE, Weiner IB (2010) The Corsini encyclopedia of psychology. Wiley, Hoboken, NJ

David M, Sutton CD (2011) Social research. An introduction. Sage, Los Angeles, CA

de Vaus DA (2002) Surveys in social research. Routledge, London

Easterby-Smith M, Thorpe R, Jackson PR (2012) Management research, 4th edn. Sage, London

Empel MV (2008) Financial services in Europe. An introductory overview. European law collection, 3rd edn. Kluwer Law International, Alphen aan den Rijn, the Netherlands

Fasnacht D (2009) Open innovation in the financial services. Growing through openness, flexibility and customer integration. Springer, Berlin

Field AP (2013) Discovering statistics using IBM SPSS statistics. And sex and drugs and rock 'n' roll. Sage, London

Fowler FJ (2009) Survey research methods. Sage, Thousand Oaks, CA

Frank A (2007) On the value of survey-based research in finance. Alternation 14(1):243–261

Frankfort-Nachmias C, Leon-Guerrero A (2011) Social statistics for a diverse society. Pine Forge Press, Thousand Oaks, CA

Fuller WA (2009) Sampling statistics. Wiley, Hoboken, NJ

Geginat J, Morath B, Wittmann R, Knüsel P (2006) Kapitalkosten als strategisches Entscheidungskriterium. Available at http://www.rolandberger.com/expertise/functional_issues/restructuring/2006-05-03-rbsc-pub-capital.html

Graham JR, Harvey CR (2001) The theory and practice of corporate finance: evidence from the field. J Financ Econ 60(2/3):187–243

Graham JR, Harvey CR (2003) The theory and practice of corporate finance: the data. Available from http://papers.ssrn.com/sol3/papers.cfm?abstract_id=395221

Groves RM, Fowler FJ, Couper MP, Lepkowski JM, Singer E, Tourangeau R (2009) Survey methodology. Wiley, Hoboken, NJ

Hain J (2013) Einfache statistische Testverfahren. Available at http://www.uni-wuerzburg.de/fileadmin/10040800/user_upload/hain/SPSS/Testverfahren.pdf

Hermes N, Smid P, Yao L (2007) Capital budgeting practices: a comparative study of the Netherlands and China. Int Bus Rev 16(5):630–654

Iacobucci D, Churchill GA (2010) Marketing research. Methodological foundations. South-Western Cengage Learning, Mason, OH

Kline RB (2009) Becoming a behavioral science researcher. A guide to producing research that matters. Guilford Press, New York, NY

Lavrakas PJ (2008) Encyclopedia of survey research methods. Sage, Thousand Oaks, CA

Lewis-Beck MS, Bryman A, Liao TF (2004) The Sage encyclopedia of social science research methods. Sage, Thousand Oaks, CA

McLaney E, Pointon J, Thomas M, Tucker J (2004) Practitioners' perspectives on the UK cost of capital. Eur J Finance 10(2):123–138

Miller RL, Jentz GA (2010) Fundamentals of business law. Excerpted cases. South-Western Cengage Learning, Mason, OH

Miller LA, McIntire SA, Lovler RL (2011) Foundations of psychological testing. A practical approach. Sage, Thousand Oaks, CA

Moore DS, McCabe GP (2006) Introduction to the practice of statistics. WH Freeman, New York, NY

Newcomer KE, Wirtz PW (2004) Using statistics in evaluation. In: Wholey JS, Hatry HP, Newcomer KE (eds) Handbook of practical program evaluation. Wiley, Hoboken, NJ, pp 439–478

Norris G (2012) Introduction to statistics with SPSS for social science. Pearson, Harlow

Petersen C, Plenborg T, Schøler F (2006) Issues in valuation of privately held firms. J Private Equity 10(1):33–48

Reinard JC (2006) Communication research statistics. Sage, Thousand Oaks, CA

Ryan PA, Ryan GP (2002) Capital budgeting practices of the fortune 1000: how have things changed? J Bus Manag 8(4):355–364

Serita T (2008) On survey data analysis in corporate finance. J Int Econ Stud 22:97–111

Shannon ML (2004) Spurious relationship. In: Lewis-Beck MS, Bryman A, Liao TF (eds) The Sage encyclopedia of social science research methods. Sage, Thousand Oaks, CA, pp 1062–1063

Siegel AF (2012) Practical business statistics. Academic, Burlington, MA

Smith T, Walsh K (2013) Why the CAPM is half-right and everything else is wrong. Abacus 49:73–78

Sterba SK, Foster ME (2008) Self-selected sample. In: Lavrakas PJ (ed) Encyclopedia of survey research methods. Sage, Thousand Oaks, CA

Stopher PR (2012) Collecting, managing, and assessing data using sample surveys. Cambridge University Press, Cambridge, UK

Subrahmanyam A (2013) Comments and perspectives on 'the capital asset pricing model'. Abacus 49:79–81

Thode HC (2002) Testing for normality. Statistics, textbooks and monographs, 164th edn. Marcel Dekker, New York, NY

Truong G, Partington G, Peat M (2008) Cost-of-capital estimation and capital-budgeting practice in Australia. Aust J Manag 33(1):95–121

Utts JM, Heckard RF (2012) Mind on statistics. Brooks/Cole Cengage Learning, Boston, MA

Wholey JS, Hatry HP, Newcomer KE (2004) Handbook of practical program evaluation. Wiley, Hoboken, NJ

Zachrau M (2013) LinkedIn holt auf, XING immer noch Spitze in DACH. Available from http://www.ant-marketing.org/2013/01/08/linkedin-holt-auf-xing-immer-noch-spitze-in-dach/

Chapter 8
Conclusion and Contribution to Knowledge

In the final chapter of this thesis, the outcome and the contribution to knowledge from all stages of this research are outlined and summarised. In doing so, both the findings from the qualitative interviews and the findings from the quantitative company survey are taken into account in order to arrive at an overall conclusion that integrates the results from the different methods. Furthermore, in this chapter, the limitations of the research are pointed out. Moreover, the implications of this research for theory, practice and further research are discussed.

This chapter starts with the presentation of the final research outcome (Sect. 8.1), followed by an explanation of how this thesis contributes to the body of knowledge (Sect. 8.2). Next, the limitations of the research (Sect. 8.3) are discussed. Subsequently, implications for practice (Sect. 8.4) and for theory and further research (Sect. 8.5) are discussed. The thesis is closed with a brief overall conclusion in Sect. 8.6.

8.1 Research Outcome

8.1.1 Overview and Synthesis of Previous Literature

One challenge in very specific topics like the one addressed in this thesis is to identify relevant primary literature, as secondary literature such as the textbooks by Brealey et al. (2009), Damodaran (2011) and Arnold (2008) only deal with cost-of-capital on an introductory level.

For this thesis, relevant primary literature was compiled from different sources and systematically discussed, compared and synthesised in two chapters (see Chaps. 2 and 3). In doing so, information on cost-of-capital was also extracted from studies on related topics such as capital budgeting.

As a final conclusion and result of this comprehensive literature review, a literature classification framework has been developed (see Fig. 8.1). This framework classifies previous literature in the field and can also be used to locate this thesis within the existing body of knowledge.

The framework classifies literature in two dimensions: In the columns, the different fields of research or sub-topics are shown. In the rows, the method used by the respective researchers can be seen.[1] The literature matrix shows that there is a relationship between the sub-topic and the methods used in previous literature. The following sub-topics were identified in the literature review:

1. Determination techniques for *company* cost-of-capital: Research in this area addresses the development and evaluation of cost-of-capital estimation techniques. The major focus is on the estimation of cost of equity with the CAPM and alternative models such as the APT or option-based models (see Sect. 2.1). This type of research question is dealt with theoretically and with the help of large sample analysis of financial market data.
2. Determination techniques for *business unit* cost-of-capital deal with the question of how cost-of-capital can be estimated for non-listed entities and business units when no capital market information is available (see Sects. 2.3 and 2.4). These issues are addressed with a similar methodology to the one for company cost-of-capital.
3. Cost-of-capital *practices of companies* (see Chap. 3): When it comes to the question of whether and how practitioners apply the techniques, internal data from companies has to be collected. Therefore, survey and interview designs are used to conduct research on this sub-topic (see Sect. 3.1.2).

This study contributes to the third field of the literature framework by providing new empirical results for Germany and in the context of Managerial Finance. Moreover, as can be seen in the figure, with a mixed methods approach, a new methodology in the field was used.

8.1.2 New Empirical Results on Cost-of-Capital Practices

In this study, new empirical results for cost-of-capital practices in Germany in the context of Managerial Finance were obtained. The investigation was based on proposition P1 and hypothesis H1 (*"There is a theory-practice gap in cost-of-capital methods"*), which is supported by the results of this thesis. In this section, these original results are briefly summarised, taking into account the findings from all stages of this research. Moreover, a final conclusion concerning the status quo of cost-of-capital practices in the German real economy sector will be drawn.

---

[1] The content of Fig. 8.1 is not comprehensive in terms of the pieces of literature that are listed. It only gives examples of seminal pieces of literature that were discussed in the literature review.

METHOD			FIELD OF RESEARCH: Determination of company cost-of-capital	Determination of business units cost-of-capital: Comparable company approach	Determination of business units cost-of-capital: Analytical approaches	Determination of business units cost-of-capital: Practitioner approaches	Cost-of-capital practices of companies
Theoretical			Markowitz 1952, Lintner 1965, Sharpe 1964, Ross 1967, McNulty 2002	Brigham 1977, Van Horne 1977, Hamada 1972, Conine et al 1985	Bowman et al 1979, Conine et al 1982, Gordon et al 1974, Lev 1974		***This study***
Empirical	Quantitative	Financial data analysis	Fama & French 1993, Armstrong 2011	Boquist et al 1983, Erhardt et al 1991, Ingram et al 2010, Chua et al 2006, Fuller et al 1981, Bowman et al 2006, Cummins et al 2005	Ball et al 1969, Beaver et al 1970, Bildersee 1975, Thompson et al 1976, Toms et al 2005	Bufka et al 2004	
Empirical	Quantitative	Survey					Al Mutairi et al 2009, Arnold et al 2000, Baker et al 2011, Bennouna et al 2010, Black et al 2002, Block 2003,Brounen et al 2004, Chazi et al 2010, Cohen 2007, Graham et al 2001, Hermes et al 2007, McLaney et al 2004, Ryan et al 2002, Truong et al 2008
Empirical	Quantitative	Interviews					Petersen et al 2006
Empirical	Qualitative	Interviews					Steinle et al 2007
Empirical	Mixed Methods	Interviews + Survey					***This study***

Fig. 8.1 Literature classification framework

Conclusions on the influencing factors of cost-of-capital practices are made in the subsequent two sections.

The first theme of cost-of-capital practices that was examined both in the expert interviews and the company survey concerns which **determination techniques** are used to calculate cost-of-capital and cost of equity. On the *company group level*, this question has previously been investigated by several studies in other countries (see Sect. 3.2). In line with prior results (e.g. Al Mutairi et al. 2012; Brunzell et al. 2011; Truong et al. 2008), this study finds that WACC and CAPM are the standard procedures to determine the cost-of-capital (see Sect. 7.4.1). However, a substantial number of companies do not determine their cost-of-capital at all. For determination of cost-of-capital on *BU level*, there are fewer prior results (see Sect. 3.3). This study reveals that only approximately 50 % of the companies explicitly determine their cost-of-capital on BU level and only approximately 30 % determine cost of equity on BU level (see Sect. 7.4.2). Confirming prior results from other countries, only a few companies use objective methods such as the CCA (Block 2003).

Concerning cost-of-capital practices in **performance measurement and value-based management**, there have been very limited prior results. In this thesis, a first step examined whether companies use *capital-oriented performance measures*, i.e. for instance capital, value-based metrics or absolute capital measures. In the expert interviews (see Sect. 6.4.1), a preliminary finding was that value-based measures are generally only calculated in large companies and are primarily used for external representation purposes. The limited relevance of the value-based metrics for smaller companies has also been confirmed by the quantitative results from the company survey (see Sect. 7.5.2). The relevance of capital return measures (e.g. ROCE) were found to be higher in the survey than expected from the expert interviews, being the most important capital-oriented performance measures, with approximately 60 % of the companies using the measures (see Sect. 7.4.3). Finally, research was conducted on the question of whether companies set *explicit capital return targets*, which would indicate an awareness of cost-of-capital even if no cost-of-capital rate is explicitly calculated. It was found that approximately half of the companies set return targets (see Sect. 7.4.3). Contrary to what is suggested by theory, only a minority of companies use the calculated cost-of-capital rate.

In the third area of interest of this thesis—**capital allocation and capital budgeting**—the results from the company survey have confirmed the findings from the expert interviews. In terms of using differentiated hurdle rates, most of the companies follow the recommendations by theory and differentiate their hurdle rates, e.g. by business units or geographical regions. Prior to this research, mixed results were obtained for this question. This study confirms some results (Bennouna et al. 2010), but contrasts with other studies (Chazi et al. 2010; Graham and Harvey 2003), reporting that most of the companies use the overall company hurdle rate for all projects. With regard to how the hurdle rates are determined, this study's results show that only approximately 40 % of the companies use calculated cost-of-capital rates as hurdle rates.

8.1 Research Outcome

Overall, it can be concluded that the results of this study are generally in line with prior findings of related studies from different countries, although comparisons between studies should generally be made with caution (see Sect. 3.1.3) and this study has examined additional issues that were not included in the prior studies (in particular performance measurement and value-based management). This study's results show that there is a certain theory-practice gap in Germany in cost-of-capital practices in the context of Managerial Finance. The gap tends to increase from group to BU or local level. Moreover, it is larger in performance measurement and value-based management than in capital budgeting. However, it can be reported that especially in larger companies, cost-of-capital practices are already sophisticated and satisfactory overall from a theoretical point of view. In particular, the use of capital-oriented performance measures shows that companies are conscious of cost-of-capital even if they might not explicitly calculate a rate.

8.1.3 Influencing Factors of Cost-of-Capital Practices

Based on proposition P2 ("*There are systematic differences between companies that explain differences in cost-of-capital practices*"), a number of possible influencing factors of cost-of-capital practices were identified in the qualitative expert interviews that were conducted for this thesis. They were subsequently expressed as hypotheses and tested quantitatively with the help of a company survey. As Table 8.1 summarises, three of the factors had to be rejected, while five are (partially) supported by the quantitative results.

In this section, this thesis's results concerning influencing factors are briefly summarised and compared to prior results. Furthermore, some of the factors are revised based on the quantitative results in order to obtain the final factors which will enter into the final model in the subsequent section.

Table 8.1 Summary and revision of influencing factors

Hypothesis	Factor	Support	Final revised factor
H2	Company size	Supported	Company size
H3	Industry sector	Rejected	–
H4	Stock market listing	Supported	Stock market listing
H5	Investor types	Rejected	
H6	Perceived cost-benefit	Partially supported	Perceived cost-benefit
H7	Top management background	Rejected	–
H8	Corporate culture	Partially supported	Influence of finance and accounting function
H9	Organisational structure	Partially supported	Level of centralisation

Company size (H2) was commonly mentioned by the candidates in the expert interviews as a possible influence on cost-of-capital practices (see Sect. 6.4.2). This idea was supported by the quantitative results of the company survey (see Sect. 7.5.2). In the data, company size is positively correlated with the use of objective determination techniques such as the CAPM. These results are in line with findings of previous studies (see Sect. 3.4). In particular, a correlation between cost of equity determination techniques such as the CAPM and the size factor has previously been identified (Al Mutairi et al. 2012; Chazi et al. 2010; Graham and Harvey 2001). Regarding capital budgeting, the data revealed that large companies are more likely to use methods like IRR and NPV and to differentiate hurdle rates by BU, geographical location or individual projects. These results are in line with the findings of Baker et al. (2011). In the data reported by Graham and Harvey (2001), large companies are more likely to use differentiated discount rates. Other authors do not find comparable size effects in their data; however, there is no contradictory evidence either. In this study, it was additionally shown that larger companies are more likely to use value-based measures, set explicit return targets and use calculated cost-of-capital rates in performance measurement. This aspect has not been considered in prior research.

The company size factor has been confirmed by the survey results and will be included in the final model.

Industry (H2) as an influencing factor was mentioned by three interviewees (see section 6.4.2). In order to test the factor quantitatively, two variables were used. First, a broad sector variable was used, which only showed a few significant relationships when controlling for stock market listing (see Sect. 7.6.2.2). In the U.S., Graham and Harvey (2001), who also used a broad classification consisting of "manufacturing" and "other", also found some significant relationships. Second, for the manufacturing sector, a more detailed industry classification was used, which showed few significant relationships. The importance of the industry factor seems to be similar to the results of the study by Al Mutairi et al. (2012), who distinguish between seven industry sectors.

Overall, the influence seems to be relatively weak, so hypothesis H2 was rejected and the factor is not further considered in the development of the final model.

Stock market listing (H3) can be reported as a very significant factor. This confirms previous findings from the U.S. by Graham and Harvey (2001), who report that non-listed entities are less likely to apply the CAPM.

Consequently, stock market listing is considered as a factor in the final model.

Regarding **investor types (H4)**, a result of the expert interviews was that cost-of-capital practices might be influenced by the type of investor, as, for instance, family investors have different requirements than financial investors (see Sect. 6.4.2). This aspect has not been examined in prior research except for management ownership (Al Mutairi et al. 2012; Graham and Harvey 2001). This study has gone beyond prior studies and analysed the influence of six different investor types on cost-of-capital practices. However, quantitatively this relationship could not be clearly shown. The significant relationships that were initially identified mostly

8.1 Research Outcome

disappeared when controlling for stock market listing and company size (see Sects. 7.6.2.2 and 7.6.2.3).

Therefore, the hypothesis was rejected and the factor is not included in the final model.

Perceived cost-benefit (H6) as an influencing factor of cost-of-capital practices was identified in expert interviews for this thesis (see Sect. 6.4.2) and has not previously been considered by other authors in comparable quantitative studies. Therefore, no comparison with prior results can be made. The idea that methods are only applied if the perceived benefit is higher than the perceived cost was measured with the help of five survey items. The items that are associated with cost show negative relationships with the application of certain cost-of-capital techniques, while the items associated with benefit show positive relationships (see relationship matrix in Sect. 7.5.1). However, controlling for stock market listing and company size, it results that some of the relationships were spurious.

Overall, the factor remains partially supported and is included in the model without changes.

Based on the interview candidates' perception that **top management (H7)** exercises influence over cost-of-capital methods, an attempt was made to relate cost-of-capital practices to systematic characteristics of management. Two variables were examined: CEO background and Finance knowledge of the top management. Previous studies (Al Mutairi et al. 2012; Baker et al. 2011; Graham and Harvey 2001) have examined the influence of the CEO's degree (MBA, PhD etc.), but this was considered less relevant for Germany in this study. However, the dependency of cost-of-capital practices on systematic differences of managers was controversial in the expert interviews. Also, in light of the company survey, no sufficient quantitative evidence that supports this idea can be reported (Sect. (Sect. 7.5.7).

Consequently, the hypothesis related to the management factor was rejected and the factor is not included in the final model.

In the expert interviews, several aspects of **corporate culture (H8)** were mentioned that might have an influence on cost-of-capital practices. In the company survey (see Sect. 7.5.8), a significant influence on cost-of-capital practices can be reported for the cultural dimension *influence of the Finance and Accounting function*. The prior studies discussed in this thesis have not considered issues related to corporate culture.

For integration into the final model of cost-of-capital practices, the corporate culture factor is revised and considered as *influence of the Finance and Accounting function*.

With regard to **organisational structure (H9)**, some theoretical considerations were brought up by some consultants in the expert interviews (see Sect. 6.4.2). As a result, different variables concerning organisational structure were examined in the company survey. Controlling for stock market listing and company size, only one factor—the level of centralisation—is significant (see Sect. 7.6.2.2 and 7.6.2.3). In prior studies, no comparable relationships were identified.

Based on the quantitative results, the organisational structure factor is adjusted and taken into account as *level of centralisation*.

8.1.4 Final Model of Cost-of-Capital Practices

In the previous section, the final five influencing factors that result from a synthesis of the qualitative and quantitative findings of this research were presented. In this section, the last step in the development of an explanatory model is taken: the relationships between the final model's factors are modelled and explained theoretically. In doing so, both statistical insights from the analysis of the company survey and assumptions of causal relationships derived from qualitative insights are taken into account.

In Fig. 8.2, the final model of cost-of-capital practices is presented. The strongest influencing factors on cost-of-capital practices are illustrated in bold letters and thick lines. Relationships between influencing factors are illustrated as dotted lines.

This research shows that **company size** has a positive effect on cost-of-capital practices, i.e. the larger a company, the more sophisticated the methods that are applied. The reason for this relationship is that larger companies have more resources, i.e. more staff and more financial resources to charge external experts such as management consultants with the improvement of their methods. Moreover, large companies tend to have more financial specialist knowledge because of a higher absolute number of staff and many highly skilled employees who have previously worked in consulting or banking. Additionally, large companies often have more formalised processes which have a positive influence on the use of objective techniques.

The positive effect of company size on cost-of-capital practices is even reinforced by its interconnections with other influencing factors. Large companies

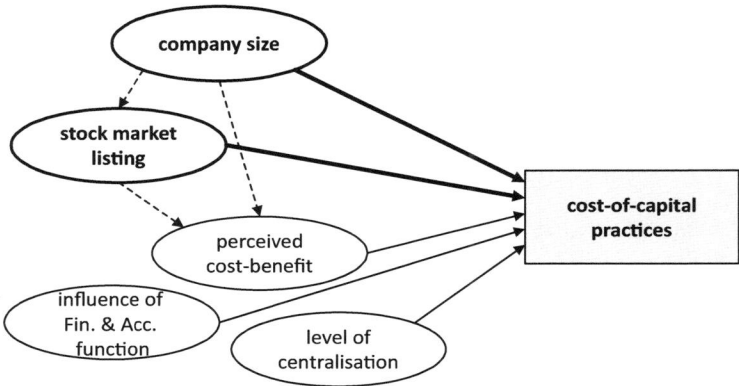

Fig. 8.2 Final model of cost-of-capital practices

are more likely to be stock market listed and the perceived benefit of sophisticated cost-of-capital methods is generally higher in large companies.

Another important influencing factor is **stock market listing**, which also has a positive effect on cost-of-capital practices. Reasons are high information requirements that have to be fulfilled by listed companies, since they have to publish extensive financial data. Even if they are not obliged to publish certain cost-of-capital information, the level of transparency and sophistication of financial methods is generally higher than in non-listed companies. Additionally, listed companies are subject to more pressure to generate adequate returns on the capital invested in the company. One reason for this is the high influence of professional investors such as institutional investors.

Apart from these direct effects, the perceived benefit in relation to the costs of sophisticated methods is higher in stock market listed companies. This might be related to the information and publication requirements of listed companies but also to their greater financial knowledge.

Perceived cost-benefit influences cost-of-capital practices as follows: the perceived cost associated with the calculation of figures and use of sophisticated methods has a negative influence on cost-of-capital practices. Perceived cost includes items like time invested by employees, but also direct costs for consultants and information providers. In contrast, perceived benefits of sophisticated cost-of-capital techniques have a positive effect on cost-of-capital practices. Perceived benefit in particular refers to the question of whether the application of sophisticated techniques makes sense from the point of view of the company.

The higher the **influence of the Finance and Accounting function** within the organisation, the more sophisticated the cost-of-capital methods applied. This could be due to the fact that the organisation in general is more focused on financial figures. Another reason could be that Finance and Accounting professionals are more likely to see benefits of using sophisticated cost-of-capital methods. Only if the influence of the function in the organisation is sufficient can they enforce the use of more sophisticated techniques.

Finally, the **level of centralisation** of the organisation influences cost-of-capital practices. As discussed in the literature review in Sect. 2.2.3, decentralisation tendencies in organisations can increase agency problems. This study finds that the factor can work in either direction. On the one hand, the use of sophisticated determination techniques for cost-of-capital is less likely with a higher level of centralisation. A possible theoretical explanation could be that with more centralisation (i.e. less decentralisation), formal methods to control the business units are less important, since the principal-agent problem is less of a concern. On the other hand, in capital budgeting, the use of hurdle rates differentiated by BU, type of project or individual projects is positively influenced by a high level of centralisation. A possible reason for this could be that investment projects are all controlled by the holding organisation in centralised company groups. Thus, given the overview of all investment projects, risk-adjusted hurdle rates can be used.

8.2 Contribution to the Body of Knowledge

This thesis contributes to the body of knowledge in a number of ways, which are summarised in Table 8.2. The table is sorted by type of contribution. For each contribution, the related research gap which has been identified in Sect. 3.5.2 is indicated.[2]

The *literature review* of this thesis has contributed to knowledge by offering a comprehensive collection of primary literature that deals with the determination of divisional cost-of-capital. Moreover, previous empirical results on companies' cost-of-capital practices were extracted from a large number of studies on related topics. Using these studies, this thesis has generated meta-level knowledge by comparing previous results on cost-of-capital practices both quantitatively and qualitatively. Subsequently, research gaps were derived from the analysis of previous studies. Finally, a two-dimensional literature classification framework for the field was developed and presented in Sect. 8.1.1.

The qualitative and quantitative *empirical results* provided by this study are the most important contribution of this thesis and have addressed a number of research gaps in the field. The study provides detailed empirical results on cost-of-capital practices focused on the German real economy sector for the first time. Additionally, the focus on performance measurement and value-based management is a major contribution to knowledge. Furthermore, the extent to which influencing factors of cost-of-capital practices were analysed qualitatively and quantitatively constitutes an original contribution to knowledge.

Based on this study's empirical findings, the author has developed a *model* to explain companies' cost-of-capital practices, which is another major contribution. Based on the hypotheses that were formulated, five influencing factors could be identified and confirmed. The model contributes to a better understanding of the theory-practice gap in cost-of-capital practices and why there are large differences between the practices of different companies. In contrast to previous studies, the empirical results were not only analysed descriptively or based on bivariate analysis. Instead, relationships among influencing factors were also taken into account in order to build the model on solid statistical grounds.

Based on the qualitative results obtained from the expert interviews, this thesis could make a contribution to *theory* by theoretically explaining the underlying effects and reasons behind the influencing factors in the final model of cost-of-capital practices.

Finally, the author has developed and refined a number of data analysis *methods* during the analysis of the qualitative and quantitative data for this study. These include a qualitative data analysis approach as well as new visualisation methods to present qualitative and quantitative data in matrix formats. In particular, the relationship matrix, which can be used to create a holistic overview of bivariate

---

[2] Please note that the contribution of the literature review is not based on a previously identified research gap, as the gaps were derived from the literature review.

8.2 Contribution to the Body of Knowledge

Table 8.2 Summary of contribution to knowledge

Type of contribution	Contribution	Research gap	Implication of contribution	Reference
Literature review	Compilation, classification and criticism of literature on determination of BU cost-of-capital		Minor	Sect. 2.4
	Compilation of papers that include findings on cost-of-capital practices		Minor	Sect. 3.1.1, Table 3.1
	Numerical comparison of previous results on company cost-of-capital practices		Minor	Sect. 3.2, Fig. 3.2, Fig. 3.3, Fig. 3.4, Fig. 3.5
	Discussion of previous results on BU cost-of-capital practices		Minor	Sect. 3.3, Fig. 3.6, Fig. 3.7, Fig. 3.8, Fig. 3.9
	Comparison of previous results on influencing factors		Minor	Sect. 3.4.2, Table 3.5
	Identification of research gaps		Minor	Sect. 3.5.2, Table 3.7
	Development of literature classification framework		Minor	Sect. 8.1.1, Fig. 8.1
Empirical results	Qualitative findings on cost-of-capital practices	Reasons for theory-practice gap; Lack of theory to explain determinants/influencing factors	Minor	Sect. 6.4.1, Sect. 8.1.2
	Qualitative findings on influencing factors	Determinants of cost-of-capital practices; Lack of theory to explain determinants/influencing factors	Major	Sect. 6.4.2, Sect. 8.1.3
	Quantitative findings on company cost-of-capital practices in German real economy sector	Results for real economy sector in Germany; Mixed results on application of CAPM	Major	Sect. 7.4.1, Sect. 8.1.2, Fig. 7.11, Fig. 7.12
	Quantitative findings on BU cost-of-capital	Results for real economy sector in Germany; Results on	Major	Sect. 7.4.2, Sect. 8.1.2 Fig. 7.14,

(continued)

Table 8.2 (continued)

Type of contribution	Contribution	Research gap	Implication of contribution	Reference
		business unit cost-of-capital		Fig. 7.15, Fig. 7.16
	Focused empirical results concerning cost-of-capital practices in performance measurement	Results for real economy sector in Germany; Results for area of performance measurement and value-based management	Major	Sect. 7.4.3, Sect. 8.1.2, Fig. 7.17, Fig. 7.18
	Quantitative findings concerning influencing factors	Determinants of cost-of-capital practices	Major	Sect. 7.5, Sect. 7.6, Sect. 8.1.3, Fig. 7.21, Fig. 7.30, Fig. 7.31
Model-building	Support of hypotheses concerning influencing factors	Determinants of cost-of-capital practices	Major	Sect. 8.1.3, Table 8.1
	Final model of cost-of-capital practices	Determinants of cost-of-capital practices; Lack of theory to explain determinants/influencing factors	Major	Sect. 8.1.4, Fig. 8.2
Theory-building	Qualitative explanation and interpretation of interdependences in final model	Lack of theory to explain determinants/influencing factors	Major	Sect. 8.1.4
Method development	Development of data analysis approach for qualitative data		Minor	Sect. 6.2.7, Fig. 4.2
	Development of new form of data presentation for qualitative data		Minor	Fig. 6.5, Fig. 6.6, Fig. 6.7, Fig. 6.8
	Development of new form of data presentation for quantitative data (relationship matrix)		Minor	Fig. 7.21
	Development of new form of data presentation for quantitative data (elaboration analysis)		Minor	Fig. 7.30, Fig. 7.31

8.3 Limitations of the Research

There are some aspects of this research that might place limitations on the outcomes. First of all, the research might not be generalizable beyond the deliberate delimitations of scope (see Sect.1.2.3). These include a geographical dimension (Germany) and a sector dimension (real economy sector).

Moreover, there are some aspects of the research design which are potentially an issue. As discussed in Sect. 7.2.5, the sampling approach of the company survey does not allow for generalisations beyond the sample cases from a statistical point of view. However, the analysis of the sample composition (see Sect. 7.3.2) in terms of companies of different sizes and investor structures shows that an adequate representation of different companies is ensured. Moreover, the results of those aspects of the research that prior studies have already examined in different contexts appear similar, which indicates that the sample describes the population well.

Furthermore, to protect the respondents' privacy and confidential data, no details on companies could be disclosed and the analysis was only conducted on an aggregated level. However, for illustration and interpretation of the findings, a discussion of individual cases would have been helpful at some points.

8.4 Implications for Practice

This study has shown that there is still a substantial theory-practice gap in cost-of-capital considerations. This means that there is a large improvement potential for the companies if they want to follow the recommendations of theory. Areas that provide large improvement potential are, for instance, the explicit determination of cost-of-capital on BU level, the use of explicit return targets in performance measurement and the calculation of value-based measures.

In particular, it is recommended that the responsible persons in companies are trained in terms of the following issues: First of all, there should be an understanding of the basic idea of cost-of-capital, i.e. that capital invested in a business creates an opportunity cost and should be remunerated with an adequate return in order to compensate for the risk. Second, the importance of differentiating cost-of-capital within an organisation in order to account for different risk of projects and BUs should be emphasised. It is important to understand the consequences of using non-differentiated rates, e.g. a misallocation of capital within the organisation (see Sect. 2.2.2.2). Finally, the technical use of objective methods to determine cost of equity such as the CAPM or the CCA could be further trained, especially in SMEs.

8.5 Implications for Theory and Further Research

As discussed in the previous section, the theory-practice gap revealed in this study implies that practitioners should move their cost-of-capital practices toward the suggestions by theory in order to improve their business.

On the other hand, the *theory-practice gap* can also have implications for theories and the academics that deal with them. The reason for the theory-practice gap is not only the lack of knowledge among practitioners, but also that the perceived benefit of the methods does not seem to be very high among practitioners. This could have two implications for academics: First, the knowledge and understanding of the theoretical models needs to be increased among practitioners through stronger consideration in teaching and textbooks. Second, it could mean that the theoretical models themselves should be reconsidered from an application point of view. As pointed out in the literature review (see Sect. 2.2.1.2), the development of the methods is largely driven by research dealing with investment theory and stock market data, such as Roll and Ross (1984) or Fama and French (1993). Instead, research could be increasingly done from a Managerial Finance perspective.

Apart from this general discussion about the responsibility for a theory-practice gap, the topic offers more potential for further research. First of all, this research question could be examined beyond the explicit delimitations of this research; in particular, it would be interesting to repeat this research in *other countries*. As pointed out in Sect. 3.1.1, the study by Graham and Harvey (2001), which had a different focus, was replicated in several countries, e.g. by Black et al. (2002) and Chazi et al. (2010). The replication studies provide interesting comparisons between countries. Also, studies that include several countries, such as the work of Brounen et al. (2004), could provide interesting insights into the influencing factors of cost-of-capital practices.

Second, this study has generated some original findings in terms of *influencing factors* which go beyond previous findings. These should be triangulated and tested for their robustness in further studies. This includes in particular the perceived cost-benefit factor and the influence of a cultural dimension on companies' cost-of-capital practices. Moreover, it could also be interesting to conduct research on these influencing factors in related contexts such as Management Accounting. Additionally, more research could be conducted on the interdependence of influencing factors.

Although this thesis has filled some of the gaps that were identified from the literature review, the following gap that was excluded from the scope of the thesis remains: There is little knowledge about how exactly the cost-of-capital models are applied by practitioners, e.g. which parameters they use in the CAPM. Although some studies (Al Mutairi et al. 2012; KPMG International 2010) deal with this issue, there is certainly more potential for research into this aspect.

Another question that was not considered in this research is the influence of cost-of-capital practices on firms' performance, which was also identified as a potential subject for further research by Al Mutairi et al. (2012). As discussed in the literature review (see Sect. 2.2.2.2), from a theoretical point of view it is expected that the use of non-differentiated cost-of-capital rates in capital allocation results in misallocation of capital and hence lower performance. This issue is examined in the study by Geginat et al. (2006). However, as argued in Sect. 3.3.4, another research design using actual financial data instead of an estimation of the effect by a survey respondent might be helpful to gain better insights into this issue.

Concerning methods, the following research design could provide additional insights into the topic: First, a longitudinal design to examine the development of the theory-practice gap over time might be interesting. Second, in order to gain deeper insights into the functioning of the influencing factors, a case study approach in one or multiple companies might be interesting.

8.6 Conclusion

The aim of this thesis was to examine and explain the cost-of-capital practices of German companies in the context of Managerial Finance. This included the objectives to investigate how companies use and determine cost-of-capital, to develop a model that explains the cost-of-capital practices and to theoretically explain the reasons that underlie the companies' behaviour.

In this final chapter, it was shown that based on a compilation and synthesis of existing literature, research gaps had been identified and new empirical results had been obtained. As a final result, a new model to explain companies' cost-of-capital practices was presented, taking into account five influencing factors that were identified using a mixed methods approach based on a post-positivist research philosophy.

This thesis has argued from a theoretical standpoint, advocating the use of sophisticated cost-of-capital methods in practice. At the same time, it was stressed that the results of this thesis also have implications for theory and further development of cost-of-capital techniques and models.

This thesis has contributed to a better understanding of the theory-practice gap in cost-of-capital practices. Nevertheless, there remains a lot of research potential in the area, which offers many exciting opportunities for future research projects for the author and for other researchers.

References

Al Mutairi M, Tian G, Tan A (2009) Corporate finance practice in Kuwait: a survey to confront theory with practice. In: 22nd Australasian finance and banking conference 2009 (available from SSRN)

Al Mutairi M, Tian G, Hasan H, Tan A (2012) Corporate governance and corporate finance practices in a Kuwait stock exchange market listed firm: a survey to confront theory with practice. Corp Gov 12(5):595–615

Armstrong CS, Core JE, Taylor DJ, Verrecchia RE (2011) When does information asymmetry affect the cost of capital? J Account Res 49(1):1–38

Arnold G (2008) Corporate financial management. Financial Times Prentice Hall, Harlow

Arnold G, Hatzopoulos PD (2000) The theory-practice gap in capital budgeting: evidence from the United Kingdom. J Bus Finance Account 27(5/6):603–626

Baker HK, English P (2011) Capital budgeting valuation. Financial analysis for today's investment projects. Wiley, Hoboken, NJ

Baker HK, Martin GS (2011) Capital structure and corporate financing decisions. Theory, evidence, and practice. Essential perspectives. Wiley, Hoboken, NJ

Baker HK, Dutta S, Saadi S (2011) Corporate finance practices in Canada: where do we stand? Multinatl Finance J 15(3/4):157–192

Ball R, Brown P (1969) An empirical evaluation of accounting income numbers. J Account Res 6(2):300–323

Beaver W, Kettler P, Scholes M (1970) The association between market determined and accounting determined risk measures. Account Rev 10(2):654–682

Bennouna K, Meredith GG, Marchant T (2010) Improved capital budgeting decision making: evidence from Canada. Manag Decis 48(2):225–247

Bildersee JS (1975) The association between a market-determined measure of risk and alternative measures of risk. Account Rev 50(1):81–98

Black C, Parry J, Anderson H, Bennett JA (2002) Are New Zealand chief financial officers the 'country cousins' of their American counterparts? Univ Auckl Bus Rev 4(1):1–11

Block S (2003) Divisional cost of capital: a study of its use by major U.S. firms. Eng Econ 48(4):345–362

Boquist JA, Moore WT (1983) Estimating the systematic risk of an industry segment: a mathematical programming approach. Financ Manag 12(4):11–18

Bowman RG (1979) The theoretical relationship between systematic risk and financial (accounting) variables. J Financ 34(3):617–630

Bowman RG, Bush SR (2006) Using comparable companies to estimate the betas of private companies. J Appl Financ 16(2):71–81

Brealey RA, Myers SC, Allen F (2009) Principles of corporate finance. McGraw-Hill, Boston, MA

Brigham EF (1975) Hurdle rates for screening capital expenditure proposals. Financ Manag 4(3):17–26

Brounen D, de Jong A, Koedijk K (2004) Corporate finance in Europe: confronting theory with practice. Financ Manag 33(4):71–101

Brunzell T, Liljeblom E, Vaihekoski M (2011) Determinants of capital budgeting methods and hurdle rates in Nordic firms. Account Financ 53(1):85–110

Bufka J, Kemper O, Schiereck D (2004) A note on estimating the divisional cost of capital for diversified companies: an empirical evaluation of heuristic-based approaches. Eur J Financ 10(1):68–88

Chazi A, Terra PRS, Zanella FC (2010) Theory versus practice: perspectives of Middle Eastern financial managers. Eur Bus Rev 22(2):195–221

Chua J, Chang PC, Wu Z (2006) The full-information approach for estimating divisional betas: implementation issues and tests. J Appl Financ 16(1):53–61

Cohen L, Manion L, Morrison K (2007) Research methods in education. Routledge, London

Conine TE Jr (1982) On the theoretical relationship between business risk and systematic risk. J Bus Financ Account 9(2):199–205

Conine TE Jr, Tamarkin M (1985) Divisional cost of capital estimation: adjusting for leverage. Financ Manag 14(1):54–58

Cummins DJ, Phillips RD (2005) Estimating the cost of equity capital for property-liability insurers. J Risk Insur 72(3):441–478

Damodaran A (2011) Applied corporate finance. Wiley, Hoboken, NJ

Ehrhardt MC, Bhagwat YN (1991) A full-information approach for estimating divisional betas. Financ Manag 20(2):60–69

Fama EF, French KR (1993) Common risk factors in the returns of stocks and bonds. J Financ Econ 33(1):3–56

Fuller RJ, Kerr HS (1981) Estimating the divisional cost of capital: an analysis of the pure-play technique. J Financ 36(5):997–1009

Geginat J, Morath B, Wittmann R, Knüsel P (2006) Kapitalkosten als strategisches Entscheidungskriterium. Available at http://www.rolandberger.com/expertise/functional_issues/restructuring/2006-05-03-rbsc-pub-capital.html

Gordon MJ, Halpern PJ (1974) Cost of capital for a division of a firm. J Financ 29(4):1153–1164

Graham JR, Harvey CR (2001) The theory and practice of corporate finance: evidence from the field. J Financ Econ 60(2/3):187–243

Graham JR, Harvey CR (2003) The theory and practice of corporate finance: the data. Available from: http://papers.ssrn.com/sol3/papers.cfm?abstract_id=395221

Hamada RS (1972) The effect of the firm's capital structure on the systematic risk of common stock. J Financ 27(2):435–452

Hermes N, Smid P, Yao L (2007) Capital budgeting practices: a comparative study of the Netherlands and China. Int Bus Rev 16(5):630–654

Ingram M, Margetis S (2010) A practical method to estimate the cost of equity capital for a firm using cluster analysis. Manag Financ 36(2):160–167

KPMG International (2010) Cost of capital and impairment test study 2009. Empirical survey of companies in Germany, the Netherlands, Austria, Switzerland and Spain. Available from: http://www.kpmg.de/WasWirTun/17368.htm

Lev B (1974) On the association between operating leverage and risk. J Financ Quant Anal 9(4):627–641

Lintner J (1965) The valuation of risk assets and the selection of risky investments in stock portfolios and capital budgets. Rev Econ Stat 47(1):13–37

Markowitz H (1952) Portfolio selection. J Financ 7(1):77–91

McLaney E, Pointon J, Thomas M, Tucker J (2004) Practitioners' perspectives on the UK cost of capital. Eur J Financ 10(2):123–138

McNulty JJ, Yeh TD, Schulze WS, Lubatkin MH (2002) What's your real cost of capital? Harv Bus Rev 80(10):114–121

Petersen C, Plenborg T, Schøler F (2006) Issues in valuation of privately held firms. J Priv Equity 10(1):33–48

Roll R, Ross S (1984) The arbitrage pricing theory approach to strategic portfolio planning. Financ Anal J 4(3):14–26

Ross S (1976) The arbitrage theory of capital asset pricing. J Econ Theory 13(3):341–360

Ryan PA, Ryan GP (2002) Capital budgeting practices of the fortune 1000: how have things changed? J Bus Manag 8(4):355–364

Sharpe WF (1964) Capital asset prices: a theory of market equilibrium under conditions of risk. J Financ 19(3):425–442

Steinle C, Krummaker S, Lehmann G (2007) Bestimmung von Kapitalkosten in diversifizierten Unternehmungen: Verfahrensvergleiche und Anwendungsempfehlungen. Z Controlling Manag 51(3):204–218

Thompson DJ (1976) Sources of systematic risk in common stocks. J Bus 49(2):173–189

Toms S, Salama A, Nguyen DT (2005) The association between accounting and market-based risk measures. University of York Working Paper

Truong G, Partington G, Peat M (2008) Cost-of-capital estimation and capital-budgeting practice in Australia. Aust J Manag 33(1):95–121

Chapter 9
Appendix

9.1 List of Codes in Qualitative Data Analysis

Code no.	Description	Meaning
001	Availability of cost positions on BU level	Data availability for business units or project (problem: figures are available for legal organizational structure only, which might be different from management structure)
002	Availability of assets on BU level	Data availability for business units or project (problem: figures are available for legal organizational structure only, which might be different from management structure)
003	Hierarchical level to be controlled	For which management level do cost-of-capital targets/return targets make sense?
004	Possibility to influence cost of equity	General issue: is it possible to influence cost of equity at all?
005	Investor specifications concerning methods	Investors determine which figures should be calculated and reported
006	Size as a proxy for investor specifications	Larger companies have different cost-of-capital practices because they have different investor structures
007	Asset intensity as a determinant	Sophisticated cost-of-capital practices make more sense for companies with higher amounts of assets, i.e. with more capital needs. For instance, service company vs. manufacturing
008	Stock market listing as a proxy for investor specifications	Listed companies have different cost-of-capital practices because investors require different methods
009	Understandability by creator of reports	The person who prepares the reports should understand how to calculate and interpret the figures

(continued)

Code no.	Description	Meaning
010	Understandability by recipient of reports	The person who receives the reports should understand how to interpret the figures
011	Understanding of possibilities to influence figure	Managers that are evaluated according to a certain figure should understand how to influence it
012	Methods depend on field of application	E.g. different cost-of-capital practices in Financial Accounting than in performance management
013	Company size influences methods	Larger companies have more professional methods
014	Different risk structures of segments/projects	If the risk of segments is different, it is important to differentiate cost-of-capital
015	Methods are influenced by regulation	In certain fields of application (e.g. IFRS), there are regulations regarding how to calculate certain measures
016	Difficulty to obtain market values of capital	For WACC weights, market values of equity and debt are needed, which are sometimes not available
017	Size of department influences methods	Larger departments have more possibilities
018	Difficulty to find comparable companies	For comparable company approach, often listed companies that can be used as proxies are not available
019	Capital market orientation influences methods	Capital market oriented companies are more likely to use sophisticated techniques
020	Connections between business units	Companies with different business units that are not directly linked are more likely to apply sophisticated methods
021	Data availability in general	As a precondition to calculate certain figures
022	Enough manpower is necessary	In order to do differentiated analyses and calculate complex measures, staff resources are needed.
023	Size of company is related to manpower	Larger companies have more resources to do calculations and analyses
024	Heterogeneity of business units influences methods	More diversified businesses apply more sophisticated methods
025	Ownership structure influences methods	E.g. founder vs. financial investor; founders focus less on financial figures
026	Qualified staff are necessary	Theoretical knowledge is required to apply certain methods (e.g. CAPM)
027	Cost/benefit of calculation	Calculation of certain figures creates costs; there has to be an appropriate benefit from it in order that the method is applied
028	Simple methods are more often used	Simple methods are more popular among companies than complex methods
029	Return targets are determined by shareholders	Shareholders set financial targets (as opposed to cost-of-capital determination techniques)
030	Management determines return/profit targets	Management subjectively sets targets as opposed to using cost-of-capital determination techniques

(continued)

9.1 List of Codes in Qualitative Data Analysis   235

Code no.	Description	Meaning
031	Calculation models are used to make targets plausible	*They have no influence on decisions: Instead, the parameters in the models are set in a way that achieves the desired outcome*
032	Freedom in using the methods	*The flexibility provided by cost-of-capital models is a benefit for companies*
033	Size is related to degree of standardization	*Larger companies have a higher degree of standardization and formal procedures*
034	Stock market listing correlates with size	*Stock market listed companies are large; Larger companies are more likely to be stock market listed*
035	Interest/calculation affinity of the client	*If the management likes 'calculation games', the company is more likely to apply sophisticated methods*
036	VBM serves primarily for external communication	*Value-based measures are often only calculated for external reports and not used for internal management*
037	Industry influences methods	*Cost-of-capital practices are different between industries*
038	Openness to innovations	*If companies are not open to innovations, they do not introduce new methods*
039	Corporate culture in general influences methods	*Corporate culture has an influence on cost-of-capital practices*
040	Freedom in calculation of indicators is problematic	*The flexibility in cost-of-capital models increases complexity and gives way to manipulation*
041	Conservative corporate culture	*Conservative companies do not introduce new methods very easily*
042	Complexity of calculation	*Due to the complexity of cost-of-capital techniques, they are often not applied*
043	Relevant information is determined by recipient	*The figures that are reported are those that are requested by management and not those that the controller finds interesting*
044	Background of board members	*Board members with background different from Finance might not be so interested in advanced methods*
045	Technology/innovation culture *vs.* financial culture	*In some companies, technological innovations are more important than financial figures and vice versa*
046	Harmony-orientation *vs.* financial culture	*In some companies, harmony is more important than financial figures and vice versa*
047	Impulses by new CEO	*With the start of a new CEO, new methods and processes are introduced*
048	Influence of Finance function	*Degree of influence of the Finance function compared to other departments within the organisation*
049	Awareness of the idea that capital creates cost	*Many people are not aware that capital creates opportunity costs and has to be remunerated*
050	Lack of implementation on operational level	*Criticism against cost-of-capital concepts: rates are only determined on top levels but there is no real implementation of the concept through the organisation*

(continued)

Code no.	Description	Meaning
051	Complexity of company structure	*If structure is too complex, no sophisticated treatment of cost-of-capital might be possible*

9.2 Assignment of Codes to Categories in Qualitative Data Analysis

Category	Codes
Data availability	001, 002, 016, 018, 021
Investor specifications	005, 029
Company size	006, 013, 023, 033
Staff Resources	026, 022, 017
Industry	007, 037
Fields of application	012
Company structure	014, 020, 024, 051
Ownership structure	025
Cost/benefit of calculation	027
Corporate culture	038, 039, 041, 045, 046, 048
Capital market orientation	008, 019, 034
Subject complexity	009, 010, 028, 042, 011
Scope for creativity in methods	032, 040
Management	030, 035, 043, 044, 047
Purposes of applying methods	031, 036
Regulation	015
Rest/unallocated	003, 004, 049, 050

9.3 Questionnaire

1 Country, sector and industry

Which country is the headquarters of your company located in?
☐ Germany
☐ Other (_____)

Which sector does your company operate in?
☐ Manufacturing
☐ Retail / wholesale / services
☐ Other (_____)

Which of the following industries / product areas best describe your company?
(only manufacturing companies)

☐ Food products, beverages, tobacco
☐ Wood products
☐ Metal products (except Machinery)
☐ Automotive / motor vehicles
☐ Pharmaceutical products

☐ Textile and leather products
☐ Paper products
☐ Machinery and equipment
☐ Other transportation
☐ Print and media products

☐ Rubber and plastic products
☐ Chemical products
☐ Electrical equipment
☐ Optical and precision equipment
☐ Other (_____)

---

2 Cost-of-capital practices

2.1 Determination of cost-of-capital

Does your company determine <u>cost-of-capital</u> on a company <u>group</u> level?	yes ☐ no ☐				
If yes, how relevant are the following methods for your company?	not relevant				very relevant
a. Weighted Average Cost of Capital (WACC)	☐	☐	☐	☐	☐
b. Other (_____)	☐	☐	☐	☐	☐

Does your company determine <u>cost of equity</u> on a company <u>group</u> level?	yes ☐ no ☐				
If yes, how relevant are the following methods for your company?	not relevant				very relevant
a. Capital Asset Pricing Model (CAPM)	☐	☐	☐	☐	☐
b. Other capital market models	☐	☐	☐	☐	☐
c. Historical returns on the company's stock	☐	☐	☐	☐	☐
d. Targets set by management	☐	☐	☐	☐	☐
e. Targets set by investors / owners	☐	☐	☐	☐	☐
f. Other (_____)	☐	☐	☐	☐	☐

Does your company determine <u>cost-of-capital</u> specifically on the level of <u>subsidiaries, business units, segments, product lines, projects or regions</u>?	yes ☐ no ☐				
If yes, how relevant are the following methods for your company?	not relevant				very relevant
a. Weighted Average Cost of Capital (WACC)	☐	☐	☐	☐	☐
b. Adjusting the overall company group WACC	☐	☐	☐	☐	☐
c. Targets set by management	☐	☐	☐	☐	☐
d. Targets set by investors / owners	☐	☐	☐	☐	☐
e. Other (_____)	☐	☐	☐	☐	☐

Does your company determine <u>cost of equity</u> specifically on the level of <u>subsidiaries, business units, segments, product lines, projects or regions</u>?	yes ☐ no ☐				
If yes, how relevant are the following methods for your company?	not relevant				very relevant
a. Using cost of equity / betas of comparable companies	☐	☐	☐	☐	☐
b. Adjusting the company group cost of equity / beta	☐	☐	☐	☐	☐
c. Using qualitative approaches (e.g. scoring models)	☐	☐	☐	☐	☐
d. Targets set by management	☐	☐	☐	☐	☐
e. Targets set by investors / owners	☐	☐	☐	☐	☐
f. Other (_____)	☐	☐	☐	☐	☐

9.3 Questionnaire

2.2 Performance management and cost-of-capital

Which of the following indicators does your company include in the reporting to evaluate the performance of the company group or its subsidiaries, business units, segments, regions etc.?	Company group	Business unit, segments, regions etc.
a. Revenues / sales	☐	☐
b. Return on sales	☐	☐
c. Profit measures, e.g. EBIT	☐	☐
d. Value-based measures, e.g. EVA	☐	☐
e. Capital return measures, e.g. ROI, ROCE etc.	☐	☐
f. Absolute capital measures, e.g. Net Assets, Working Capital	☐	☐
g. Cost of debt, e.g. interest expenses	☐	☐
h. Other (_____)	☐	☐

Does your company define explicit capital return targets, e.g. a minimum ROI, ROCE, ROE etc. for the company group?	yes ☐ no ☐				
If yes, how relevant are the following methods for your company to set targets?	not relevant				very relevant
a. Using the calculated cost-of-capital rate	☐	☐	☐	☐	☐
b. Specification by management	☐	☐	☐	☐	☐
c. Specification by investors / owners	☐	☐	☐	☐	☐
d. Specification by Controlling / Finance department	☐	☐	☐	☐	☐
e. Other (_____)	☐	☐	☐	☐	☐

Does your company define explicit capital return targets, e.g. a minimum ROI, ROCE etc. for its business units, segments, regions etc.?	yes ☐ no ☐				
If yes, how relevant are the following methods for your company to set targets?	not relevant				very relevant
a. Using the cost-of-capital rate	☐	☐	☐	☐	☐
b. Specification by management	☐	☐	☐	☐	☐
c. Specification by investors / owners	☐	☐	☐	☐	☐
d. Specification by Controlling / Finance department	☐	☐	☐	☐	☐
e. Other (_____)	☐	☐	☐	☐	☐

2.3 Investments and cost-of-capital

When deciding which investments to pursue, how relevant are the following evaluation techniques for your company?	not relevant				very relevant
a. Cost comparison	☐	☐	☐	☐	☐
b. Earnings comparison	☐	☐	☐	☐	☐
c. Accounting return / Return on Investment (ROI)	☐	☐	☐	☐	☐
d. Payback period	☐	☐	☐	☐	☐
e. Net Present Value (NPV) / Discounted Cash Flow (DCF)	☐	☐	☐	☐	☐
f. Internal Rate of Return (IRR)	☐	☐	☐	☐	☐
g. Discounted payback period	☐	☐	☐	☐	☐
h. Qualitative assessment	☐	☐	☐	☐	☐
i. Value-based methods (e.g. EVA)	☐	☐	☐	☐	☐
j. Other (_____)	☐	☐	☐	☐	☐

When evaluating projects, how frequently does your company use the following hurdle rates or discount rates?	never				always
a. Identical hurdle rate for all projects (group-wide)	☐	☐	☐	☐	☐
b. Hurdle rates differentiated by business units or lines of business	☐	☐	☐	☐	☐
c. Hurdle rates differentiated by geographical location	☐	☐	☐	☐	☐
d. Hurdle rates differentiated by type of project (e.g. replacement or enhancement)	☐	☐	☐	☐	☐
e. Hurdle rates differentiated by individual projects	☐	☐	☐	☐	☐

How relevant are the following methods to determine hurdle rates, minimum returns or discount rates for investment projects for your company?	not relevant				very relevant
a. Cost-of-capital calculation	☐	☐	☐	☐	☐
b. Specification by management	☐	☐	☐	☐	☐
c. Specification by investors / owners	☐	☐	☐	☐	☐
d. Specification by Controlling/Finance	☐	☐	☐	☐	☐
e. Other (_____)	☐	☐	☐	☐	☐

How frequently does your company use the following methods to account for different risk in project evaluation?	never				always
a. Different cash flow or earnings estimations	☐	☐	☐	☐	☐
b. Different hurdle rates	☐	☐	☐	☐	☐
e. Other (_____)	☐	☐	☐	☐	☐

3 Influencing factors

3.1 Cost and benefit of cost-of-capital in Managerial Finance

What do you believe is the prevailing opinion / view in your company in relation to the following statements?	Strongly disagree				Strongly agree
a. The determination of cost-of-capital is very complex	☐	☐	☐	☐	☐
b. The calculation of cost-of-capital figures is costly	☐	☐	☐	☐	☐
c. Overall, the cost to calculate differentiated cost-of-capital is higher than the benefit	☐	☐	☐	☐	☐
d. It is important that an adequate return on the company owners' capital is generated in the business	☐	☐	☐	☐	☐
e. Differentiating hurdle rates for investments depending on the risk makes sense	☐	☐	☐	☐	☐

9.3 Questionnaire

3.2 Company data: Size and investors

Please indicate the size of your company (group figures).

a. Revenues / sales in kEUR   b. Number of employees

_____   _____

Is your company listed on the stock exchange?	yes ☐	no ☐
Has your company issued debt securities, e.g. bonds?	yes ☐	no ☐
Does your company report under IFRS?	yes ☐	no ☐

What is the structure of ownership of your company?

	N/A	0-10%	11-25%	26-50%	51-75%	>75%
a. Individual private investors or families	☐	☐	☐	☐	☐	☐
b. Institutional investors, e.g. banks, funds etc.	☐	☐	☐	☐	☐	☐
c. Private equity investors	☐	☐	☐	☐	☐	☐
d. Corporate / strategic investors	☐	☐	☐	☐	☐	☐
e. Management ownership	☐	☐	☐	☐	☐	☐
f. Free float	☐	☐	☐	☐	☐	☐
g. Other (_____)	☐	☐	☐	☐	☐	☐

3.3 Company data: Organisational structure

What is the primary organisational structure of your company group that is used in reporting?
☐ Legal structure
☐ Business units or product lines
☐ Regions or countries
☐ Other (_____)

How would you describe the structure of your company?	low				high
a. Degree of centralisation	☐	☐	☐	☐	☐
b. Heterogeneity of local units (legal entities, business units etc.) in terms of business model / risk	☐	☐	☐	☐	☐
c. Complexity of the organisational structure	☐	☐	☐	☐	☐

3.4 Company data: Management and corporate culture

What is the main professional and/or educational background of your CEO?
☐ Engineering / Science   ☐ Marketing / Sales   ☐ Finance / Accounting
☐ General Management   ☐ Human Resources   ☐ Logistics / Production
☐ Other (_____)

Would you agree or disagree with the following statements?	Strongly disagree				Strongly agree
a. Our top management possesses sufficient knowledge of finance and accounting topics.	☐	☐	☐	☐	☐
b. Our company is open to innovations in management.	☐	☐	☐	☐	☐
c. Our company is very financial and number-driven.	☐	☐	☐	☐	☐
d. In our company, the influence of the Controlling / Finance department is very high.	☐	☐	☐	☐	☐
e. Our corporate culture is rather conservative.	☐	☐	☐	☐	☐

3.5 Further data

Which of the following best describes the department or function you work in?
☐ Financial Accounting   ☐ Management Accounting   ☐ Finance / Treasury
☐ Board / Management
Which of the following best describes your position?
☐ Junior Staff   ☐ Junior management
☐ Senior Staff   ☐ Middle management
☐ Senior management

What is the name of your company? (group)
_____

If you would like a copy of the analysed results please provide your Email:
_____

9.4 Descriptive Statistics of Ordinal and Ratio Variables

Category	Variable	Mean	Median	Mode	Std. Deviation	Skewness	Kurtosis	Minimum	Maximum
Group level	Weighted Average Cost of Capital (WACC)	3.86	4.00	5.00	1.334	-1.035	-.161	1.00	5.00
Group level	Capital Asset Pricing Model (CAPM)	3.59	4.00	5.00	1.458	-.645	-1.020	1.00	5.00
Group level	Other capital market models	2.00	1.50	1.00	1.198	.847	-.518	1.00	5.00
Group level	Historical returns on the company's stock	2.05	2.00	1.00	1.138	.706	-.461	1.00	5.00
Group level	Targets set by management	3.28	4.00	4[a]	1.457	-.347	-1.253	1.00	5.00
Group level	Targets set by investors / owners	2.94	3.00	1.00	1.466	-.101	-1.354	1.00	5.00
BU level	Weighted Average Cost of Capital (WACC)	3.74	4.00	5.00	1.326	-.732	-.619	1.00	5.00
BU level	Adjusting the overall company group WACC	2.86	3.00	4.00	1.294	-.142	-1.155	1.00	5.00
BU level	Targets set by management	3.15	4.00	1.00	1.606	-.288	-1.520	1.00	5.00
BU level	Targets set by investors / owners	2.67	2.00	1.00	1.457	.351	-1.290	1.00	5.00
BU level	Using cost of equity / betas of comparable companies	3.00	3.00	1.00	1.563	-.125	-1.553	1.00	5.00
BU level	Adjusting the company group cost of equity / beta	2.70	3.00	1.00	1.535	.177	-1.451	1.00	5.00
BU level	Using qualitative approaches (e.g. scoring models)	1.74	1.00	1.00	1.023	1.267	.509	1.00	4.00
BU level	Targets set by management	3.27	4.00	4.00	1.413	-.509	-.987	1.00	5.00
BU level	Targets set by investors / owners	2.83	3.00	1.00	1.464	.097	-1.361	1.00	5.00
P.M. Group	Using the calculated cost-of-capital rate	3.40	4.00	5.00	1.483	-.465	-1.227	1.00	5.00
P.M. Group	Specification by management	4.02	4.00	4.00	1.041	-1.340	1.659	1.00	5.00
P.M. Group	Specification by investors / owners	3.34	4.00	4.00	1.389	-.419	-1.074	1.00	5.00
P.M. Group	Specification by Controlling / Finance department	3.36	4.00	4.00	1.171	-.480	-.477	1.00	5.00
P.M. BU	Using the cost-of-capital rate	3.42	4.00	5.00	1.628	-.490	-1.427	1.00	5.00
P.M. BU	Specification by management	3.86	4.00	4.00	1.159	-1.082	.461	1.00	5.00
P.M. BU	Specification by investors / owners	2.68	2.00	1.00	1.492	.211	-1.506	1.00	5.00
P.M. BU	Specification by Controlling / Finance department	3.19	3.00	4.00	1.355	-.280	-1.067	1.00	5.00
Capital budgeting	Identical hurdle rate for all projects (group-wide)	2.54	2.00	1.00	1.596	.433	-1.431	1.00	5.00
Capital budgeting	Hurdle rates differentiated by business units or lines of business	2.32	2.00	1.00	1.498	.618	-1.184	1.00	5.00
Capital budgeting	Hurdle rates differentiated by geographical location	2.42	1.50	1.00	1.622	.543	-1.403	1.00	5.00
Capital budgeting	Hurdle rates differentiated by type of project (e.g. replacement or enhancement)	2.04	1.00	1.00	1.392	.950	-.637	1.00	5.00
Capital budgeting	Hurdle rates differentiated by individual projects	1.88	1.00	1.00	1.229	1.195	.244	1.00	5.00
Capital budgeting	Cost-of-capital calculation	2.85	3.00	1.00	1.653	.102	-1.665	1.00	5.00
Capital budgeting	Specification by management	3.07	3.00	1.00	1.510	-.207	-1.373	1.00	5.00
Capital budgeting	Specification by investors / owners	2.19	1.00	1.00	1.441	.720	-1.024	1.00	5.00
Capital budgeting	Specification by Controlling/Finance	2.78	3.00	1.00	1.389	-.104	-1.327	1.00	5.00
Cost-benefit	The determination of cost-of-capital is very complex	3.55	4.00	3[a]	1.170	-.337	-.831	1.00	5.00
Cost-benefit	The calculation of cost-of-capital figures is costly	2.45	2.00	2.00	1.166	.393	-.802	1.00	5.00
Cost-benefit	Overall, the cost to calculate differentiated cost-of-capital is higher than the benefit	2.87	3.00	4.00	1.260	.015	-1.086	1.00	5.00
Cost-benefit	It is important that an adequate return on the company owners' capital is generated in the business	4.01	5.00	5.00	1.267	-1.109	.030	1.00	5.00
Cost-benefit	Differentiating hurdle rates for investments depending on the risk makes sense	3.18	3.00	3.00	1.268	-.091	-.885	1.00	5.00
Investors	Individual private investors or families	3.92	4.00	6.00	1.972	-.276	-1.595	1.00	6.00
Investors	Institutional investors, e.g. banks, funds etc.	2.32	2.00	2.00	1.435	1.243	.841	1.00	6.00
Investors	Financial investors, e.g. Private Equity	1.98	2.00	1.00	1.276	1.665	2.435	1.00	6.00
Investors	Corporate / strategic investors	2.09	2.00	1.00	1.558	1.605	1.523	1.00	6.00
Investors	Management ownership	2.05	2.00	2.00	1.275	2.076	4.197	1.00	6.00
Investors	Free float	2.84	3.00	1.00	1.683	.536	-.891	1.00	6.00
Org. struct.	Degree of centralisation	3.46	4.00	4.00	1.170	-.677	.325	0.00	5.00
Org. struct.	Heterogeneity of local units (legal entities, business units etc.) in terms of business model / risk	3.13	3.00	4.00	1.385	-.512	-.389	0.00	5.00
Org. struct.	Complexity of the organisational structure	3.04	3.00	3.00	1.335	-.328	-.429	0.00	5.00
Mgt	Our company is open to innovations in management.	3.41	4.00	4.00	1.153	-.181	-1.060	1.00	5.00
Culture	Our company is very financial and number-driven.	3.46	4.00	4.00	1.060	-.312	-.610	1.00	5.00
Culture	In our company, the influence of the Controlling / Finance department is very high.	3.37	3.00	3.00	1.022	-.063	-.699	1.00	5.00
Culture	Our corporate culture is rather conservative.	3.46	4.00	4.00	1.188	-.447	-.621	1.00	5.00
Size	Revenues	2.67	3.00	3.00	1.17431	.168	-.781	1.00	5.00
Size	Employees	3.01	3.00	3.00	1.20889	-.021	-.919	1.00	5.00

9.5 Relationship Matrix Controlling for Stock Market Listing

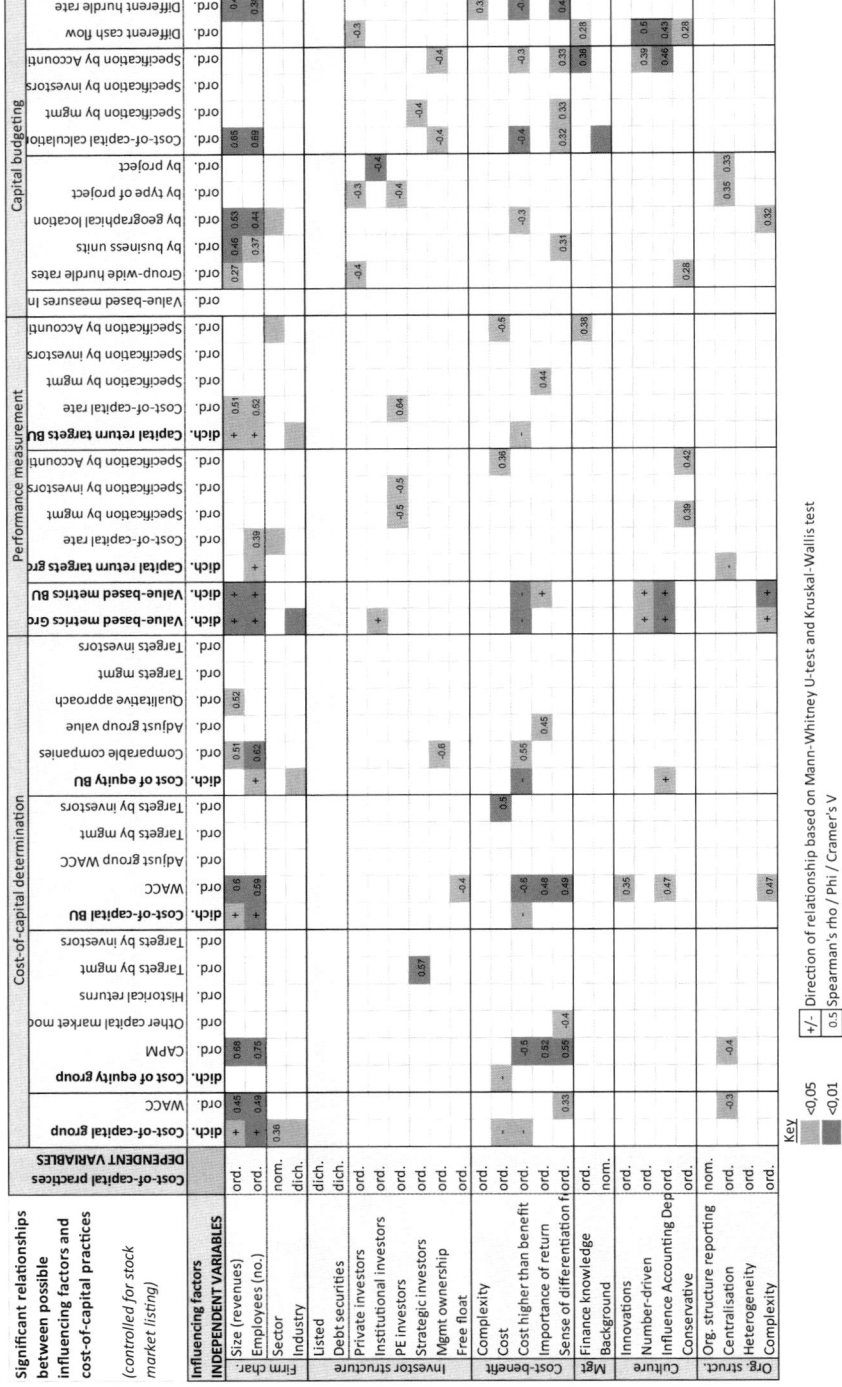

9.6 Relationship Matrix Controlling for Company Size

Printed by Printforce, the Netherlands